THE MULTILINGUAL TURN

"This important contribution to educational linguistics . . . adds a much-needed social perspective to the theory of SLA, English language teaching, and bilingual education. It takes a useful and needed step in moving beyond the monolingual and psycholinguistic biases of researchers in SLA and TESOL."

Bernard Spolsky, Bar-Ilan University, Israel

"Boundary-breaking, with wonderful width as well as originality, this book is at the cutting edge. The star-studded list of chapter authors are THE experts in their fields of study."

Colin Baker, Bangor University, UK

"The critical approach to SLA, TESOL, bi- and multilingual education raises much needed questions about the usefulness of subject-bounded approaches to second language teaching. The case for multidisciplinary frameworks is well-made."

Naz Rassool, The University of Reading, UK

Drawing on the latest developments in bilingual and multilingual research, *The Multilingual Turn* offers a critique of, and alternative to, still-dominant monolingual theories, pedagogies, and practices in SLA, TESOL, and bilingual education. Critics of the "monolingual bias" argue that notions such as the idealized native speaker, and related concepts of interlanguage, language competence, and fossilization, have framed these fields inextricably in relation to monolingual speaker norms. In contrast, these critics advocate an approach that emphasizes the multiple competencies of bi/multilingual learners as the basis for successful language teaching and learning.

This volume g the issue of multilingualism
more centrally g, making more permeable its

key subdisciplinary boundaries—particularly, those between SLA, TESOL, and bilingual education. It addresses this issue head on, bringing together key international scholars in SLA, TESOL, and bilingual education to explore from cutting-edge interdisciplinary perspectives what a more critical multilingual perspective might mean for theory, pedagogy, and practice in each of these fields.

Stephen May is Professor of Education in Te Puna Wānanga and Deputy Dean Research in the Faculty of Education, The University of Auckland, New Zealand. He is editor of the interdisciplinary journal *Ethnicities* and Associate Editor of the journal *Language Policy.*

THE MULTILINGUAL TURN

Implications for SLA, TESOL and Bilingual Education

Edited by Stephen May

Routledge
Taylor & Francis Group
NEW YORK AND LONDON

First published 2014
by Routledge
711 Third Avenue, New York, NY 10017

Simultaneously published in the UK
by Routledge
2 Park Square, Milton Park, Abingdon, Oxon OX14 4RN

*Routledge is an imprint of the Taylor & Francis Group,
an informa business*

© 2014 Taylor & Francis

Library of Congress Cataloging-in-Publication Data

The multilingual turn : implications for SLA, TESOL and bilingual
    education / Edited by Stephen May.
        pages cm
    Includes bibliographical references and index.
    1. Second language acquisition—Study and teaching. 2. Education,
Bilingual. 3. Multicultural education. I. May, Stephen, 1962– editor of
compilation.
    P118.2.M86 2013
    418.0071—dc23
    2013003826

ISBN: 978-0-415-53431-4 (hbk)
ISBN: 978-0-415-53432-1 (pbk)
ISBN: 978-0-203-11349-3 (ebk)

Typeset in Bembo
by Apex CoVantage, LLC

MIX
Paper from
responsible sources
FSC   FSC® C013056
www.fsc.org

Printed and bound in Great Britain by
TJ International Ltd, Padstow, Cornwall

In memory of David Corson (1945–2001), one of the pioneering boundary crossers in our field

CONTENTS

PREFACE

This volume began (as most things do) with a conversation. After Lourdes Ortega had given a keynote address, "The Bilingual Turn in SLA," at the Annual AAAL Conference in Atlanta in 2010, I contacted her to discuss synergies with my own work on the disciplinary constraints of SLA, TESOL, and bilingual education. This initial conversation expanded to include others and led, in turn, to my chairing a colloquium at AAAL in Boston in 2012 that involved many of the contributors herein.

But there is a far earlier antecedent that I also would like to acknowledge. David Corson, to whom this volume is dedicated, was a key, and still relatively rare, exemplar of an applied linguistics scholar committed both to theoretical revisionism and a determined interdisciplinarity. Along with Jim Cummins, his work in the 1980s and 1990s specifically bridged the TESOL and bilingual education fields and unpacked the related first and second language (L1/L2) divide, all with an underpinning commitment to social justice. His untimely death robbed applied linguistics of his keen intellectual insights and, in an academic context increasingly preoccupied with recency, so too the prescience and importance of his work has since been largely lost to sight. On a personal note, David was my postgraduate advisor in the 1980s and was a central figure in mentoring my early academic career. Indeed, my own academic interests, commitments, and inter-disciplinarity have been very much shaped by his example. For that, I hope this current volume constitutes something of a debt repaid.

Meanwhile, in getting us to this point, some other thanks are also due. To my friends and colleagues represented herein for their willingness to contribute to this project in the first instance and, more importantly, for actually making it happen (the two aren't always the same, especially with edited volumes). To Claire Kramsch and Colin Baker for their lucid, constructive, and critical review commentaries on early versions of each chapter in the volume. And finally, to my redoubtable editor, Naomi Silverman, for keeping me to task throughout, despite my often-heroic efforts at procrastination and/or circumlocution, traits for which I am widely and justly renowned.

Stephen May
Faculty of Education,
University of Auckland, New Zealand
January 2013

INTRODUCING THE "MULTILINGUAL TURN"

Stephen May

Multilingualism, it seems, is the topic du jour—at least in critical applied linguistics. Driven by globalization, and what Vertovec (2007) has described as "superdiversity," critical applied linguists have increasingly turned their attention to the dynamic, hybrid, and transnational linguistic repertoires of multilingual (often migrant) speakers in rapidly diversifying urban conurbations worldwide. Such repertoires have been described by Makoni and Pennycook (2012) as "lingua franca multilingualism," where "languages are so deeply intertwined and fused into each other that the level of fluidity renders it difficult to determine any boundaries that may indicate that there are different languages involved" (Makoni & Pennycook, 2012, p. 447). Other comparable terms include Rampton's (2011) "contemporary urban vernaculars," Canagarajah's (2011) "codemeshing," Creese et al.'s (2011) "flexible bilingualism," Pennycook's (2010) "metrolingualism," García's (2009) "translanguaging," and Jørgensen's (2008) "polylingual languaging," to name but a few.

The terminological proliferation notwithstanding, the increasing focus on superdiverse linguistic contexts is welcome. It has usefully foregrounded multilingualism, rather than monolingualism, as the new norm of applied linguistic and sociolinguistic analysis. It has increasingly challenged bounded, unitary, and reified conceptions of languages and related notions of "native speaker" and "mother tongue," arguing instead for the more complex fluid understandings of "voice" (Makoni & Pennycook, 2007, 2012), "language as social practice" (Heller, 2007), and a related "sociolinguistics of mobile resources" (Blommaert, 2010). And, following from both, it has highlighted the need for more nuanced ethnographic understandings of the complex multilingual repertoires of speakers in urban environments, along with their locatedness, scale (Blommaert, 2010), flow, and circulation (Heller, 2011) in a globalized world. As Makoni and Pennycook (2012) summarize it in their recent discussion of the notion of "metrolingualism," the aim of this new, critical, urban applied linguistics is to describe "the ways in which people of different and mixed backgrounds use, play with and negotiate identities through language" (Makoni & Pennycook, 2012, p. 449).

But there are also a number of ironies in this sudden "turn" towards multilingualism. The first, of course, is that urban multilingualism is not solely the product of late modernity but has been present in earlier periods of history, particularly prior to the advent of nationalism and the nation-state (Canagarajah & Liyanage, 2012; May, 2012). Likewise, Western applied linguistics' recent "discovery" of multilingualism reveals its own lack of historicity and not a little ethnocentrism. After all, scholars from beyond the West have long argued for just such an examination of multilingualism, albeit more broadly than in just urban contexts, and a related contesting of the monolingual norms that still underpin the study of language acquisition and use (the distinction itself reflecting this). Indeed, as I discuss in Chapter 1, Yamuna Kachru and Shikaripur Sridhar mounted just such a critique nearly 20 years ago, albeit with little effect on the wider field at that time.

And this brings us to the next irony: Despite an increasing interest in, and engagement with, multilingualism, "mainstream" applied linguistics remains to this day largely untouched, uninterested, and unperturbed by such developments. We see this most clearly in second language acquisition (SLA), but also in much of the TESOL industry, both of which continue to treat the acquisition of an additional language (most often, English) as an ideally hermetic process uncontaminated by knowledge and use of one's other languages. A final related irony is that those working within mainstream SLA and TESOL can continue to blithely ignore this turn towards multilingualism precisely because it remains corralled within a "critical applied linguistics" with which they seldom engage (or, when they do, take seriously).

This volume is an initial attempt to resituate the issue of multilingualism more centrally in applied linguistics and, in so doing, to make more permeable some of its key subdisciplinary boundaries—particularly, those between SLA, TESOL, and bilingual education. The chapters can be said to focus, respectively, on SLA (May; Ortega; Block), TESOL (Canagarajah; Norton; Leung), and bilingual education (García & Flores; Li Wei; Blackledge, Creese, & Takhi). That said, this demarcation is itself inevitably somewhat arbitrary—no more, in effect, than a useful heuristic—since all chapters traverse a range of issues and transgress a number of boundaries. Throughout, we have problematized the normative ascendancy of monolingualism underpinning the study of language acquisition and use and related educational and assessment practices. However, such is the ongoing hegemony of monolingualism in these fields; try as we might, we have not wholly escaped from the established terminology associated with it—most notably, the still ubiquitous terms of "native speaker" and, of course, "language" itself. The volume is also still focused predominantly on Western contexts, an ongoing legacy of the hegemony of Western applied linguistics. However, we hope that the volume at least provides the basis for further academic discussion of multilingualism across a much wider range of contexts in the coming years (see also Conteh & Meier, in press).

In Chapter 1, I examine why, despite the long-standing critique of the "monolingual bias" in SLA and TESOL, so little progress has been made in developing, as a first step, a more additive approach to bi/multilingualism. By drawing on Bourdieu's notion of field and Bernstein's concepts of classification and framing, I argue that the construction of SLA and TESOL as academic disciplines and the dominance of linguistic–cognitive approaches within them actively delimits the possibilities of developing a more additive bilingual approach, although it does not foreclose it. By way of example, I conclude by discussing LEAP (Language Enhancing the Achievement of Pasifika), a major web-based professional development resource for teachers, which integrates research in bilingualism and bilingual education with second language teaching and learning. LEAP thus provides a still rare international exemplar that takes seriously the challenge of developing an additive bilingual pedagogy for SLA and TESOL. It could also potentially be developed further to incorporate the latest theoretical developments underpinning a more dynamic fluid understanding of bi/multilingualism since additive bilingualism can be criticized in turn for reinforcing, rather than undermining, the discreteness of linguistic boundaries.

In Chapter 2, Lourdes Ortega argues that both nativeness and monolingualism should be abandoned as organizing principles in the study of additional language learning, particularly within her own community of linguistic–cognitive SLA scholars. She first examines the ideological roots of the monolingual bias in linguistic–cognitive SLA work and highlights the serious validity and ethical problems that ensue when late bilingualism is investigated as the psycholinguistic process of developing monolingual competence a second time around in life. Ortega argues instead for a strategic theoretical commitment to usage-based linguistics (UBL) as a means of resituating the SLA field. For Ortega, UBL can help SLA researchers in three important ways by encouraging: a shift of the explanatory burden from birth to history and experience; a focus on the link between language input affordances and learning success; and an analytical treatment of linguistic development as self-referenced, nonteleological, and unfinished. An acknowledgement of its inherent monolingualism, coupled with a strategic commitment to UBL, is crucial for an epistemic reorientation of linguistic–cognitive SLA, away from explaining why bilinguals are not native speakers (i.e., monolinguals) and towards understanding the psycholinguistic mechanisms and consequences of becoming bi/multilingual later in life.

David Block, in Chapter 3, develops and extends his earlier sociocultural critique of the monolingual bias inherent in linguistic–cognitive SLA to include an additional call to address directly the issues of embodiment and multimodality. He first examines, drawing on Bourdieu and Merleau-Ponty, how embodiment is inextricably linked to language acquisition and use, providing a range of culturally specific examples. Drawing on Gee, Hymes, and Goffman, among others, he then argues that multimodality—including, but not limited to, proxemics, posture, and gesture—must be addressed more seriously by linguistic–cognitive SLA scholars, again, providing a range of illustrative examples from different cultural contexts. In combination, he thus advocates for both a multilingual and multimodal turn to SLA.

In Chapter 4, Suresh Canagarajah argues for a practice-based view of language and competence as the best means of examining the linguistics of contact (where speakers of different languages come into contact with each other and attempt to negotiate communication in such contexts successfully) and the related uses of language varieties in such contexts as complex, fluid, and mobile semiotic resources. By way of example, Canagarajah examines what he describes as the "translingual practice" of adult African skilled migrants in the United States, Britain, Australia, and South Africa in their interactions with and uses of English. He explores how these multilingual migrants develop a more complex language awareness and metalinguistic competence through practice—a "performative competence" that does not treat languages as separate but rather takes their multilingual repertoire as a starting point. What is emphasized is thus the repertoire—the way the different language resources constitute an integrated ever-expanding competence in such contact zones—combining effective language use and learning in the process.

Bonny Norton, in Chapter 5, examines four multilingual contexts where participants are negotiating the often-complex connections between literacy, identity, and language teaching. These include students' resistant reading of texts in South Africa, the appeal of *Archie* comics among multilingual young people in Canada, the perceptions of literacy among Pakistani students and the influence of English on their learner identities, and the use of digital literacy among multilingual students in Uganda. Drawing on the notion of "investment," she explores the socially and historically constructed relationship of the learners in each of these contexts to the target language (English) and how their complex multilingual identities inform and mediate their language learning. Each of the contexts she examines suggests that meaning making is facilitated when learners are in a position of relative power within a given literacy event and when learners' social, cultural, and linguistic identities are validated in the teaching and learning process.

In Chapter 6, Constant Leung presents a reflexive examination of the notion of communicative competence in English Language Teaching (ELT). In particular, he explores the continuing ambiguities between certified communicative competence—via proficiency test scores, for example—and the observed capacity of English language learners to communicate in context. He examines critically the Common European Framework of Reference for Languages, a number of internationally marketed textbooks, and English (as a subject) in the National Curriculum of England, all of which are ostensibly predicated on the notion of communicative competence. He then draws on spoken interaction within linguistically diverse classrooms in London in order to explore the match (and mismatch) between these conventional understandings of communicative competence and multilingual classroom learning. In so doing, he highlights the importance of adding the notion of students' "participatory involvement" to language knowledge so as to better reflect the complexities of communicative competence in multilingual learning contexts.

Ofelia García and Nelson Flores, in Chapter 7, focus on the Common Core State Standards (CCSS) now adopted by nearly all U.S. states. The CCSS present an integrated model of learning where language/literacy and content overlap significantly. CCSS also emphasizes languaging as action and practice, rather than language as a system, with a related emphasis on participatory involvement leading to understanding and more complex language use. As such, they argue, the CCSS could actively accommodate and draw on the rapidly increasing linguistic diversity in U.S. classrooms, and the associated complex "translanguaging" practices of bi/multilingual students, in the teaching and learning process, although it currently does not do so. García and Flores outline what an alternative "Bilingual Common Core State Standards" (BCCSS) might comprise. First, a BCCSS would provide different progressions of what bilingual students are able to do using English, and in their languages other than English, in order to meet standards. Second, it would legitimate translanguaging pedagogical strategies as a scaffold for learning English, and, finally, it would need to be aligned with assessments that separate language proficiency from content knowledge.

In Chapter 8, Li Wei examines Chinese-language "complementary schools" in Britain, which teach bi/multilingual students on a voluntary basis and within local community contexts outside of normal school hours. The chapter is underpinned by data on classroom interactions in six schools (three Mandarin and three Cantonese language schools) located in three British cities. Li Wei focuses, in particular, on the co-learning of both language and cultural practices that occurs between the teachers and students in these classrooms. Co-learning, he argues, challenges the usual unequal power relationships between teachers and students by fostering a more dynamic and participatory engagement in knowledge construction in the classroom. Co-learning also allows both teachers and students to draw on their multilingual resources and related funds of knowledge in the teaching and learning process.

In Chapter 9, Adrian Blackledge, Angela Creese, and Jaspreet Kaur Takhi employ Bakhtin's notion of "heteroglossia" to argue for an understanding of multilingualism that dispenses with any vestigial attachment to discrete language boundaries. Drawing on Bakhtin's related notions of indexicality, tension-filled interaction, and multivoicedness, they examine data from one classroom lesson in a Panjabi complementary school in Birmingham, England. In so doing, they highlight the fluidity of multilingual language practices therein, along with the significance of language play—including stylization, parody, and pastiche—and student identities in the teaching and learning context. They conclude by arguing for the importance of an understanding of multilingualism that balances imperatives towards standardization, centralization, and correctness alongside the acceptance of linguistic signs and voices, which index students' localities, social histories, circumstances, and complex, dynamic, bi/multilingual identities.

The volume ends with a brief afterword on where all this might (or should) take us next.

References

Blommaert, J. (2010). *The sociolinguistics of globalization.* New York, NY: Cambridge University Press.

Canagarajah, A. S. (2011). Codemeshing in academic writing: Identifying teachable strategies of translanguaging. *The Modern Language Journal, 95,* 401–417.

Canagarajah, A. S., & Liyanage, I. (2012). Lessons from pre-colonial multilingualism. In M. Martin-Jones, A. Blackledge, & A. Creese (Eds.), *The Routledge handbook of multilingualism* (pp. 49–65). London, UK: Routledge.

Conteh, J., & Meier, G. (Eds.) (in press) *The multilingual turn in languages education.* Manuscript submitted for publication. Clevedon, UK: Multilingual Matters.

Creese, A., Blackledge, A., Barac, T., Bhatt, A., Hamid S., Li, W., . . . Yagcioglu, D. (2011). Separate and flexible bilingualism in complementary schools: Multiple language practices in interrelationship. *Journal of Pragmatics, 43*(5), 1196–1208.

García, O. (2009). *Bilingual education in the 21st century: A global perspective.* Malden, MA: Blackwell/Wiley.

Heller, M. (2007). Bilingualism as ideology and practice. In M. Heller (Ed.), *Bilingualism: A social approach* (pp. 1–22). Basingstoke, UK: Palgrave Macmillan.

Heller, M. (2011). *Paths to post-nationalism: A critical ethnography of language and identity.* Oxford, UK: Oxford University Press.

Jørgensen, J. N. (2008). Poly-lingual languaging around and among children and adolescents. *International Journal of Multilingualism, 5*(3), 161–176.

Makoni, S., & Pennycook, A. (2007). Disinventing and reconstituting languages. In S. Makoni & A. Pennycook (Eds.), *Disinventing and reconstituting languages* (pp. 1–41). Clevedon, UK: Multilingual Matters.

Makoni, S., & Pennycook, A. (2012). Disinventing multilingualism: From monological multilingualism to multilingua francas. In M. Martin-Jones, A. Blackledge, & A. Creese (Eds.), *The Routledge handbook of multilingualism* (pp. 439–453). New York, NY: Routledge.

May, S. (2012). *Language and minority rights: Ethnicity, nationalism and the politics of language* (2nd ed.). New York, NY: Routledge.

Pennycook, A. (2010). *Language as a local practice.* New York, NY: Routledge.

Rampton, B. (2011). From "multi-ethnic adolescent heteroglossia" to "contemporary urban vernaculars". *Language & Communication, 31,* 276–294.

Vertovec, S. (2007). Super-diversity and its implications. *Ethnic and Racial Studies, 30*(6), 1024–1054.

1

DISCIPLINARY DIVIDES, KNOWLEDGE CONSTRUCTION, AND THE MULTILINGUAL TURN

Stephen May

The subject is initially established by the silence through which power speaks. (Bernstein, 1990, p. 28)

Writing in the early 1990s on the "monolingual bias" inherent in second language acquisition (SLA) research, Yamuna Kachru (1994) despondently observed that, up until that point, "few attempts [had] been made to gather evidence [of second language acquisition] from stable contexts of bi-/multilingualism in Africa, Asia, Europe and Latin America" (Kachru, 1994, p. 796). Rather, she argued, the Chomskyan notion of the idealized native speaker, and related concepts of interlanguage, language competence, and fossilization, has framed the SLA research field inextricably in relation to monolingual speaker norms.

In making this critique, there is no allied requirement to assume that these monolingual norms are unidimensional or that monolingual speakers do not themselves demonstrate a range of linguistic competencies in relation to them (cf. Ellis, 2008; Rothman, 2008; see also Rampton 1990). Indeed, this is precisely the point that Kachru (1994) is making: Monolingual bias occurs because the notion of monolingual norms as an invariant standard presupposes monolingualism to be the unmarked, unexamined category and "native speaker" competence to be a uniform benchmark in relation to second language learning. In so doing, the existing bi/multilingual repertoires of learners were, in her view, either ignored or perceived in explicitly deficit terms. So too, by extension, were the fluid and overlapping language uses, and related linguistic and sociocultural competencies, of multilingual communities.

Commenting on fossilization as the dominant explanation in SLA for learner "errors," Kachru (1994) notes, for example, that "[w]hatever the psycholinguistic validity of the notion, it is irrelevant to situations in which a second or an additional language has definite societal roles in the linguistic repertoire of its users" (Kachru, 1994, p. 797). More broadly, Kachru argues that the conception in the SLA literature that acquiring a second or additional language meant being able to then use it in the same way as monolingual speakers simply ignores the extensive existing literature on bi/multilingualism. This literature "has demonstrated that all the languages in the multilinguals' repertoire complement one another to produce the type of composite language competence that suits their needs" (Kachru, 1994, p. 797). A sociolinguistic perspective of what competent bi/multilinguals do with different codes in their repertoire is thus quite different from the narrow psycholinguistic perspective that focuses on the acquisitional stages of learners, as reflected in notions such as fossilization and interlanguage. "The two perspectives come into conflict," she concludes, "when language attitudes and considerations of power and control begin to play a role in the debate" (Kachru, 1994, p. 798).

In the same issue of *TESOL Quarterly,* Sridhar (1994) expands on Kachru's (1994) overarching concerns when he observes:

> Given that the aim of SLA is bilingualism, one would expect SLA theories to build on theories of bilingualism and use the natural laboratory of bilingual communities worldwide. With rare exceptions, the dominant models of SLA scarcely refer to this resource. (Sridhar, 1994, p. 800)

Moreover, if they did, Sridhar argues, they would realize that typically in multilingual communities the second language (L2) is used along with, not in place of, the first language (L1). "The relevant model of bilingualism is an additive one, not replacive" (Sridhar, 1994, p. 800). By extension, the notion of a duplicative model of bilingualism as the target of SLA—acquiring native-like competence in two languages, in the Bloomfield (1933) sense—needs to be replaced with a more complementary model of bilingualism, recognizing, as with Kachru (1994), that "a bilingual acquires as much competence in the two (or more) languages as is needed and that all of the languages together serve the full range of communicative needs" (Sridhar, 1994, p. 802). Adopting an additive bilingual approach, Sridhar concludes, would avoid the "negative characterization of the overwhelming majority of L2 acquirers and users . . . as speakers of *interlanguages* . . . that is, as failed monolinguals rather than successful bilinguals . . . Such theories condemn vibrant second languages and their speakers to a permanent subaltern state" (Sridhar, 1994, p. 802). It would also avoid the L1/L2 dichotomization in SLA and the related pathologizing of language transfer, mixed systems, convergence, and the interpenetration of systems, which are all central to language interaction in the ecology of multilingualism.

The additive bilingual model has subsequently been criticized, in turn, for reinforcing, albeit unwillingly, a conception of languages, and their use by bi/multilinguals, as distinct and delineable. Rather, as the chapters in this volume outline, bi/multilingualism is a significantly more complex, dynamic, and porous phenomenon than this, reflecting the multiple discursive practices adopted by bi/multilinguals across the full range of modalities, in a wide range of contexts, and with many different interlocutors. This more dynamic, reciprocal, and permeable conception of bi/multilingualism is perhaps highlighted most clearly in recent discussions of dynamic bilingualism and translanguaging (see Blackledge, Creese, & Takhi, this volume; García & Flores, this volume; see also García, 2009). Nonetheless, the notion of additive bilingualism advanced by Sridhar (1994), and subsequently championed by other critics (see below), still presents a strikingly different basis for analyzing language learning than the monolingual norms, and related dismissal and/or subtractive views of bilingualism, found within mainstream SLA.

Kachru (1994) and Sridhar (1994) were not the first to make these observations. Ben Rampton (1987) had earlier pointed out, for example, that what is regularly described as code-switching in sociolinguistics somehow "winds up as interference in SLA" (Rampton, 1987, p. 55). Rampton argues in the same article that "IL [interlanguage] scholarship . . . runs the risk of remaining restrictively preoccupied with the space between the speaker and his [sic] grammar, rather than with the relationship between speakers and the world around them" (Rampton, 1987, p. 49). Rampton's nascent critique accords with other early work, such as that of Auer (1984), Beebe (1980), Bley-Vroman (1983), and Tarone (1988), which, along with Kachru and Sridhar, collectively laid the groundwork for what Block (2003) terms the subsequent "social turn" in, or sociocultural critique of, SLA, more fully developed from the late 1990s onwards (see below for further discussion).

Nor have Kachru (1994) and Sridhar (1994) been the last to voice these criticisms (see, e.g., Block, 2003; Ortega, 2009). However, their critical commentary is notable, and worth revisiting, for two reasons: its prescience and directness at that time in the early 1990s, and more discouragingly, for how little apparent effect/impact it has had on subsequent developments in SLA and related TESOL pedagogy and practice, at least until very recently (see below). Of course, this does not mean that the discipline has been silent on these issues in the interim. Rather, as we shall see, it is that the ongoing critique of the monolingual bias in "traditional" or "mainstream" SLA and TESOL continues to be resolutely ignored by its key proponents within these fields.[1]

The emergence of a distinctive sociocultural view of SLA expanded the critique of the cognitive and psycholinguistic preoccupations of mainstream SLA—described by Ortega (this volume) as "linguistic–cognitive" SLA—via a range of key contributions (or interventions) from the late 1990s onwards.[2] In this sense, it has proved a useful precursor to the *multilingual turn* explored in this volume. Sociocultural commentators have consistently argued for the replacement of the deficit terminology that still characterizes linguistic–cognitive SLA. Leung, Harris, and Rampton (1997), for example, argue that the terms "native speaker" and "mother tongue" should be replaced with the terms "language expertise," "language inheritance," and "language affiliation." Cook (1999, 2002a,

2008) advocates for the notion of "multicompetence" to describe bi/multilingual speakers (and for the notion of second language users, rather than learners; see also Ortega, this volume; Block, this volume). And Block (2003), directly echoing Kachru (1994) and Sridhar (1994), problematizes the L1/L2 distinction itself, given that the latter presupposes the sequential addition of a second language, rather than, as is far more common, the simultaneous multiple-language-learning contexts evident in multilingual environments.[3]

The ongoing monolingual bias of SLA, reflected in the notions of interlanguage and fossilization, has also garnered specific critical attention. For example, in Firth and Wagner's (1997) influential critique of mainstream linguistic–cognitive SLA research, they reiterate "the prevailing monolingual orientation in SLA" and the implication that "interactions with NS [Native Speakers] are seen to be the 'preferred' conditions for SLA to occur" (Firth & Wagner, 1997, p. 292). In contrast, they argue that many of the world's English speakers are not English "learners" in this traditional SLA sense, but rather multicompetent English users (cf. Cook, 2002b) who employ English as a lingua franca in multiple varying ways in their daily lives for a range of purposes and in a variety of social settings (see also Canagarajah, this volume; Norton, this volume). Following from this, they press for further SLA investigations into "everyday L2 use" (Firth & Wagner, 1997, p. 292; see also Leung et al., 1997), a challenge that has begun to be picked up by recent welcome sociolinguistic work exploring directly the implications of language learning in multilingual contexts.[4] This current volume aims to contribute further to these important developments.

But, meanwhile, mainstream SLA theorizing continues on much as it ever has. Aside from a flurry of controversy and counter-response generated by Firth and Wagner's (1997) arguments, a point to which I will return, ongoing developments in mainstream SLA appear largely impervious to and/or uninterested in seriously addressing these critiques. As Zuengler and Miller (2006) assert, the proponents of linguistic–cognitive SLA, and proponents of a more socially situated and critical SLA, are so ontologically disparate and professionally divided as to remain in "parallel SLA worlds" (Zuengler & Miller, 2006, p. 35). This is starkly illustrated by an *AILA Review* of SLA that came out in the same year (Bardovi-Harlig & Dörnyei, 2006), which, while purporting to address new developments in the field, manifestly failed to engage substantively with anything beyond linguistic–cognitive SLA. Another example is highlighted by Jenkins (2006), who argues that standard (read: cognitive/psycholinguistic) texts on SLA, such as Lightbown and Spada (2006), Littlewood (2004), and Mitchell and Myles (2004), "still frame as interlanguage any L2 output which deviates from the nativelike and assume that full mastery of any language means that of its NSs" (Jenkins, 2006, p. 144; cf. Gardner & Wagner, 2004). Similarly, fossilization remains a key concept that continues to be regularly promoted in such texts (as in, e.g., Han & Selinker, 2005), as well as in teacher training courses. The only notable exception here is the work of Lourdes Ortega, who has in recent years become increasingly critical of this ongoing (resistant/entrenched) monolingual bias in SLA (see especially, Ortega 2009, 2010) and who extends her critique in this current volume. That said, the fact that she remains the only linguistic–cognitive SLA scholar so identified in the current volume highlights the ongoing exceptionalism of her critique within traditional/mainstream SLA.

Much the same pattern can be seen in the TESOL field. Comparable socio-cultural and critical critiques of TESOL have also clearly emerged in the last two decades. These have focused on the (multiple) identities of language learners, including gender, race, ethnicity, and sexuality, and their necessary embeddedness in wider social contexts of power and inequality.[5] Alongside this have been critical accounts of the hegemonic influence of English as the current lingua mundi or international language vis-à-vis other languages and the complex articulations that attend TESOL in an increasingly globalized world dominated by English.[6]

This critical work has also tried specifically "to connect the microrelations of TESOL—classrooms, teaching approaches, interactions—with broader social and political relations" (Pennycook, 1999, p. 331; see also Leung, 2005). The pedagogical implications are not always clear here—a weakness of critical pedagogy more generally (May & Sleeter, 2010)—but they do at least allow for both problematizing existing TESOL practice and developing what Pennycook (1999) terms a wider "pedagogy of engagement": "An approach to TESOL that sees such issues as gender, race, class, sexuality and postcolonialism as so fundamental to identity and language that they need to form the basis of curricular organization and pedagogy" (Pennycook, 1999, p. 340). How one implements such an approach in the classroom is, of course, the nub of the challenge.

And yet, despite these developments, the relative novelty of adopting an additive bilingual approach to TESOL also remains demonstrably apparent. Canagarajah (2006), for example, in his review of TESOL as a discipline at 40 years, could still remark: "It is clear that teaching English in a manner that complements rather than competes with local languages and local interests, *leading to additive bilingualism,* is the *new* challenge (Canagarajah, 2006, p. 25; emphases added). In proceeding to outline what this might entail, he argues that:

> Teaching English as an international language needs to be conducted with multilateral participation. Teachers in different communities have to devise curricula and pedagogies that have local relevance. Teaching materials have to accommodate the values and needs of diverse settings, with sufficient complexity granted to local knowledge. . . . We need to learn from diverse traditions of professionalization in different communities to develop a richer TESOL discourse. (Canagarajah, 2006, p. 27)

Canagarajah's (2006) argument at that time still seemed more aspirational than anything else, even when other "traditions of professionalization" have been actively mined, as Canagarajah avers (although, see Canagarajah this volume;

Leung, this volume, for further developments). Areas such as bilingualism and bilingual education, for example, have clearly intersected in the past with both SLA and TESOL. The early seminal work of Jim Cummins (1976, 1977, 1979) is a case in point here, as are subsequent attempts to develop and explore their implications more fully in both Cummins's later work (see, for example, 2000, 2003) and that of the late David Corson (1998, 2000).[7] But such attempts at disciplinary cross-fertilization have to date again proved to be the exception rather than the rule. Even when cross-fertilization has occurred, as in Corson's work, such attempts often remain radically underappreciated, falling through, or between, disciplinary gaps (May, 2002). And, of course, TESOL pedagogy and practice continue to be dominated by communicative language teaching (CLT) and its latest manifestation, task-based teaching and learning (TBLT)—both of which are still predicated largely on mainstream SLA principles (Leung, 2005, this volume). *Plus ça change, plus c'est la même chose.*

Why has so little apparent progress been made then in developing an additive bilingual approach to SLA and TESOL, let alone an approach underpinned by more dynamic conceptions of bi/multilingualism? In what follows, I argue that this is because disciplines and their subdisciplines, such as SLA and TESOL, themselves construct, validate, contain, and exclude particular forms of knowledge. This process is, in turn, the result of their disciplinary histories and the academic hierarchies established within them, as well as in relation to other disciplines. I examine these issues via Pierre Bourdieu's notions of "habitus" and "field"—and more importantly, their inextricable interconnection and interaction—as well as Basil Bernstein's closely related notions of classification and framing.

Field, Habitus, and Practice

Bourdieu is best known for his notion of habitus—that is, those embodied dispositions—or ways of viewing and living in the world—that influence, shape, and even frame our choices and actions. However, in order to fully understand the implications of habitus, we need first to understand Bourdieu's less discussed, but equally important, notion of "field," as the two concepts are intrinsically related. Bourdieu defines field thus:

> [as] a network, or configuration of objective relations between positions. These positions are objectively defined, in their existence and in the determinations they impose upon their occupants, agents or institutions, by their present and potential situation (situs) in the structure of the distribution of species of power (or capital) whose possession commands access to the specific profits that are at stake in the field. (Bourdieu & Wacquant, 1992, p. 97)

According to Bourdieu, a field is a specific site of economic, cultural, and/or intellectual reproduction, with its own "logic of practice"—which is "specific and irreducible to those that regulate other fields" (Bourdieu & Wacquant, 1992, p. 97). Central to the logic of practice in any given field are the types of capital (economic, cultural, intellectual) that are valued, recognized, and/or rewarded within it. Fields are thus structured (and structuring) spaces that are "characterised by their own distinctive properties, by distinctive forms of capital" (Thompson, 1991, p. 15), over which those engaged in the field compete for maximum advantage. In this sense too, fields are essentially relational—any individual or collective action undertaken in the field will have implications (positive and/or negative) for all others within that field. They are also intrinsically competitive spaces or arenas of struggle. Fields, as such, continuously reflect (changing) positions of relative dominance and/or subordination in determining what counts as capital in the field, including established norms and boundaries. As Swartz (1997) outlines: "Fields are 'tightly coupled'. . . relational configurations where change in one position shifts the boundaries among all other positions. Field struggle [thus] pits those in dominant positions against those in subordinate positions" (Swartz, 1997, p. 124). On this basis, Swartz argues, "[t]he struggle for position in fields opposes those who are able to exercise some degree of monopoly power *over the definition and distribution of capital* [emphasis added] and others who attempt to usurp the advantages" (Swartz, 1997, p. 124).

Bourdieu argues that this contest over the definition and distribution of forms of capital within particular fields can be described in relation to the countervailing forces of orthodoxy and heterodoxy. These opposing, but nonetheless dialectally related, strategies also presuppose what Bourdieu terms an "illusio"—a belief or acceptance about the worth of the game of a field and that the field of struggle is worth pursuing in the first place (Bourdieu, 1990). Fields act as "structuring structures" that shape (but do not determine) agents' actions and identities in their pursuit of, and/or contest over, the accepted forms of capital within that field and the related status (economic, social, and/or intellectual) associated with them. The resulting practices in the field are thus a combination of the interrelationship between the structure of the relevant field and the habitus of the agents involved (Bourdieu, 1984).[8]

Prominent commentators on Bourdieu have often dismissed his notion of habitus as overly deterministic.[9] However, when explored in direct conjunction with field, a more nuanced and sophisticated analysis of habitus becomes possible. Fields clearly *do* form individual habitus in influential ways and also clearly influence and even shape what are deemed to be acceptable/unacceptable practices within each field. However, the complex recursive articulation of field, habitus, and practice means that the reproductive processes within a given field, while powerfully reinforced, are never wholly determinative nor are related norms and boundaries, respectively, sacrosanct or hermetic. As such, they *may* change over time, both internally as a result of ongoing struggle or contestation and externally in relation to their relationship to/articulation with other (related) fields of practice.

The degree of balance between reproduction and transformation, and the related degree of porosity, within and across particular fields is in the end, as Heller (2008) argues, an empirical question. I will return to this point shortly when I reexamine SLA and TESOL as specific examples of Bourdieu's notion of "intellectual [or academic] fields." Before doing so, however, I wish to explore how Bourdieu's articulatory understanding of field, habitus, and practice is broadly similar to Bernstein's notions of "classification" and "framing," and also to the latter's related discussion of academic disciplines. This allows us to develop a (more) reflexive account of the construction, maintenance, and (potential) transformation of academic disciplines such as SLA and TESOL. This is a necessary precursor, in turn, to understanding more fully the challenges and potentialities of repositioning both these fields in relation to adopting a more positive and dynamic understanding of bi/multilingualism, with which this volume is centrally concerned.

Developing a Reflexive View of Academic Disciplines

Bernstein was particularly interested in exploring both the social organization and status hierarchies of academic subjects or disciplines, as well as their participants (see, e.g., Bernstein 1990, 2000). Central to these explorations are his notions of classification and framing.

"Classification" describes the boundaries that are established both within, and between, academic disciplines or subjects. These encompass "relations between categories, where these categories are between agencies, between discourses, between practices" (Bernstein, 2000, p. 6). "Framing" refers to "the locus of control over pedagogic communication and its context" (Bernstein, 2000, p. 6). Pedagogic communication, for Bernstein, is any "sustained process whereby somebody acquires new forms or develops existing *forms of conduct, knowledge, practice and criteria* [emphasis added] from somebody or something deemed to be an appropriate provider and evaluator" (Bernstein, 2000, p. 78).

Bernstein (2000) applies these conceptual tools to an analysis of the establishment of distinct academic disciplines from the 19th century onwards and their subsequent organization into self-regulating communities, or what he terms "singulars" (Becher & Trowler, 2001). Singulars, for Bernstein, are characterized by strong boundary maintenance (classification), which are supported culturally (via professional associations, networks, and writing) and psychologically (in students, teachers, and researchers). As a result, "singulars develop strong autonomous self-sealing and narcissistic identities" (Bernstein, 2000, p. 54). Singulars are also framed by "three interrelated rules: distributive rules, recontextualizing rules and evaluative rules" (Bernstein, 2000, p. 114).

"Distributive rules" determine whose, or what, research is deemed acceptable, valued, and/or legitimate within the particular academic discipline (singular). "Recontextualizing rules" regulate how teachers enact the accepted/acceptable research—particularly, via textbooks, syllabi, and examinations—which, in turn, define the "evaluative rules," providing "for acquirers the principles for the production of what counts as the legitimate text" (Bernstein, 2000, p. xiv). Legitimate texts include the usual staples of academic production—journal articles, books and book chapters, theses, etc.,—which, again, recursively reinforce the underlying rubric of accepted/acceptable (disciplinary) knowledge.

Bernstein's analysis, in combination with Bourdieu's, helps to explain why academic disciplines, and particular subdisciplines such as SLA and TESOL, are so often defined (and confined) by a narrowly derived set of research assumptions, approaches, and related models of teaching and learning. Such analyses also explain why such disciplines are equally resistant to change. After all, fundamental changes in the classification and framing of knowledge also necessarily involve significant shifts in the structure and distribution of power and in principles of control—that is, in who controls, and what counts as, disciplinary knowledge.

The only potential exceptions here, as Bernstein (2000) argues, are interdisciplinary and/or applied fields, which he describes as "regions." For Bernstein, regions are "created by a recontextualising [and, one might add, expansion] of singulars" (Bernstein, 2000, p. 9). The idea of regions thus allows for (at least the possibility of) a more reflexive, porous understanding of the origins and dominant research principles underlying particular academic disciplines. In the first instance, such reflexivity provides the basis for critically analyzing the normative research questions and understandings previously established within disciplines. As Becher and Trowler (2001) suggest, in their discussion of the construction of academic disciplines, "[a] detailed analysis of disciplinary discourse . . . can help not only to bring out characteristic cultural features of disciplines but also to highlight various aspects of the knowledge domains to which they relate" (Becher & Trowler, 2001, p. 46). By this, they argue, it is possible "to discern differences in the modes in which arguments are generated, developed, expressed and reported, and to tease out the epistemological implications of the ways in which others' work is evaluated" (Becher & Trowler, 2001, p. 46).

From this, lines of inquiry previously thought unthinkable in these disciplines can be pursued. These new lines of inquiry can be drawn from related disciplines. As Becher and Trowler (2001) again observe of this:

> It often happens that adjoining disciplinary groups lay claim to the same pieces of intellectual territory. This does not necessarily entail a conflict between them. In some cases, depending on the nature of the claimants and the disposition of the no man's land, it may involve a straightforward division of interest; in others it may mark a growing unification of ideas and approaches. (Becher & Trowler, 2001, p. 60)

Greater interdisciplinarity thus opens up the possibilities of reconceptualizing and/or reconfiguring existing disciplines in order to overcome theoretical and research impasses (Albright, 2008), particularly where these impasses arise directly from existing disciplinary hierarchies of power and control.

Reexamining Disciplinary Debates in SLA

In light of the critical conceptual analyses and insights offered by Bourdieu and Bernstein, how might we reconceptualize the apparent impasse reached in SLA and TESOL with respect to developing a more additive, even dynamic, bilingual approach to second language learners? More importantly, perhaps, how might we achieve a more interdisciplinary approach that allows for the possibility of a way forward? Let me first address these key questions via a reexamination of pertinent disciplinary debates within SLA. In particular, I want to explore the controversy surrounding Firth and Wagner's (1997) critique of SLA, discussed earlier, and the subsequent concerted defense, and rearticulation of, traditional or mainstream (read: linguistic–cognitive) approaches.

Firth and Wagner's robust critique of mainstream SLA created something of a firestorm when it was published in 1997. In their article, published in *The Modern Language Journal,* they directly questioned the Chomskyan/psycholinguistic bias in SLA, arguing that its preoccupation with analyzing language learning as an inherently individualistic, mechanistic, and thus decontextualized process devalued and/or simply ignored the importance of wider social context and language (in) use. Such an approach, they argued, "fails to account in a satisfactory way for interactional and sociolinguistic dimensions of language. As such, it is flawed, and obviates insight into the nature of language, most centrally the use of second- or foreign-language (S/FL) speakers" (Firth & Wagner, 1997, p. 285). Firth and Wagner advocated instead for a dismantling of the field's ongoing bifurcation of language "acquisition" (cognitive/internal) and language "use," arguing for an analytical approach that was concerned with "how language is used *as it is being acquired through interaction,* and used resourcefully, contingently, and contextually" (Firth & Wagner, 1997, p. 296). Recasting the SLA field along these lines also included, as has already been discussed, a fundamental questioning and reconsideration of the usefulness of such terms as "interlanguage" and "fossilization."

Mainstream SLA theorists—the target of Firth and Wagner's (1997) criticisms—were, to say the least, not amused. The counter-response, and related defense, of the existing field of SLA was quick and equally robust. The nub of these rejoinders (see, e.g., Gass, 1998; Long, 1997) was simply to dismiss the Firth and Wagner critique, reasserting the language acquisition/use divide in the process. Long (1997), for example, directly rejects Firth and Wagner's above assertion for its lack of relevance to the "core" activities of SLA research:

> SLA, as the name indicates, is the study of L2 acquisition, not (except indirectly) of "the nature of language" in general or "most centrally the language use of second or foreign language speakers"—especially not "most centrally"—interesting though those subjects may be. (Long, 1997, p. 318)

He proceeds to elaborate along these lines, as follows:

> More important than whether we are guilty as charged, however, is the deeper underlying issue [Firth and Wagner] wish to raise: the very nature of the SLA beast. Whether [they] like it or not (they do not), *most SLA researchers* [emphasis added] view the object of inquiry as in large part an internal, mental process: the acquisition of new (linguistic) knowledge. And I would say, with good reason. (Long, 1997, p. 319)

Long concludes his response by stating his ongoing "skepticism as to whether greater insights into SL *use* will *necessarily* have much to say about SL *acquisition*" (Long, 1997, p. 322).

The brusque (some would say, intemperate) reassertion of the primacy of a linguistic–cognitive view in these rejoinders is also consistently linked directly to maintaining the academic seriousness of the discipline (in contradistinction, one assumes, to a social/critical perspective; see also below). Some years later, Long and Doughty (2003), for example, could argue the following:

> For SLA to achieve the *stability, stimulation,* and *research funding* to *survive* as a *viable* [emphases added] field of inquiry, it needs an intellectual and institutional home that is to some degree autonomous and separate from the disciplines and departments that currently offer shelter. Cognitive science is the logical choice. (Long & Doughty, 2003, p. 869)

The re-invocation of a scientific at the expense of a more social approach to SLA reflects and reinforces existing academic hierarchies, both within the SLA field and in conjunction with other disciplines. But more than that, it is also deeply imbricated with the advent of structural linguistics itself. Bourdieu (1982, 1991), for example, is particularly scathing of the preoccupation in modern linguistics with analyzing language in isolation from the social conditions in which it is used and mounts what Heller (2008) describes as a "furious . . . attack on a linguistics that insists on understanding language as a reified system, rather than as social practice embedded in the construction of relations of power" (Heller, 2008, p. 57). As Bourdieu (1991) comments ironically of this process:

> bracketing out the social . . . allows language or any other symbolic object to be treated like an end in itself, [this] contributed considerably to the success of structural linguistics, for it endowed the "pure" exercises that characterise a purely internal and formal analysis with the charm of a game devoid of consequences. (Bourdieu, 1991, p. 34)

For Bourdieu (1991), the inherent formalism of so much modern linguistics rests on the central distinction between the internal form of the language—a "language system" in effect—and its outworking in speech. This distinction, in turn, arises from the conception of language as a "universal treasure," freely available to all—a view that was first articulated by Auguste Comte and subsequently adopted by the founding fathers of modern linguistics, Ferdinand de Saussure and Noam Chomsky. De Saussure (1974) invokes the distinction via his celebrated comparison between "langue" and "parole," while Chomsky's (1972) notions of "competence" and "performance" reflect a similar conception. Of course, this is not to suggest that de Saussure and Chomsky's conceptions are indistinguishable. Chomsky's model is clearly more dynamic in its attempt to incorporate the generative capacities of competent speakers and this distinction has been further clarified with the move away by generative linguists from analyzing idealized speakers/hearers to a focus on the direct investigation of the principles of universal grammar. The latter at least now allows for the *possibility* of including bilingual speakers and code-switching as governed by such principles (Auer, 2007). Nonetheless, both approaches still rest on the notion that language can be constituted as an autonomous and homogeneous object amenable to linguistic study (Thompson, 1991).

An allied critique of this preoccupation with linguistic formalism at the expense of a wider analysis of the social and political conditions in which language comes to be used can also be found in Vološinov (1929/1973, pp. 77–82) and Mey (1985). Vološinov argued cogently against the "abstract objectivism" of structural linguistics, as represented by de Saussure, suggesting it created a radical disjuncture between the idea of a language system and actual language history (see also Blackledge, Creese, & Takhi, this volume). Mey likewise observes:

> that linguistic models, no matter how innocent and theoretical they may seem to be, not only have distinct economical, social and political presuppositions, but also consequences . . . Linguistic (and other) inequalities don't cease to exist simply because their socioeconomic causes are swept under the linguistic rug. (Mey, 1985, p. 26)

Bourdieu (1991) describes the resulting orthodoxy, which posits a particular set of linguistic practices as a normative model of "correct" usage, as the "illusion of linguistic communism that haunts all linguistic theory" (Bourdieu, 1991, p. 43).

The notion of language as autonomous and homogeneous is not solely the product of a cognitivist construction of the discipline of linguistics and a related attempt to raise its scientific status—a process that Block (1996, 2003) accurately describes as "science envy." It is also a historical product of the wider politics of nationalism and nation building over the last few centuries (Auer, 2007; Makoni & Pennycook, 2007; May, 2011, 2012). Distinct, clearly definable languages were reified and treated post hoc as natural facts, despite the (actual) fact that they were deliberately constructed, standardized, and regulated over time by new nation-states (Bauman & Briggs, 2003). As Bourdieu (1991) observes of this process:

In order for one mode of expression among others (a particular language in the case of bilingualism, a particular use of language in the case of a society divided into classes) to *impose* itself as the only legitimate one, the linguistic market has to be *unified* [emphases added] and the different dialects (of class, region or ethnic group) have to be measured practically against the legitimate language or usage. Integration into a single "linguistic community" [aka the modern nation-state], which is the product of the political domination that is endlessly reproduced by institutions capable of imposing universal recognition of the dominant language, is the condition for the establishment of relations of linguistic domination. (Bourdieu, 1991, pp. 46–47)

And yet, as Bourdieu (1991) argues, by ignoring the sociohistorical conditions that have established this particular set of linguistic practices as dominant and legitimate in the first place, this dominant and legitimate language—this victorious language, in effect—is simply taken for granted by linguists (Thompson, 1991; see also Mühlhäusler, 1996):

To speak of *the* language, without further specification, as linguists do, is tacitly to accept the *official* definition of the *official* language of a political unit. This language is the one which, within the territorial limits of that unit, imposes itself on the whole population as the only legitimate language . . . The official language is bound up with the state, both in its genesis and its social uses . . . this state language becomes the theoretical norm against which all linguistic practices are objectively measured. (Bourdieu, 1991, p. 45)

This combination of scientism and nationalist ideology helps then to explain why adopting a more positive and dynamic conception of bi/multilingualism within SLA and TESOL has proven to be so difficult. As Auer (2007) argues, bi/multilingual talk, including code-switching, challenges directly the autonomous, homogeneous view of language underpinning structural linguistics and, by extension, linguistic–cognitive SLA and related TESOL theory and practice. It "blurs the line between language A and language B, but also between 'langue' and 'parole', between linguistic systems and their uses, between knowledge and practice. It questions the starting point of linguistics as a whole" (Auer, 2007, p. 320). In short, he concludes, "the assumption of bound linguistic systems as the object of linguistic research is [fundamentally] questioned by bilingual practices" (Auer, 2007, p. 337; cf. Blommaert, 2010). "Translanguaging," which incorporates but also specifically goes beyond code-switching (see Blackledge et al., this volume; García, 2009; García & Flores, this volume), is a further recent elaboration of this dynamic and permeable conception of bi/multilinguals and their (complex) language practices.

On this basis, is it any wonder then about the ongoing imperative among many in mainstream SLA and TESOL to continue to treat bi/multilingualism as a form of individual aberration and bi/multilingual learners as deficient in relation to monolinguals? If we return to Bourdieu's idea of fields as "arenas in which there [are] struggles to define what [is] most important, and thus to gain advantage, as individuals and groups, *by defining what is most valuable*" (Collins, 2008, p. 365), we can see just what is at stake: *who and what controls and defines the field in question*. Long's earlier assertion that "most SLA researchers" support a view of language acquisition as purely an internal process suggests as much. Orthodoxy (or hegemony), by definition, is not easily contested. Central to this struggle are the forms of academic and political capital associated with the field and whether these can be modified or replaced. Also central to the success of the latter is the degree to which the relative autonomy of fields can be challenged and made more porous and reflexive. As Heller (2008) observes of this, "[i]t is an empirical question as to how closed [fields] may be, that is, how reproductive of current arrangements of difference and inequality; or, conversely, how open they may be to forms of social action aimed at, and perhaps achieving, social change" (Heller, 2008, p. 50).

And this returns us the notion of greater interdisciplinarity as the basis for effecting any substantive transformational change. In relation to addressing the ongoing monolingual bias in SLA and TESOL, this must involve in the first instance exploring more fully the potential synergies among SLA, TESOL, and research in bilingualism and bilingual education, as well as in relation to more social and critical conceptions within and across each of these disciplinary areas. By way of example, I conclude by discussing a recent research-informed, web-based, professional development resource, LEAP (Language Enhancing the Achievement of Pasifika, http://leap.tki.org.nz; New Zealand Ministry of Education, 2007), which attempts to do just that.

LEAP: Crossing the Borderlands of Bilingual, SLA, and TESOL Research

Before discussing the LEAP resource itself, let me first briefly contextualize it within the broader educational and societal context in which it was developed. New Zealand, a country of 4 million people, is predominantly English speaking—indeed, nearly 80% of its population are monolingual English speakers (Statistics New Zealand, 2007). Given this, the education system in New Zealand, and the vast majority of teachers therein, have relatively little direct knowledge of, or engagement with, bi/multilingualism and its relationship to teaching and learning. The only notable exception here is in the field of Maori-medium education, which has emerged over the last 30 years as a key educational intervention in the revitalization of the indigenous Maori language (see May, 2004 for an overview). However, Maori-medium education stands somewhat apart from the "mainstream" (English-medium) context. There is very little crossover between their respective teaching forces, and knowledge of bilingual/immersion pedagogies is largely limited to the Maori-medium education sector. Bilingual/immersion education options for other language speakers are paltry and restricted to a small number of individual schools (May, 2005).

A similar lack of crossover can be found within mainstream schools between generalist teachers, on the one hand, and TESOL specialists on the other. Generalist teachers adopt an almost uniformly monolingual English approach to teaching and learning in their classrooms, irrespective of student language background. For students from home-language backgrounds other than English, there is limited TESOL support available, although the model adopted in most New Zealand schools is an ESL (English second language) pullout approach, staffed by separately trained TESOL teachers (Franken & McComish, 2003; May, Hill, & Tiakiwai, 2004). Because students are withdrawn from the classroom for specialist ESL instruction, generalist teachers are thus not exposed to second language teaching and learning approaches. Meanwhile, the ESL pullout model itself perpetuates a subtractive view of students' bilingualism, given that there is little, if any, recourse to students' home languages in the instructional process. This stands in contrast to integrated ESL programs, for example, that draw on bilingual assistants within mainstream classrooms and encourage the use of L1 as a basis/scaffold for learning (Leung, 2007; see also below).

A key constituency in New Zealand that is affected—often deleteriously—by this monolingual/subtractive ESL approach in mainstream classrooms are Pasifika students. Pasifika is the pan-ethnic term currently used to describe Pacific Island migrants to New Zealand from the principal islands of Samoa, Tonga, Cook Islands, Niue, Tokelau, Fiji, and Tuvalu, as well as other Pacific nations. Pasifika migration to New Zealand has been occurring in significant numbers since the 1960s and, as a result, at the time of the last census (2006) Pasifika peoples comprised 6.9% (265,974) of the total New Zealand population. Nearly half of those (131,100) identified as Samoan. The next largest grouping, Cook Islands Maori, was considerably smaller at 58,011 (22%), with Tongan following at 50,478 (19%) and Niuean at 22,473 (8%). All other New Zealand Pasifika communities have less than 10,000 members each, including Fijian, 9,861, Tokelauan, 6,819, and Tuvaluan 2,625 (Statistics New Zealand, 2007).

Pasifika peoples were initially encouraged to migrate in the 1960s to fill labor shortages and were treated subsequently as a source of cheap and ready manual labor, working mostly in the unskilled manufacturing and service sectors (Macpherson, Spoonley, & Anae, 2001; see also Macpherson, 1996). However, these sectors were hardest hit in the economic decline of the 1980s and 1990s. As a result, Pasifika in New Zealand have been consistently overrepresented among the unemployed, lower-skilled workers, and low-income earners—that is, in the lowest socioeconomic and employment indices. The same pattern can be found in education. Despite high parental and student aspirations, Pasifika students fare consistently less well educationally than other New Zealand students in compulsory schooling

(Jones, 1991; Nash, 2000). There have been recent improvements in school and tertiary qualification levels for Pasifika students (Newell & Perry, 2006), albeit off a low base. However, Pasifika students remain disproportionately represented in the lowest English-literacy achievement levels as measured by international literacy assessments such as PISA (Marshall, Caygill, & May, 2008), a trend that continues into adulthood (New Zealand Ministry of Education, 2001).

The experiences of Pasifika peoples in New Zealand are thus not dissimilar to those of many low socioeconomic migrant groups elsewhere, particularly with respect to delimited employment and educational opportunities and, with respect to the latter, very little, if any, accommodation of their language varieties in the teaching and learning context. What is also similar is the long-standing construction of their relative lack of educational achievement in specifically deficit terms. For many years, the differential pattern of educational achievement was "explained" by educational policy makers and teachers via deficit constructions of Pasifika family or community backgrounds and/or by a subtractive view of their bilingualism (Kennedy & Dewar, 1997; Nakhid, 2003). It is only in recent years that there has been a shift in focus to acknowledge that the schooling that Pasifika students experience might be a key contributory factor to their educational underachievement (Coxon, Anae, Mara, Wendt-Samu, & Finau, 2002; May, 2005; May, Hill, & Tiakiwai, 2004). Even here though, this recognition has not as yet extended to rethinking the dominant model of monolingual English language provision, supplemented by limited ESL pullout support.

Be that as it may, in 2003, the New Zealand Ministry of Education, increasingly concerned by the apparent intractability of differential Pasifika educational achievement, commissioned a research team, led by the author,[10] to examine the teaching and learning experiences of bilingual Pasifika students in mainstream (English-medium) classrooms. The specific aim of the project was to develop a research-informed professional development resource for New Zealand teachers working in mainstream (English-medium) schools, focusing on enhancing their teaching practices with bilingual Pasifika students and, by extension, improving (bilingual Pasifika) student learning. The three-year funded project (2004–2006) resulted in the subsequent development of an interactive web-based resource, entitled LEAP (Language Enhancing the Achievement of Pasifika) (New Zealand Ministry of Education, 2007).

LEAP is interesting, and unusual, for two reasons. First, it *integrates* research on bilingualism, SLA, and TESOL in order to provide an additive approach to issues of SLA and TESOL in English-medium teaching and learning contexts. More recent conceptions of dynamic bilingualism and translanguaging were not directly addressed at the time of its development, although the principles underpinning them are implicitly endorsed in the resource's emphasis on the complexity of bilingualism and bilingual practices, as well as the notion that a bi/multilingual's linguistic repertoire is a fundamental source of, not an obstacle to, effective language teaching and learning. This approach is in direct contrast with most existing

SLA/TESOL courses that, even when they do incorporate discussion of bi/multilingual education, usually do so as a separate/discrete section. As has already been highlighted, these courses seldom, if ever, apply additive bilingual principles, let alone dynamic notions of bilingualism, to existing SLA/TESOL practices. LEAP attempts precisely that. In so doing, it is a still rare example internationally of a resource that addresses/redresses directly the long-standing criticism of the monolingual bias in SLA and TESOL.

Second, it is an equally rare example of an interactive web-based resource for teachers that is both explicitly research informed and directly accessible to teachers. The latter has been achieved by developing LEAP on the principles of activity theory (Leont'ev, 1981; Shulman, 1987) and by providing over 50 individual "inquiries" for teachers, working in *both* elementary *and* high school contexts, to explore issues pertinent to the teaching and learning experiences of bilingual (Pasifika) students. These inquiries include supporting material and related investigations that teachers can complete, either individually or collectively as part of a professional development group.

The teacher-based inquiries sit within five broad thematic sections. The first section explores the historical background of Pasifika in New Zealand, including a central focus on their language backgrounds, bilingualism, and related educational experiences. While necessarily contextual, the experiences of Pasifika peoples in New Zealand can also easily be extrapolated to other migrant/minority language communities in comparable positions. For example, a central concern of this section is to address/contest directly the wider politics of ethnicity and language, and related attitudes about bilingualism, that are apparent in English-dominant contexts such as New Zealand. Drawing directly on Jim Cummins's (2000) question as to why bilingualism is good for the rich but not for the poor, the section deconstructs the regular dichotomization of bilingualism in relation to the perceived status of the languages in question, with circumstantial bilingual speakers, predominantly migrants who speak a low status L1, perceived in overtly subtractive bilingual terms, while elective bilinguals who are learning so-called prestige languages are viewed in additive terms. More broadly, the often-unquestioned monolingual (English) language and education polices that follow from this distinction are explored and critiqued. Particular critical attention is given here to the unnecessary and erroneous presumptions that the maintenance of minority languages in English-dominant contexts is problematic and that the learning of English for those language speakers is (or should be) a zero-sum game.

The second section ("Being bilingual") extends this perspective by addressing directly the ongoing deficit misconceptions surrounding bilingualism, and bilingual learners, for speakers of minority languages—again, particularly apparent in (but not exclusive to) English-dominant contexts (Fishman, 1992; May, 2008). By this, the section also aims to extend the limited knowledge base of New Zealand's generalist (and predominantly English monolingual) teachers with respect to the relationship between bilingualism and learning. Again, while the focus is specifically on bilingual Pasifika students, many of the themes explored clearly pertain to other bi/multilingual learners as well. The construction of bilingualism as a complex language continuum, often shaped by the degree to which individual bilingual speakers are free/able to use their respective languages in the wider society and, if so, in what language domains, is specifically addressed. A key theme throughout this section is the importance of adopting an explicitly positive view of bilingual learners, and their multiple linguistic repertoires, as the basis for their long-term educational success. While the context remains focused on English-medium classrooms, principles and practices encouraging and/or incorporating L1 use, to the degree possible, are foregrounded for classroom teachers.

Section 3 ("What helps students to learn") examines the complex links between identity and learning, with particular attention given to how to foster positive student identities and actively recognize/incorporate the home (family and community) background of students in the teaching and learning process. Following from this, how to strengthen the home–school relationship is also explored. Section 4 ("Language and school") provides teachers with a wide range of SLA and TESOL principles and practices that (can) support language acquisition *and* use *within* an additive bilingual framework. The final section ("Supporting language development") explores the wider principles attendant upon language and literacy across the curriculum and the curricular- and wider-school change processes needed to implement such approaches effectively (May, 2007).

Throughout the LEAP resource, illustrative examples, including videos of actual classroom practices, are also provided. These examples of practice were often drawn from the few schools in New Zealand, outside the Maori-medium sector, that were already directly familiar with bilingual education processes. The New Zealand Ministry of Education, consonant with its wider lack of interest in providing bilingual education outside of Maori-medium education (May, 2005), was initially reticent about the inclusion of such examples (on the basis, one assumes, that this might "promote" bilingual education). However, the research team successfully argued that drawing on practice examples from existing bilingual schools made good pedagogical sense even though the LEAP resource was directed at English-medium contexts, since such schools were in the best position to demonstrate the educational advantages of bi/multilingualism for students.

Conclusion

LEAP thus provides a concrete exemplar of a major, research-informed, professional development resource that specifically incorporates an additive bilingual approach to the education of bilingual learners in English-medium contexts. It could also subsequently be modified/extended to provide a more dynamic conception of bilingualism in light of more recent theoretical developments in this area. But even what it has achieved to date has necessarily involved adopting a cross-disciplinary, or "regional" approach (á la Bernstein) to second language teaching and learning—a still rare occurrence, given the hermetic nature of disciplinary boundaries. As I have argued consistently in this chapter, only by this can the subtractive bilingual orientation that still so permeates SLA and TESOL—a result, in turn, of the ongoing dominance of linguistic–cognitive approaches to the discipline(s)—be effectively challenged, contested, and disrupted.

However, as I have also argued, this disciplinary construction of SLA and TESOL is itself located within a wider nexus of nationalism and nation-building that constructs societal monolingualism as the norm and on which monolingual educational (and wider public) policies are subsequently based. No wonder then that subtractive constructions of bilingualism are so hard to shift, particularly in relation to those communities of speakers, often migrants, whose language varieties, and the complex language practices attending their bi/multilingualism, are not accorded high status in the wider society. Nor should it surprise us that misconceptions about bi/multilingualism within education and the wider society for these (and other) bilingual learners remain so pervasive and apparently intractable—particularly in, but by no means limited to, English-dominant contexts.

And this highlights the wider, perhaps central, sociopolitical challenge attendant upon *any* promotion of bi/multilingualism as a core linguistic resource, whether in education or more broadly. This challenge is succinctly encapsulated in the following observation by Mary McGroarty (2006): "Advocates for positive language and education policies must constantly articulate the value of bilingualism, and . . . do so in varied terms that respond to a protean environment of public discussion" (McGroarty, 2006, pp. 5–6). LEAP attempts to do just that, providing a small window of opportunity for addressing and *redressing* the long-standing monolingual bias in SLA and TESOL. It may well be a small step forward, and more recent theoretical developments in the study of bi/multilingualism suggest that it needs to be revisited and revised on an ongoing basis. But it nonetheless remains an important example of how we might more seriously address the multifaceted nature of bi/multilingualism and its (positive) impact on teaching and learning. And, given just what is at stake for bi/multilingual learners, not before time.

Notes

An earlier version of this chapter was first published in *Linguistics and Education, 22*(3), 233–247, as *The Disciplinary Constraints of SLA and TESOL: Additive Bilingualism and Second Language Acquisition, Teaching and Learning.* I am grateful to Elsevier for permission to publish this revised and updated version here.

1. The notions of traditional and mainstream are in quotations marks for a reason, as will be explored in the following section on the construction of disciplines.
2. For other sociocultural critiques of SLA, see, for example, Block (2003); Cook (2002b); Firth and Wagner (1997); Lantolf (2000); Seeley and Carter (2004); and Seidlhofer (2003).
3. Although Jenkins (2006) notes that many of these sociocultural commentators still accept, at least at some level, the native speaker (NS) target of mainstream SLA researchers—particularly in their failure to address directly the increasing (legitimate) use of English as a lingua franca (ELF) rather than as a foreign language (EFL). Thus, while

rejecting the *necessity* of judging nonnative speakers (NNS) by NS speaker norms, as for example does Vivian Cook (2002a, 2002b), the distinction between NNS/NS still remains largely intact (see also, Canagarajah, this volume; Leung, this volume; Norton, this volume).

4. See, for example, Blackledge (2005); Blommaert (2005); Canagarajah (2005); Dewaele, Housen, and Li (2003); Freeland and Patrick (2004); Jenkins (2006, 2007); Makoni and Pennycook (2007); Pavlenko and Blackledge (2004).
5. See, for example, Block (2003); Corson (2000); Heller (1999); Kubota and Lin (2006); Norton (1997, 2000); Rampton (1995). See also Norton, this volume.
6. See, for example, Block and Cameron (2008); Blommaert (2010); Holborow (1999); Macedo, Dendrinos, and Gounari (2003); May (2012); Pennycook (1994, 1998, 2010); Phillipson (1992, 2010).
7. See, for example, Corson (1993, 1998, 2000); Cummins (1996, 2000, 2003).
8. In arguably his most influential publication, *Distinction*, Bourdieu (1984) specifically asserts that practices can be reduced to neither habitus nor field but rather develop from their "interrelationship." He summarizes this as follows: "[(habitus) (capital) + field = practice" (Bourdieu, 1984, p. 101).
9. See, for example, among others: Giroux (1983); Jenkins (2003). For critiques of this persistent misreading of Bourdieu, see Albright and Luke (2008); Calhoun, LiPuma, and Postone (1993); Grenfell (2011); Harker and May (1993); Swartz (1997).
10. The other core members of the research team were Margaret Franken and Johanne McComish.

References

Albright, J. (2008). Problematics and generative possibilities. In J. Albright and A. Luke (Eds.), *Pierre Bourdieu and literacy education* (pp. 11–32). New York, NY: Routledge.

Albright, J., & Luke, A. (Eds.). (2008). *Pierre Bourdieu and literacy education*. New York, NY: Routledge.

Auer, P. (1984). *Bilingual conversation*. Amsterdam, The Netherlands: John Benjamins.

Auer, P. (2007). The monolingual bias in bilingualism research, or: Why bilingual talk is (still) a challenge for linguistics. In M. Heller (Ed.), *Bilingualism: A social approach* (pp. 320–339). London, UK: Palgrave.

Bardovi-Harlig, K., & Dörnyei, Z. (Eds.). (2006). Themes in SLA research. *AILA Review, 19*.

Bauman, R., & Briggs, C. (2003). *Voices of modernity: Language ideologies and the politics of inequality*. Cambridge, UK: Cambridge University Press.

Becher, T., & Trowler, P. (2001). *Academic tribes and territories: Intellectual enquiry and the culture of disciplines* (2nd ed.). Philadelphia, PA: Open University Press.

Beebe, L. (1980). Sociolinguistic variation and styleshifting in second language acquisition. *Language Learning, 30*(2), 433–447.

Bernstein, B. (1990). *The structuring of pedagogic discourse, Vol. 4: Class, codes and control*. London, UK: Routledge.

Bernstein, B. (2000). *Pedagogy, symbolic control and identity: Theory, research, critique*. Lanham, MA: Rowman & Littlefield.

Blackledge, A. (2005). *Discourse and power in a multilingual world*. Amsterdam, The Netherlands: John Benjamins.

Bley-Vroman, R. (1983). The comparative fallacy in interlanguage studies: The case of systematicity. *Language Learning, 33*(1), 1–17.

Block, D. (1996). Not so fast: Some thoughts on theory culling, relativism, accepted findings and the heart and soul of SLA. *Applied Linguistics, 17*(1), 63–83.

Block, D. (2003). *The social turn in second language acquisition.* Edinburgh, UK: Edinburgh University Press.

Block, D., & Cameron, D. (Eds.) (2008). *Globalization and language teaching.* New York, NY: Routledge.

Blommaert, J. (2005). Situating language rights: English and Swahili in Tanzania revisited. *Journal of Sociolinguistics, 9*(3), 390–417.

Blommaert, J. (2010). *The sociolinguistics of globalization.* New York, NY: Cambridge University Press.

Bloomfield, L. (1933). *Language.* New York, NY: Holt, Rinehart, & Winston.

Bourdieu, P. (1982). *Ce que parler veut dire: L'économie des échanges linguistiques.* Paris, France: Arthème Fayard.

Bourdieu, P. (1984). *Distinction: A social critique of the judgement of taste.* Cambridge, MA: Harvard University Press.

Bourdieu, P. (1990). *The logic of practice.* Cambridge, UK: Polity Press.

Bourdieu, P. (1991). *Language and symbolic power.* Trans. G. Raymond & M. Adamson. Cambridge, UK: Polity Press.

Bourdieu, P., & Wacquant, L. (1992). *An invitation to reflexive sociology.* Chicago, IL: University of Chicago Press.

Calhoun, C., LiPuma, E., & Postone, M. (Eds.). (1993). *Bourdieu: Critical perspectives.* Cambridge, UK: Polity Press.

Canagarajah, A. S. (2005). Dilemmas in planning English/vernacular relations in post-colonial communities. *Journal of Sociolinguistics, 9*(3), 418–447.

Canagarajah, A. S. (2006). TESOL at forty: What are the issues? *TESOL Quarterly, 40*(1), 9–34.

Chomsky, N. (1972). *Language and the mind.* New York, NY: Harcourt Brace Jovanovich.

Collins, J. (2008). Postscript. In J. Albright & A. Luke (Eds.), *Pierre Bourdieu and literacy education* (pp. 363–373). New York, NY: Routledge.

Cook, V. (1999). Going beyond the native speaker in language teaching. *TESOL Quarterly, 33*(2), 185–209.

Cook, V. (2002a). Background to the L2 user. In V. Cook (Ed.), *Portraits of the L2 user* (pp. 1–28). Clevedon, UK: Multilingual Matters.

Cook, V. (Ed.). (2002b). *Portraits of the L2 user.* Clevedon, UK: Multilingual Matters.

Cook, V. (2008). Multi-competence: Black hole or wormhole for second language acquisition research? In Z. Han (Ed.), *Understanding second language process* (pp. 16–26). Clevedon, UK: Multilingual Matters.

Corson, D. (1993). *Language, minority education and gender: Linking social justice and power.* Clevedon, UK: Multilingual Matters.

Corson, D. (1998). *Changing education for diversity.* Buckingham, UK: Open University Press.

Corson, D. (2000). *Language, diversity and education.* Mahwah, NJ: Lawrence Erlbaum.

Coxon, E., Anae, M., Mara, D., Wendt-Samu, T., & Finau, C. (2002). *Literature review on Pacific education issues: Final report.* Wellington, NZ: New Zealand Ministry of Education. Retrieved from http://www.educationcounts.govt.nz/publications/pasifika_education/27772/8

Cummins, J. (1976). The influence of bilingualism on cognitive growth: A synthesis of research findings and explanatory hypotheses. *Working Papers on Bilingualism, 9*, 1–43.

Cummins, J. (1977). Cognitive factors associated with the attainment of intermediate levels of bilingual skills. *The Modern Language Journal, 61*(1), 3–12.

Cummins, J. (1979). Linguistic interdependence and the educational development of bilingual children. *Review of Educational Research, 49*(2), 222–259.

Cummins, J. (1996). *Negotiating identities: Education for empowerment in a diverse society.* Toronto, UK: California Association for Bilingual Education.

Cummins, J. (2000). *Language, power and pedagogy: Bilingual children in the crossfire.* Clevedon, UK: Multilingual Matters.

Cummins, J. (2003). Bilingual education. In J. Bourne & E. Reid (Eds.), *Language education: World yearbook of education* (pp. 3–19). London, UK: Evans Bros.

De Saussure, F. (1974). *Course in general linguistics.* (W. Baskin, Trans.). London, UK: Fontana.

Dewaele, J.-M., Housen, A., & Li, W. (Eds.). (2003). *Bilingualism: Beyond basic principles.* Clevedon, UK: Multilingual Matters.

Ellis, E. (2008). Defining and investigating monolingualism. *Sociolinguistic Studies, 2*(3), 311–330.

Firth, A., & Wagner, J. (1997). On discourse, communication and (some) fundamental concepts in SLA research. *The Modern Language Journal, 81,* 285–300.

Fishman, J. (1992). The displaced anxieties of Anglo-Americans. In J. Crawford (Ed.), *Language loyalties: A source book on the Official English controversy* (pp. 165–170). Chicago, IL: University of Chicago Press.

Franken, M., & McComish, J. (2003). *Improving English language outcomes for students receiving ESOL services in New Zealand schools.* Wellington, NZ: New Zealand Ministry of Education.

Freeland, J., & Patrick, D. (2004). *Language rights and language "survival": A sociolinguistic exploration.* Manchester, UK: St Jerome Publishing.

García, O. (2009). *Bilingual education in the 21st century: A global perspective.* Malden, MA: Blackwell/Wiley.

Gardner, R., & Wagner, J. (2004). *Second language conversations.* London, UK: Continuum.

Gass, S. (1998). Apples or oranges: Or, why apples are not oranges and don't need to be. A response to Firth and Wagner. *The Modern Language Journal, 82*(1), 83–90.

Giroux, H. (1983). Theories of reproduction and resistance in the new sociology of education. *Harvard Educational Review, 53,* 257–293.

Grenfell, M. (2011). *Bourdieu, language and linguistics.* London, UK: Continuum.

Han, Z., & Selinker, L. (2005). Fossilization in L2 learners. In E. Hinkel (Ed.), *Handbook of research in second language teaching and learning.* Mahwah, NJ: Lawrence Erlbaum.

Harker, R., & May, S. (1993). Code and habitus: Comparing the accounts of Bernstein and Bourdieu. *British Journal of Sociology of Education, 14*(2), 169–178.

Heller, M. (1999). *Linguistic minorities and modernity: A sociolinguistic ethnography.* New York, NY: Longman.

Heller, M. (2008). Bourdieu and literacy education. In J. Albright & A. Luke (Eds.), *Pierre Bourdieu and literacy education* (pp. 50–67). New York, NY: Routledge.

Holborow, M. (1999). *The politics of English: A Marxist view of language.* London, UK: Sage.

Jenkins, J. (2006). Points of view and blind spots: ELF and SLA. *International Journal of Applied Linguistics, 16*(2), 137–162.

Jenkins, J. (2007). *English as a lingua franca: Attitude and identity.* Oxford, UK: Oxford University Press.

Jenkins, R. (2003). *Pierre Bourdieu* (2nd ed.). London, UK: Routledge.

Jones, A. (1991). *"At school I've got a chance". Culture/privilege: Pacific Islands and Pakeha girls at school.* Palmerston North, NZ: Dunmore Press.

Kachru, Y. (1994). Monolingual bias in SLA research. *TESOL Quarterly, 28*(4), 795–800.

Kennedy, S., & Dewar, S. (1997). *Non-English speaking background students: A study of programmes and support in New Zealand schools.* Wellington, NZ New Zealand Ministry of Education.

Kubota, R., & Lin, A. (Eds.). (2006). Race and TESOL [Special issue]. *TESOL Quarterly*, *40*(3).

Lantolf, J. (Ed.). (2000). *Sociocultural theory and second language learning*. Oxford, UK: Oxford University Press.

Leont'ev, A. N. (1981). The problem of activity in Soviet psychology. In J. V. Wertsch (Ed.), *The concept of activity in Soviet psychology* (pp. 37–71). Armonk, NY: Sharpe.

Leung, C. (2005). Convivial communication: Recontextualizing communicative competence. *International Journal of Applied Linguistics*, *15*(2), 119–144.

Leung, C. (2007). Integrating school-aged ESL learners into the mainstream curriculum. In J. Cummins & C. Davison (Eds.), *International handbook of English language teaching* (Vol. 15, Part 1, Section 2, pp. 249–269). New York, NY: Springer.

Leung, C., Harris, R., & Rampton, B. (1997). The idealized native speaker, reified ethnicities, and classroom realities. *TESOL Quarterly*, *31*(3), 543–560.

Lightbown, P., & Spada, N. (2006). *How languages are learned* (3rd ed.). Oxford, UK: Oxford University Press.

Littlewood, W. (2004). Second language learning. In A. Davies & C. Elder (Eds.), *The handbook of applied linguistics* (pp. 501–524). Oxford, UK: Blackwell.

Long, M. (1997). Construct validity in SLA research: A response to Firth and Wagner. *The Modern Language Journal*, *81*(3), 318–323.

Long, M., & Doughty, C. (2003). SLA and cognitive science. In C. Doughty & M. Long (Eds.), *The handbook of second language acquisition* (pp. 866–870). Oxford, UK: Wiley Blackwell.

Macedo, D., Dendrinos, B., & Gounari, P. (2003). *The hegemony of English*. Boulder, CO: Paradigm Publishers.

Macpherson, C. (1996). Pacific Islands identity and community. In P. Spoonley, C. Macpherson, & D. Pearson (Eds.), *Nga Patai: Racism and ethnic relations in Aotearoa/New Zealand* (pp. 124–143). Palmerston North, NZ: Dunmore Press.

Macpherson, C., Spoonley, P., & Anae, M. (2001). *Tangata o te moana nui: The evolving identities of Pacific Peoples in Aotearoa/New Zealand*. Palmerston North, NZ: Dunmore Press.

Makoni, S., & Pennycook, A. (Eds.). (2007). *Disinventing and reconstituting languages*. Clevedon, UK: Multilingual Matters.

Marshall, N., Caygill, R., & May, S. (2008). *PISA 2006 reading literacy*. Wellington, UK: New Zealand Ministry of Education.

May, S. (2002). In tribute to David Corson. *Journal of Language, Identity and Education*, *1*(1), 8–11.

May S. (2004). Medium of instruction policy in New Zealand. In J. Tollefson & A. Tsui (Eds.), *Medium of instruction policies: Which agenda? Whose agenda?* (pp. 21–41). Mahwah, NJ: Lawrence Erlbaum Associates.

May, S. (2005). Aotearoa/New Zealand: Addressing the context. *International Journal of Bilingual Education and Bilingualism*, *8*(5), 365–376.

May, S. (2007). Sustaining effective literacy practices over time in secondary schools: School organisational and change issues. *Language and Education*, *21*(5), 387–405.

May, S. (2008). Bilingual/immersion education: What the research tells us. In J. Cummins & N. Hornberger (Eds.), *Encyclopedia of language and education, 2nd ed., Vol. 5: Bilingual Education* (pp. 19–34). New York, UK: Springer.

May, S. (2011). Bourdieu and language policy. In M. Grenfell (Ed.), *Bourdieu: Language and linguistics*. London, UK: Continuum.

May. S. (2012). *Language and minority rights: Ethnicity, nationalism and the politics of language* (2nd ed.). New York, NY: Routledge.

May, S., Hill, R., & Tiakiwai, S. (2004). *Bilingual/immersion education: Indicators of good practice.* Wellington, NZ: New Zealand Ministry of Education.

May, S. & Sleeter, C. (Eds.). (2010). *Critical multiculturalism: Theory and praxis.* New York, NY: Routledge.

McGroarty, M. (2006). Neoliberal collusion or strategic simultaneity? On multiple rationales for language-in-education policies. *Language Policy, 5,* 3–13.

Mey, J. (1985). *Whose language? A study in linguistic pragmatics.* Amsterdam, The Netherlands: John Benjamins.

Mitchell, R., & Myles, F. (2004). *Second language learning theories* (2nd ed.). London, UK: Arnold.

Mühlhäusler, P. (1996). *Linguistic ecology: Language change and linguistic imperialism in the Pacific region.* London, UK: Routledge.

Nakhid, C. (2003). Comparing Pasifika students' perceptions of their schooling with the perception of non-Pasifika teachers using the "mediated dialogue" as a research methodology. *New Zealand Journal of Educational Studies, 38,* 207–226.

Nash, R. (2000). Educational inequality: The special case of Pacific students. *Social Policy Journal of New Zealand, 15,* 69–86.

New Zealand Ministry of Education. (2001). *More than words.* Wellington, NZ: New Zealand Ministry of Education.

New Zealand Ministry of Education. (2007). *Language enhancing the achievement of Pasifika* (LEAP). Retrieved from http://leap.tki.org.nz

Newell, J., & Perry, M. (2006). *Trends in the contribution of tertiary education to the accumulation of educational capital in New Zealand: 1981 to 2001* (Report prepared for the Ministry of Education). Wellington, NZ: Monitoring and Evaluation Research Associates Ltd.

Norton, B. (1997). Language, identity, and the ownership of English. *TESOL Quarterly, 31*(3), 409–429.

Norton, B. (2000). *Identity and language learning: Gender, ethnicity and educational change.* London, UK: Longman.

Ortega, L. (2009). *Understanding second language acquisition.* London, UK: Hodder Arnold.

Ortega, L. (2010, March). *The bilingual turn in SLA.* Plenary delivered at the Annual Conference of the American Association for Applied Linguistics (AAAL), Atlanta, GA.

Pavlenko, A., & Blackledge, A. (Eds.). (2004). *Negotiation of identities in multilingual contexts.* Clevedon, UK: Multilingual Matters.

Pennycook, A. (1994). *The cultural politics of English as an international language.* London, UK: Longman.

Pennycook, A. (1998). *English and the discourses of colonialism.* London, UK: Routledge.

Pennycook, A. (1999). Introduction: Critical approaches to TESOL. *TESOL Quarterly, 33*(3), 329–348.

Pennycook, A. (2010). *Language as a local practice.* New York, NY: Routledge.

Phillipson, R. (1992). *Linguistic imperialism.* Oxford, UK: Oxford University Press.

Phillipson, R. (2010). *Linguistic imperialism continued.* New York, NY: Routledge.

Rampton, B. (1987). Stylistic variability and not speaking "normal" English: some post-Labovian approaches and their implications for the study of interlanguage. In R. Ellis (Ed.), *Second language acquisition in context* (pp. 47–58). New York, NY: Prentice Hall.

Rampton, B. (1990). Displacing the native speaker. *ELT Journal, 44*(2), 97–101.

Rampton, B. (1995). *Crossing: Language and ethnicity among adolescents.* London, UK: Longman.

Rothman, J. (2008). Linguistic epistemology and the notion of monolingualism. *Sociolinguistic Studies, 2*(3), 441–457.

Seeley, A., & Carter, B. (2004). *Applied linguistics as social science.* London, UK: Continuum.

Seidlhofer, B. (Ed.). (2003). *Controversies in applied linguistics.* Oxford, UK: Oxford University Press.

Shulman, L. S. (1987). Knowledge and teaching: Foundations of the new reform. *Harvard Educational Review, 57*(1), 1–22.

Sridhar, S. (1994). A reality check for SLA theories. *TESOL Quarterly, 28*(4), 800–805.

Statistics New Zealand. (2007). *Pacific profiles 2006.* Retrieved from http://www.stats.govt.nz/Census/about-2006-census/pacific-profiles-2006/samoan-people-in-new-zealand.aspx

Swartz, D. (1997). *Culture and power: The sociology of Pierre Bourdieu.* Chicago, IL: University of Chicago Press.

Tarone, E. (1988). *Variation in interlanguage.* London, UK: Edward Arnold.

Thompson, J. (1991). Editor's introduction. In P. Bourdieu, *Language and symbolic power* (pp. 1–31). Cambridge, UK: Polity Press.

Vološinov, V. (1973). *Marxism and the philosophy of language.* Trans. L. Matejka & I. R. Titunik. Cambridge, MA: Harvard University Press (Reprinted from *Marksizm i filosofija jazyka: Osnovnye problemy sociologičeskogo metoda v nauke o jazyke*, 1929, Leningrad, Soviet Union: Priboj).

Zuengler, J., & Miller, E. R. (2006). Cognitive and sociocultural perspectives: Two parallel SLA worlds? *TESOL Quarterly, 40*(1), 35–58.

2

WAYS FORWARD FOR A BI/ MULTILINGUAL TURN IN SLA

Lourdes Ortega

Extensive critiques have mounted for over two decades now against the monolingual bias that pervades most areas of applied linguistics (see May, this volume). The bias results from the assumption that monolingualism is the default for human communication and from valuing nativeness as a superior form of language competence and the most legitimate relationship between a language and its users. These critiques are poignant in unmasking deeply negative consequences for research and praxis. Serious validity and ethical problems arise in monolingually biased research on language learning and teaching (e.g., Holliday & Aboshiha, 2009; Rampton, 1990; Seidlhofer, 2001; Shohamy, 2006), and damaging deficit approaches become unwittingly entrenched in many practices found in classrooms and schools (e.g., Cenoz & Gorter, 2011; Cummins, 2007; Edge, 2010; García, 2009; Gogolin, 1994; Higgins, Nettell, Furukawa, & Sakoda, 2012; Mantero & Herpe, 2007; Phillipson & Skutnabb-Kangas, 1986; Valdés & Figueroa, 1994). The problem has also been extensively denounced and theorized from the perspectives of critical applied linguistics, critical language policy and planning, and critical sociolinguistics (e.g., Blackledge, 2005; Clyne, 2008; Liddicoat & Crichton, 2008; Makoni & Pennycook, 2007; May, 2011). In many of these critiques, the field of second language acquisition (SLA) has been targeted explicitly as suffering in its very core, and in particularly acute ways, from the ailments that result from taking nativeness and monolingualism as natural organizing principles for the study of additional-language learning (e.g., Jenkins, 2006; Sridhar, 1994). Voices from inside SLA have not been silent on the issue either, and, in particular, scholars associated with the social turn in SLA (Block, 2003) have identified and condemned many conceptual, methodological, and ethical problems that ensue from the monolingual outlook of much ongoing SLA work (e.g., Firth & Wagner, 1997; Hall, Cheng, & Carlson, 2006; Kramsch, 2010).

How useful or necessary is it to abandon nativeness and monolingualism as organizing principles for the study of additional-language learning? I find the criticisms convincing and devastating. I concur that the monolingual bias has become unsustainable for the field of SLA, as for any other field that aspires to understand multiple-language learning as an object of inquiry and to support bi/multilingualism as a societal and individual right and asset. A bi/multilingual turn is urgently needed to replace SLA's existing research goal of explaining why late bi/multilinguals are not native speakers (by which monolinguals is often meant) with the goal of understanding the process and consequences of becoming bilingual or multilingual later in life (Ortega, 2010). This bi/multilingual turn demands an epistemic reorientation through concerted collective disciplinary action. For disciplinary changes to ensue, however, viable alternatives must be offered to replace predominant monolingual theories, constructs, and research practices. The challenge is particularly great within work in SLA that is motivated by psycholinguistic interests and seeks to investigate linguistic and cognitive dimensions of additional-language learning, or what I call linguistic–cognitive SLA, for short in this chapter. The reason is that many of the existing key constructs (e.g., interlanguage, fossilization, target-likeness and native-likeness, ultimate attainment) implicitly or explicitly assume nativeness and monolingualism as organizing principles for the study of additional-language learning. What are, then, useful entry points for linguistic–cognitive SLA researchers to break away from the straitjacket of the monolingual bias, other than completely abandoning this kind of research?

In this chapter I attempt to address this question from my insider vantage point as a member of the linguistic–cognitive SLA communities I critically examine. In doing so, I am keen to heed the additive and interdisciplinary ethos proposed by May (this volume) as a needed stance to productively confront and solve the monolingual bias problem across applied linguistic fields. I first spell out the ideological roots of the monolingual bias in linguistic–cognitive SLA work, noting some of the serious validity and ethical problems that ensue when late bilingualism is investigated as the psycholinguistic process of developing monolingual competence a second time around later in life. I then call attention to the potential of a strategic theoretical commitment to usage-based linguistics (UBL) (e.g., Bybee, 2010; Tomasello, 2003) as a deliberate move designed to support ways out of the monolingual bias and forward for a bi/multilingual turn in SLA. My hope is to promote critical thinking from within linguistic–cognitive SLA and eventually to fuel actual efforts to reconfigure the field's goals, away from explaining why bilinguals are not native speakers (i.e., monolinguals) and towards understanding the cognitive, linguistic, and psycholinguistic mechanisms and consequences of becoming bi/multilingual later in life.

The Problem in Need of a Solution: The Ideological Roots of the Monolingual Bias in SLA

Historically, linguistic–cognitive SLA researchers have not proceeded without keen, if intermittent, awareness of the threats involved in the taken-for-granted adoption of a monolingual and native-speaker normative research lens. At least three well-known critiques exist. One is the warning by Bley-Vroman (1983) against the comparative fallacy, or the deeply problematic practice of taking the idealized competence of native speakers as the golden benchmark for investigating linguistic development in an additional language. The second one is the accusation by Klein (1998) that a prevalent target deviation perspective thwarts the field's potential for having broad impact on other disciplines that study language ontogeny. The third critique, and the most encompassing and well-articulated one, is Vivian Cook's (1992, 2002, 2003) proposal of multicompetence, which squarely addressed the need for a holistic bi/multilingual prism when investigating late language learning, while also loudly and clearly denouncing the deficit approach dominant in SLA. Other well-known contributors to the debate over the critical period hypothesis in linguistic–cognitive SLA have also argued that the practice of taking monolingual native speakers as benchmarks against which to evaluate and interpret learning success lacks validity (Birdsong, 2005; Singleton, 2003). Despite these critiques, however, no fundamental corresponding change has been seen at the level of theory or research practices. It is fair to say that the majority of contemporary SLA research, and most particularly linguistic–cognitive SLA research, continues to be motivated by a construal of the disciplinary object of inquiry as "efforts by monolingual adults to add on a monolingual-like command of an additional language" (Ortega, 2009, p. 5).

One cannot but wonder why the compelling arguments by such influential SLA insiders have been so ineffective in transforming the field. Disciplinary change is always slow, of course (cf. May, this volume). While it may be the case that more time is needed for the kind of reconfiguration of the field needed to overcome the monolingual bias, I believe one reason for the lack of impact of critical perspectives is the unwillingness or inability of SLA research communities to understand the ideological roots of the monolingual bias. Language ideologies or beliefs and feelings about language(s) and discourse(s) (Blommaert, 1999; Kroskrity, 2004) are not just the purview of laypeople holding folk views of language or of dominant classes recruiting language for the promotion of self-interests. Research communities are also liable to language ideologies, as has been shown, for example, of descriptive linguistics work (Irvine & Gal, 2000; Kroskrity, 2004). In order for researchers in any field of language study to take action and redress the monolingual bias and its attendant problems, a number of implicitly held assumptions that are taken to be natural facts in dominant language ideologies must be first recognized and then unlearned.

I argue that the monolingual bias in SLA rests on a number of implicitly held beliefs about the nature of language, monolingualism, bilingualism, and nativeness (Ortega, 2010). The terms *native speaker* and *nonnative speaker* offer a useful point of entry into understanding how language ideologies work in disciplinary knowledge. These labels are used in linguistic–cognitive SLA published research as if their meanings were objective and neutral, denoting two natural categories of language users. A closer examination of the overt and implied meanings reveals a different picture.

In SLA research, the term native speaker is used to denote a language user who not only has had exposure to the language by birth—as the overt meaning of *native* would indicate—but who also has had a monolingual upbringing. It is by virtue of from-birth exposure to, and primary socialization into, only one language that the archetypical native speaker is imagined to possess a superior kind of linguistic competence, one whose purity proves itself in the absence of detectable traces of any other languages during (natural or elicited) language use. Standing as a counterpart is the term nonnative speaker, defined as a language user who has developed (or is developing) functional ability in more than one language but not from birth. A nonnative speaker is imagined as possessing (or striving to possess) a derivative and approximate kind of linguistic competence, one that betrays itself in detectable traces of other languages during (natural or elicited) language use. In short, the archetype construct of native speaker stands for a monolingual native speaker (i.e., a language user who has developed functional ability in one language only and from birth), and the archetype construct of nonnative speaker stands for a late bi/multilingual speaker (i.e., a language user who has developed, or is developing, functional ability in more than one language, not from birth but later in life). What remains outside awareness in the regular usage of these two terms by SLA researchers, however, is the fact that the two labels and their meanings undergo a process of *synecdoche* (where a part stands for the whole). Namely, the number of languages issue (monolingual, bi/multilingual) dissipates from the overt labels and their explicit meanings, and all that remains for overt recognition is the timing issue, that is, language exposure from birth (native) or later in life (nonnative). The process of synecdoche in the native/nonnative speaker labels therefore supports *erasure* (Gal & Irvine, 1995; Irvine & Gal, 2000) of the number of languages issue from these two central constructs of SLA research, with at least three important consequences.

First, by making it unnecessary to even express overtly the adjective monolingual in the native speaker label, monolingualism is taken as the implicit norm. That is, learning to function in one language only is understood as the default for the human capacity for language, against which the learning of how to function in two or more languages must be examined and understood. The comparison, therefore, is not equal but *subordinating,* because it positions bi/multilingualism as a less natural form of knowing, doing, and learning language than monolingualism. The subordinating comparison is harmful from an ethical standpoint, because it casts a deficit light on people who learn an additional language later in life. In addition, it threatens the validity of the knowledge generated under such a premise, given that much research in cognitive science and the psycholinguistics of bi/multilingualism has shown that the human brain and mind are prepared to handle more than one language from the outset (De Houwer, 2009; Werker & Byers-Heinlein, 2008).

A second consequence of the erasure relates to the fact that the bilingual or multilingual competence that otherwise is a necessary part of the meaning of

nonnative speaker, once removed from the overt labels, is forgotten. SLA researchers are then free to imagine the nonnative speaking participants in their studies as
budding monolinguals for the second time around, and their bi/multilingualism
can be excluded from study designs. More generally, then, the reality of bi/mul-
tilingualism is made invisible and thus made irrelevant to the goals of disciplinary
inquiry. As with the first consequence of the erasure, this second consequence has
implications for both the validity and the ethics of the SLA knowledge generated under such a premise. Namely, bi/multilingual competence is investigated as
monolingual (a validity non sequitur), and the bi/multilingual participants that
inhabit SLA studies, once reconstrued into aspiring monolinguals of the new
language, must be characterized by deficit by being less than a full language user
(an ethical liability).

Finally, a third consequence of erasure is that linguistic ownership by birth is
elevated to an inalienable right and advantage. That is, because nativeness is the
only overtly expressed meaning in the native and nonnative speaker labels, the
issue of birth is reinforced, making space for an ideology of language birthrights
that construes ownership by birth as the most legitimate relationship between a
language and its language users and envisions a monolingual upbringing as leading to a superior form of linguistic competence. A nested belief is that languages
themselves are discrete entities or fixed systems, a kind of real, bounded knowledge out there that is internalized and owned by speakers as a result of (either
from birth or late) learning. Language exposure from birth and primary language
socialization is seen to confer the linguistic right of legitimate ownership of a
language and the advantage of possessing the "purest" form of (monolingual)
linguistic competence, one that cannot be altered by later experiences in life.
Conversely, the ideology of linguistic birthrights also makes any form of language ownership and linguistic competence that may be developed later in life
inevitably less legitimate and less pure. The third consequence of erasure, then,
exacerbates the ethical problem of a deficit construction of nonnativeness.

The importance of the three consequences of the erasure of the issue of number of languages just identified—monolingualism is taken as the implicit norm,
the reality of bi/multilingualism is made invisible, and linguistic ownership by
birth and monolingual upbringing is elevated to an inalienable right and advantage—cannot be overstated. As I have just argued, they work interconnectedly to
spawn serious validity and ethical problems in SLA. Validity is compromised at
the broadest disciplinary level of abstraction by a misrecognition (Irvine & Gal,
2000, following Bourdieu, 1977) of the object of study in SLA as the development
of monolingual-like competence in a new language. Thus, the very goals of the
discipline are led astray by the monolingual bias, and a subtractive bilingualism
approach is uncritically embraced by SLA researchers (cf. May, this volume)—one
that clashes with the best intentions of the field to investigate and support multiple-language learning throughout the life span. Misguided by the monolingual
bias are also the questions that drive linguistic–cognitive research programs. Much

of this SLA research to date has been concerned with the question of whether adult SLA (i.e., the learning of a new additional language later in life) is the same as child first-language acquisition (i.e., the learning of a first single language from birth). Once the logic of synecdoche is undone, however, an alternative reading of this question becomes available: Is monolingual development by infants similar to, or different from, bilingual development by adults? This amounts to asking a paradoxical question that is impossible to answer, since monolingual and bilingual competences are surely different in many ways. The validity of even posing the question crumbles. Damaging ethical challenges also stand in need of redress. When an impossible idealized native speaker competence is elevated to benchmark and arbiter of learning, the monolingual speaker norm not only frames and clouds data and interpretations (a validity threat), but it casts a deficit light on the people doing the learning (an ethical challenge) who are permanently defined and characterized by their second-rate ownership of the new language, their less pure form of linguistic competence (i.e., one that betrays their bi/multilingualism), and their forever lesser rather than perfect monolingual ability (Keck & Ortega, 2011).

It is by complex ideological processes such as those sketched above, I am convinced, that the monolingual bias ultimately holds sway and blinds linguistic–cognitive SLA communities to the fact that understanding how bi/multilingualism comes about later in life must be the goal of the inquiry in SLA. An epistemic reorientation is thus needed through a bi/multilingual turn that steers the field away from the existing disciplinary goal of explaining why bilinguals are not native speakers (i.e., monolinguals) and replaces it with the goal of understanding the psycholinguistic mechanisms and consequences of becoming bilingual or multilingual later in life.

Ways Out, Ways Forward

For collective disciplinary action to break away from the monolingual bias, however, viable alternatives must be offered to replace the prevalent monolingual theories, constructs, and research practices. Socioculturally oriented SLA researchers argue that the new SLA theories brought about by what Block (2003) called the social turn are particularly well suited for the task of deconstructing and rejecting the monolingual bias in the field (e.g., Hall et al., 2006). The present volume, too, offers an additional critical SLA perspective by Block (this volume). He suggests leveraging the semiotic prism of embodied and multimodal resources of language in order to overcome the narrow focus on language that has always characterized SLA's preoccupations—to go well beyond "the lingual," as he calls it. I share the view that socially oriented theories in SLA have helped make the field epistemologically more pluralistic, and this is undoubtedly a positive development (Ortega, 2005, 2011, 2012). Many of the new social insights can be exploited to deconstruct the monolingual bias and to open up SLA research to a more bi/multilingual outlook. I also agree that broad insights into language learning beyond the lingual are crucial for a satisfactory understanding of the phenomena at stake.

But shouldn't any field strive to enable plural research programs that engage with inquiry at multiple levels of breadth and granularity, letting some programs pursue analytical, and other programs global, insights? What of SLA researchers who choose to focus not on social dimensions but on linguistic, cognitive, and psycholinguistic dimensions of additional-language learning, specifically focusing on investigating linguistic development? Should this kind of research be completely abandoned? May pessimistically notes that "the ongoing dominance of psycholinguistics in framing core disciplinary knowledge actively delimits the possibilities of developing an additive bilingual approach, although it does not foreclose it" (May, 2011, p. 233). Are there ways forward to be carved out by these SLA communities? A psycholinguistic orientation to research need not be inherently marred by the monolingual bias. In fact, no choice of ontology, epistemology, or method makes any scientific community immune from counterproductive ideologies that may need to be revised (Ortega, 2005, 2012). A sobering, well-known example is the field of bilingualism, which up until the 1970s was plagued with deficit views of its own object of study in sociolinguistic as much as psycholinguistic work. In those early years, for instance, code-switching was routinely associated by researchers with imperfect knowledge and linguistic impurity (Woolard, 2004). By contrast, contemporary research on bi/multilingualism has been able to drive out deficit views, and this has been done without abandoning psycholinguistic interests (e.g., Bialystok, 2009; Cruz-Ferreira, 2010; De Houwer, 2009; Gathercole, 2010; Kroll & De Groot, 2005). What then are viable entry points for linguistic–cognitive SLA researchers to break away from the straitjacket of the monolingual bias?

One of the ways forward is to commit to a theory that can be found to be a good fit for linguistic–cognitive SLA—because it is congruent epistemologically with the goals of understanding the linguistic, cognitive, and psycholinguistic dimensions of additional-language learning—yet places demands on knowledge generation that are ontologically and methodologically helpful in the task of breaking the ideological siege of the monolingual bias. Choice of theory can have deep consequences for the transformational possibilities of any epistemic reorientation such as that demanded by the bi/multilingual turn. Theories are blueprints that structure the formulation of large-picture questions, such as: How much of the language capacity is given by birth and fixed for the rest of life and how much is shaped or altered by experience and life history? What is language, anyway? How can its ontogeny be explained? Theories also shape the hypothesis space for potential disciplinary answers. I believe UBL offers a fruitful theoretical platform for the needed epistemic reorientation. The main reason is that it furnishes theoretical arguments for opposing many of the nested ideological presuppositions underpinning the monolingual bias in SLA by positing human sociality and need for communication on the one hand and the experience of language use in context on the other, as joint forces responsible for the emergence of language, phylogenetically, and ontogenetically. What I am proposing, then, is a deliberate strategic theoretical commitment to UBL as a helpful move that supports a desirable bi/multilingual turn for linguistic–cognitive SLA research communities.

Usage-Based Linguistics in a Nutshell

At this juncture, some general background on UBL may be useful for readers unfamiliar with it. UBL encompasses not one but many theories, and as such it is best viewed as a family of diverse interrelated approaches. These have been developed to explain grammar and language change (Bybee, 2010) and also to investigate language ontogeny as instantiated in monolingual first-language acquisition (Ambridge & Lieven, 2011; MacWhinney, 1998; Tomasello, 2003) as well as, more recently, bilingual first-language acquisition (e.g., Paradis, Nicoladis, Crago, & Genesee, 2011). UBL is thus a well-defined option for the study of language development outlined in the work just cited. At the same time, it stands alongside other functional proposals that also embrace the main tenet that language is driven by experience and thus fits the descriptor "usage-based." Such other germane, but not equivalent, proposals include cognitive linguistics (Croft, 2010; Goldberg, 2006; Langacker, 2009), emergent grammar theory (Hopper, 2007), and language emergentism and connectionism (Elman et al., 1996). UBL has also already begun to generate linguistic–cognitive SLA work (e.g., Collins & Ellis, 2009; Ellis, 2011a, 2011b; Eskildsen, 2012; Robinson & Ellis, 2008). Likewise, germane but not identical to UBL instantiations within SLA are other functional proposals about additional-language learning, including complexity theory (Larsen-Freeman, 2012), dynamic systems theory (Verspoor, de Bot, & Lowie, 2011), cognitive linguistics for SLA (Tyler, 2012), and systemic-functional linguistics for SLA (Byrnes, 2009). On their part, SLA proponents of sociocultural Vygotskian theory (e.g., Lantolf & Thorne, 2006; Swain, Kinnear, & Steinman, 2010) and conversation analysis for SLA (e.g., Kasper, 2009) would probably be sympathetic towards some usage-based elements embodied in UBL but would argue for the natural theoretical integrity of each of these epistemological lines. Nevertheless, there are also SLA cases of successfully venturing into theoretical hybridity (e.g., Eskildsen's, 2012, combination of UBL and conversation analysis).

Several important tenets characterize UBL. Grammar is an emergent property of human communication, with each language user's experience shaping language over the full life span. Language knowledge emerges from the myriad actual usage events experienced in actual local communication activity by language users. This is true of all language users, regardless of their birth status or the state or shape of their given functional competence; any individual and social act of use of language unavoidably becomes part of what transpires and emerges as *language*. Because the life history of language-usage events is different for each user, knowledge of (and performance of) language is also different across individuals. Language is inseparable from the users and the usage events that bring it about; it is an emergent phenomenon and thus a process rather than an object. Central theoretical constructs that inform UBL's ontology of language include the centrality of meaning, the continuity between lexis and grammar, and embodied cognition.[1] UBL theories of language ontogeny define learning by invoking additional constructs such as input frequency, the emergence of construction inventories, schematization by analogy, and complexity and dynamic systems learning driven by variability.[2]

In terms of its place among other available theories of language and language acquisition, UBL is often pitted against nativist and generative explanations of language learning.[3] Chomsky (2011) has recently termed UBL "the nonexistence approach," in contrast to his own "biolinguistic perspective," which views internal individual grammars as having an autonomous existence, "a normal biological system, a module of the mind/body" (Chomsky, 2011, p. 269); and knowledge of language as a genetic endowment that predates experience. Chomsky's appellation of UBL is no doubt intended to be pejorative, in disapproval of UBL's emergent and distributed view of language as a process. Of course, not just UBL researchers but also many other functional linguists and most sociolinguists would be perfectly content with the idea that language is an emergent process, not something that exists autonomously. Indeed, what is objectified and takes a life of its own is linguists' abstraction of language, as captured in linguistic descriptions, grammars, and dictionaries, and which then is co-opted for other sociopolitical and economic purposes (cf. Blackledge, Creese, & Takhi, this volume; May, this volume).

There are at least three ways in which UBL can provide linguistic–cognitive SLA researchers with a much needed theoretical apparatus and impetus to carve at least some ways out from the monolingual bias. In the final sections of this chapter, I outline each in turn.

Shifting the Explanatory Burden from Birth to History and Experience

The first way in which a theoretical commitment to UBL can support a bi/multilingual turn in linguistic–cognitive SLA is general and pertains to UBL's predisposition to accord experience and history the lion's share in explanations for the ontogeny of language. As mentioned, UBL posits that grammar is not an "out there" system but an emergent property of human communication and, furthermore, that actual language experience shapes language over the full life span (Bybee, 2010). For this reason, a theoretically congruent working hypothesis is that linguistic development is driven by changes in lived experience. This hypothesis has been pursued in a number of research programs, where differential experience among adult native users of a given language (usually, but not always, English) has been found to covary robustly and importantly with differences in: (a) working memory capacity that modulates their ability to comprehend difficult relative clauses (Wells,

Christiansen, Race, Acheson, & MacDonald, 2009); (b) ability to judge the grammaticality of passives and quantifiers (Street & Dąbrowska, 2010); (c) observed brain activity while processing language (Abutalebi, 2008; Ansari, 2012); and (d) growth of brain white matter (Carreiras et al., 2009). The differences in experience investigated across these studies have involved rather mundane facts, such as differential levels of schooling and formal education, as well as differential familiarity with print and formal genres and registers, often stemming from people's occupations and jobs. Less often, experiential changes have been investigated that stem from potentially life-changing new learning during adulthood, such as the development of literacy at age 20 or later, investigated by Carreiras et al. (2009), and even the formal study of a new language in the evidence reviewed by Abutalebi (2008). Most important to appreciate, however, is that the choice of UBL as theory, rather than some other motivation, propels the investment of empirical efforts into the elucidation of the roles played by experience in driving change and learning, banning the a priori assumption that people are uniform when it comes to language competencies by virtue of their nativeness—or, for that matter, that variability is an inherent and exclusive characteristic of nonnativeness.

The general theoretical predisposition of UBL just discussed can help SLA research communities envision the possibility of studying the relevant phenomena without relying on assumed fixed consequences of nativeness and nonnativeness and hardwired modules or biologically based critical periods need not be prioritized in empirical research programs. This can vigorously energize empirical action by linguistic–cognitive SLA researchers willing to systematically work against the ideology of linguistic birthrights and their fixity. A good example is Muñoz and Singleton's recent call for a reorientation of SLA research on age effects. These researchers have warned that "factors other than maturational should be brought more to the fore and treated more seriously" and that "to focus exclusively on maturation impoverishes and distorts discussion of the relevant issues" (Muñoz and Singleton, 2011, p. 25). They have further argued that explaining additional-language learning success as a function of age is mistaken because age is a proxy for experience. Consequently, they recommend prioritizing alternative explanations for the observed age effects, including linguistic, environmental, and extralinguistic variables and de-emphasizing age as an explanatory variable. UBL can provide sound theoretical guidance for the principled investigation of Muñoz and Singleton's claims precisely because it shifts the explanatory burden and the empirical focus from birth to history and experience.

Focusing on the Link between Language Input Affordances and Learning Success

The second way in which UBL can offer cognitive–linguistic SLA researchers fruitful ways out from the monolingual bias relates to the first one. Namely, among the many variables that can be investigated when experience is investigated, UBL researchers who focus on the ontogeny of language (MacWhinney, 1998; Tomasello, 2003) have prioritized the study of the linguistic environment, understood as the language input—the term preferred in UBL studies of bilingual and monolingual child-language acquisition—afforded in actual usage events between parents or caretakers and children. Valuable lessons can be drawn from the history of ideas that have led to the making of language input into the most important dimension of experience to be investigated in UBL child-language acquisition.

It was, in the first instance, the theoretical tenet of nativism that motivated Chomskyan generative researchers of first-language acquisition to argue that the linguistic environment surrounding the child provided evidence that was clearly insufficient to allow the induction of a grammar. In other words, in order to be able to locate knowledge of language in the mind of the child prior to any experience, the input available to the child had to be emptied from any useful language evidence. With no usable linguistic information from the input, and a resulting grammar knowledge that was said to be complete and uniform for all healthy children by year four or so of life, the only logical alternative conclusion left was an innate endowment for language. This motivated the introduction of the new construct of the poverty of the stimulus in the mid-1980s as a cornerstone of the theory (Thomas, 2002).

By the same token, when UBL researchers opposed nativism, they understood the need to empty the child's mind from any endowed knowledge and instead imbue the input back with acquisition-rich information (e.g., Behrens, 2009; Tomasello, 2003). A first key empirical task, therefore, was to demonstrate that children start off with limited linguistic competence and show hardly any prior knowledge, instead evincing a conservative approach to learning that is formulaic and piecemeal or item based. The second central empirical task was to demonstrate that the input contained rich evidentiary potential for the child to induce knowledge of language from the bottom up. Interestingly, bilingual first-language acquisition researchers have been particularly successful in establishing the link between language input affordances and bi/multilingual development. It is now accepted that the frequency and quality of actual usage patterns of the languages in the environment surrounding a bi/multilingual child predict much of the individual variation seen in the eventual relative competencies attained in her or his two (or three) languages (De Houwer, 2011; Quay, 2011). When actual levels of exposure to the child are low for one of the languages, learning may slow down because he or she will need a longer period of time in order to recruit and benefit from relevant and sufficient experience for that language; if exposure becomes minimal, development in that language may stall. These observations hold true even when comparing bi/multilinguals whose chronological age and overall months or years of use of those languages are kept constant. Moreover, the empirical link between input and development is found, not only in terms of word learning, but also with regard to grammatical development (Hoff et al., 2012), and it remains effective and consequential for the maintenance of the minority language in the bi/multilingual into adulthood (Gathercole & Thomas, 2009).

What value might there be in heeding UBL's insight that empirical investigation of the language input is of paramount importance? For one, it is clear that, when evaluating people's success or failure with language learning, SLA researchers may have underestimated the importance and precise nature of the link between affordances realized in the linguistic environment for a given learner and his or her development in the additional language. For, if such a robust relationship between *learning opportunity*—defined as sufficient and relevant language input affordances for use—and *learning success*—defined as similarly satisfactory linguistic development in all of a bilingual's languages—has been found for the learning of a single language, as well as two or more languages, from birth, why would the linguistic environment not be expected to also profoundly affect additional-language learning? If we heed UBL insights, the research burden when explaining success or failure in additional-language learning should be on demonstrating that learners have indeed had sufficient opportunity to learn, that is, that they have enjoyed linguistic affordances for usage that are reasonably sufficient in frequency, intensity, and quality to expect linguistic development in the specific areas under investigation. Under the UBL perspective, language development—whether early or later in life, whether bi/multilingual or monolingual, whether by a so-called native speaking or nonnative speaking user—is piecemeal learning, and no construction (the UBL equivalent for words and rules in formal grammars) can be learned unless sufficient exposure conditions are met (Tomasello, 2000). For any given piece of the available and possible sociolinguistic inventories of a language to be learned, a critical mass of relevant linguistic data in the person's surroundings must be experienced by the particular learner. This being so, the learning opportunities afforded in people's (learners') surrounding linguistic environment must be carefully documented and taken into account in SLA.

The imprecise nature of current operationalizations of language input exposure has been observed in SLA by others, a notable example being Flege (2009). But SLA's current idealization of learning environments into undocumented or imprecise variables (e.g., length of residence, second vs. foreign language context, and so on) becomes a formidable validity problem from the UBL perspective, given that, in theoretical terms, it is learner-contingent soundscapes and textscapes that feed into bottom-up processes of item-based learning. Thus, it would be necessary to document afforded actual usage events for each additional-language user under study via recordings and analyses of learner-directed language. Some of this work has already begun, undertaken by UBL-oriented linguistic–cognitive SLA researchers. For example, Collins, Trofimovich, White, and Horst (2009) found that teacher talk to the ESL (English as a second language) students they investigated contained low numbers of tokens of his/her determiners and regular past tense -ed verbs (only 150, 79, and 150 instances, respectively, in 110,000 words). This is precisely what would be predicted of these late-acquired structures by

UBL. However, the UBL tenet that language development is input driven and piecemeal has not yet been fully recruited for epistemic reorientation away from the monolingual bias and forward into a bi/multilingually oriented SLA. Instead, currently, all too often we simply see SLA researchers engaging in proclamations of success or failure for nonnativeness wholesale.

In the future, the full pursuit of this second theoretical UBL insight would open up two new framings for the SLA field. One framing, analogous to the framings that led to the poverty of the stimulus construct in generative theory and to the richness of the input empirical focus in UBL, is to propose that investigations of SLA must account for additional-language learning in the face of likely environmental duress involving conditions of restricted input affordances. This is supported by accumulating evidence that, in many contexts—even those that would seem to make ample exposure opportunities available to learners—additional-language users may have only limited access to meaningful opportunities for use, for a number of reasons both within their agentive choice and beyond their control (Jia & Aaronson, 2003; Kinginger, 2004; Morita, 2004; Muñoz, 2011; Norton Peirce, 1995; Toohey, 2001). The other available framing is to argue for the unique value of the study of late bilingualism, precisely for the window it offers into language learning that happens in the context of likely environmental duress and limited linguistic affordances. The linguistic environment is in itself a major area of interest in UBL theorizing and in the study of language ontogeny from a UBL perspective, and SLA knowledge about it might yield a unique nuanced light on the workings and limits of this variable in explaining linguistic development.

Analyzing Linguistic Development as Self-Referenced, Nonteleological, Unfinished

A third and final benefit of committing to UBL in linguistic–cognitive SLA investigations I would like to note has methodological–analytical value but is of no lesser importance than the other two already discussed. UBL provides conceptual and analytical tools for studying linguistic development in a self-referencing manner, freed from subordinating comparisons to targets and ideal speakers. The reason is that mapping construction-specific inventories of linguistic resources is the goal in UBL. In other words, for UBL-acquisition researchers, the interest is in investigating coexisting degrees of formulaicity and schematicity, rather than on cataloguing target-likeness and nontarget-likeness over time. More specifically, UBL looks for degrees of language schematization in the form–function units that language users are able to handle at all levels of language, from holophrases to pivot schemata (i.e., very low-scope preconstructions with just two internal parts), to item-based construction (e.g., lexical-specific islands), to most abstract constructions (Tomasello, 2003). There is, of course, a potential danger of falling back on teleologism if one were to posit that acquisition should proceed towards the most schematized or abstract end of the graded continuum as an end goal.

This danger is fully preempted by UBL's maximalism (Behrens, 2009), which holds that the inventories of constructions emerging from usage events remain widely redundant. Namely, item-specific and highly abstract encodings for the same form–meaning units will always coexist. Even when fully analyzed schemata arise from sufficient experience, fully frozen equivalents will not be pruned.

Some UBL-oriented SLA researchers, notably Larsen-Freeman (2005) and Eskildsen (2012), have already begun to articulate the theoretical insight that linguistic development, including the development of additional-language grammars, is dynamically emergent, nonteleological, and unfinished. Eskildsen, for example, shows how the language production of additional-language users can be analyzed in terms of type-token frequency, item-specific learning evinced in high-token plus low-type frequency, or schematic learning evinced in low-token plus high-type frequency, in the process dispensing with any reference to native speakers or even mature grammars. And if acquisition starts from very little prior knowledge and is piecemeal, then everything an additional-language user "can do" counts as equally worthy data—whether memorized or productive, native-like or nonnativelike, norm-conforming or nonnormative (Eskildsen & Cadierno, 2007). Eskildsen (2012) points out another equally important UBL recognition: If piecemeal acquisition is shaped by actual usage events, then all patterns in the data can have their individual usage-driven acquisitional trajectories, and variability, not conformity, is what can be expected of linguistic development, in additional languages as in first languages. If usage events can at any time affect the trajectories of individual patterns and constructions, then any given form–function mapping (i.e., formulaic and/or schematized) remains open to influence and change from use. As Larsen-Freeman (2005) put it prominently in her felicitous title, "there is no end and there is no state"—and fossilization turns into an impossible construct.

Specific analytical solutions are needed to offer ways to escape the long-honored practice of measuring and interpreting evidence against (monolingual) native-speaker competencies. The analytical tools of constructionist UBL (Tomasello, 2003) confer no small benefit to SLA researchers. They can help generate better insights into developmental explanations as well as ameliorate the deficit construction of nonnativeness. Instead of benchmarking "target" and "success" against monolingual nativeness, with the help of the UBL lens, SLA researchers might investigate self-referenced development by mapping specificity and schematicity within and across constructions over time. Instead of looking for linguistic conformity or end states, they can fully expect and capture linguistic variability and openness in additional-language learning.

Caveats and Conclusion

I began this chapter by examining the ideological roots of the monolingual bias in linguistic–cognitive SLA work, arguing that serious validity and ethical problems ensue when late bilingualism is investigated as the psycholinguistic process of developing monolingual competence a second time around in life. And I have suggested that a strategic theoretical commitment to UBL is a helpful move that can support the epistemic reorientation needed to critically re-envision the object of study and the goals of inquiry for the field, away from explaining why bilinguals are not native speakers (i.e., monolinguals) and towards understanding the psycholinguistic mechanisms and consequences of becoming bi/multilingual later in life. Before concluding, I should also voice some doubts and caveats.

The bleak picture I have painted to explain linguistic–cognitive SLA thinking about nativeness and monolingualism, I admit, may be too hermetic and idealized to be a fair or full representation of how language ideologies work. I hasten to acknowledge that "ideological systems are often neither homogeneous nor very coherent" (Hill, 2008, p. 91), and that there is always "multiplicity and contention in language ideological processes" (Kroskrity, 2004, p. 497). All of this means that we can always expect complex amalgams of apparently opposing ideologies about language within the same community (Philips, 2004), including SLA research communities. Ideological heterogeneity and multiplicity are indeed prevalent for such contested notions as monolingualism, bilingualism, and nativeness. For example, language educators as well as linguists have engaged in processes of romanticization of bi/multilingualism and demonization of monolingualism (Ellis, 2008). Nativeness, likewise, has often been a positive tool for what Spivak (1993) has called strategic essentialism, for instance, in the notion that a language without native speakers is a dead language. This metaphor was used in the 15th century to support the emancipation of Romance languages from Latin (Thomas, 2004). It is also widely used in contemporary times for the validation of indigenous and heritage language revitalization and education efforts (e.g., Anderson, 2011). A subtle form of reverse affirmative action, I believe, can explain the ideological tension found in the wide endorsement by scholars of bi/multilingualism of parental monolingual discourse practices (e.g., prioritizing the minority language into the language of choice in the bilingual home or socializing children into low levels of code-switching). This puzzling endorsement, I have come to recognize, comes from a felt need to protect the minority language of bi/multilinguals. It is well known that the minority language tends to lose out to the majority language, at least in the monolingually oriented societies typically investigated (Gathercole & Thomas, 2009). Ideological complexities notwithstanding, I remain convinced that the problem of the monolingual bias in SLA can be characterized as the nested consequences of multiple-language ideological processes. It is the work of these ideologies that give rise to the problem of construing the learning of additional languages later in life as efforts by monolingual adults to add on a monolingual-like command of a new language in an imagined world where what's given/owned by birth can never be matched or altered by experience or history.

In addition, I would be remiss if I did not mention some areas of uncertainty where the ability of UBL to support a bi/multilingual turn can be questioned and must receive further reflection and evaluation. One pending question is how UBL might support a fully bi/multilingual outlook on SLA research when, in fact, much of the acquisition work done within this orientation concerns itself with monolingual child acquisition and can thus likewise be charged with taking monolingualism as the default of the human capacity for language and communication. One answer may be for linguistic–cognitive SLA research communities to turn to UBL researchers who study child bi/multilingualism (e.g., Blom, Paradis, & Sorenson-Duncan, 2012; Gathercole, 2010; Paradis et al., 2011). These researchers, although currently in the UBL minority, may organize into a burgeoning community in the near future. Deliberately seeking interdisciplinary alliances with them, as May (this volume) argues, may serve well the cause of the bi/multilingual turn in SLA. A second doubt is whether the UBL view of language input has enough content to support a project of epistemic reorientation in SLA, particularly given its inevitable associations with the traditional computer metaphor of input–interaction–output that has been criticized by socially oriented SLA researchers such as Block (2003) and Firth and Wagner (1997). It might be that, as Block (this volume) cautions regarding recent SLA research on gesture with usage-based leanings, the SLA lens of UBL remains anchored in the lingual and does not go (or at least has not yet gone) far enough in the exploration of embodiment and multimodality and their broad consequences for language learning.

On the positive side, I note that the UBL insight about the language input is qualitatively different from, although certainly not unrelated to, the SLA computer metaphor. Namely, UBL predicts that the entire set of actual linguistic affordances experienced by a particular language user at any given time constitutes that person's opportunities for learning the language, also at any given time; that is, in UBL, learning is input driven but also always material, particular, emergent, and unfinished. A good case in point is the fully theoretically congruent integration of UBL and conversation analysis achieved by Eskildsen (2012). More important is asking whether the role accorded to the linguistic input in UBL theory might be too limited for useful transposition into SLA research programs, given that, to my knowledge, when it comes to research practices, UBL restricts itself to linguistic–quantitative accounts of the linguistic environment to the exclusion of agency, identity, and power, three constructs that demand qualitative–social investigative tools. In SLA, by contrast, it is well known that agency, identity, and power are paramount in understanding the link between opportunities for actual language use (in UBL's sense) and successful linguistic development, in both adult and child additional-language learning (e.g., Norton Peirce, 1995; Toohey, 2001). This is indeed a major pending question, and one that suggests the theoretical commitment to UBL can be only one among several needed ways to move forward for a bi/multilingual turn in SLA.

Related to this caveat are other questions for the future of UBL in SLA, which the editor of the present volume submitted to me in review (Stephen May, personal communication, November 8, 2012) and which, in turn, I would like to submit to readers: Will linguistic–cognitive SLA researchers, even if working within UBL programs, be able to relinquish the traditional view of languages as discrete, pure, self-enclosed linguistic systems attached to meanings that are nation- and culture-bound? And will SLA researchers into languages other than English be convinced by the bi/multilingual turn—that is, will they be willing to renounce to ideas of linguistic birth rights and purity or might they estimate that this move is appropriate only for research on English, as the global hybrid language par excellence but not for other languages that may be considered nation- and culture-bound? While still unanswered, these are important questions to ask as some sectors of the SLA field commit to UBL in the hope that it will serve as an emancipatory theory that supports the bi/multilingual turn.

All research communities, including SLA and linguistic–cognitive SLA communities, need to guard against the monolingual bias. The outlook of much scientific knowledge production about human language and its learning suffers from the monolingual bias because the learning and use of only one language is taken to be the most natural default for human communication by subordinating comparison to which the use of multiple languages can be understood, often as a derivative complication. Nativeness and monolingualism must be abandoned as organizing principles for the study of additional-language learning and replaced by bi/multilingual constructs, methods, and goals. The strategic commitment to UBL opens up a suitable theoretical platform from which to support this task of epistemic reorientation. Ultimately, it is by recognizing the ideological roots of the monolingual bias and by searching for viable theoretical alternatives to it that the relevant SLA research communities can begin the task of translating the insights obtained from the mounting critiques against the monolingual bias into a transformative bi/multilingual turn. Changes in ideologies go hand in hand with changes in the modus operandi by which disciplinary knowledge is generated. Both will be needed to support a re-envisioning of the object of study and the goals of inquiry for linguistic–cognitive SLA work, away from explaining why bi/multilinguals are not native speakers (i.e., monolinguals) and towards understanding the psycholinguistic mechanisms and consequences of becoming bi/multilingual later in life.

Notes

I thank Stephen May for inviting me to present an earlier version of this chapter in a colloquium at the American Association for Applied Linguistics Conference in Boston in 2012, and to him, my fellow colloquium presenters, and the audience for useful comments. I would also like to acknowledge with deep gratitude the Freiburg Institute of Advanced Studies (FRIAS) at the University of Freiburg for support to develop my thinking on this topic through a senior research fellowship in fall 2010, and especially to Peter Auer, Benedikt Szmrecsanyi, and Bernd Kortmann for their collegiality and relevant discussions during my FRIAS stay.

1. Interestingly, the last of these three UB principles, embodiment, is a core distinguishing tenet of cognitive linguistics, as Tyler (2010) notes. And the importance afforded to embodiment makes UBL appropriate in principle for the broadening of SLA research beyond the "lingual" that Block, this volume, calls for.
2. Accessible overviews of main theoretical UBL tenets as they apply to language acquisition can be found in Behrens (2009); Diessel (2007); Ellis (2011a, 2011b); and Zyzik (2009).
3. For example, in monolingual first-language acquisition, see the UBL-friendly comparative treatment by Ambridge and Lieven (2011), and in SLA, see the useful comparison by Zyzik (2009).

References

Abutalebi, J. (2008). Neural processing of second language representation and control. *Acta Psychologica, 128*, 466–478.

Ambridge, B., & Lieven, E. (2011). *Child language acquisition: Contrasting theoretical approaches.* Cambridge, UK: Cambridge University Press.

Anderson, G. D. S. (2011). Language hotspots: What (applied) linguistics and education should do about language endangerment in the twenty-first century. *Language and Education, 25*, 273–289.

Ansari, D. (2012). Culture and education: New frontiers in brain plasticity. *Trends in Cognitive Science, 16*, 93–95.

Behrens, H. (2009). Usage-based and emergentist approaches to language acquisition. *Linguistics, 47*, 383–411.

Bialystok, E. (2009). Bilingualism: The good, the bad, and the indifferent. *Bilingualism: Language and Cognition, 12*, 3–11.

Birdsong, D. P. (2005). Nativelikeness and non-nativelikeness in L2A research. *International Review of Applied Linguistics, 43*, 319–328.

Blackledge, A. J. (2005). *Discourse and power in a multilingual world.* Amsterdam, The Netherlands: John Benjamin.

Bley-Vroman, R. (1983). The comparative fallacy in interlanguage studies: The case of systematicity. *Language Learning, 33*, 1–17.

Block, D. (2003). *The social turn in second language acquisition.* Washington, DC: Georgetown University Press.

Blom, E., Paradis, J., & Sorenson-Duncan, T. (2012). Effects of input properties, vocabulary size and L1 on the development of third person singular −s in child L2 English. *Language Learning, 62*(3), 965–994.

Blommaert, J. (Ed.). (1999). *Language ideological debates.* Berlin, Germany: Mouton de Gruyter.

Bourdieu, P. (1977). *Outline of a theory of practice.* Cambridge, UK: Cambridge University Press.

Bybee, J. L. (2010). *Language, usage and cognition.* Cambridge, UK: Cambridge University Press.

Byrnes, H. (Ed.). (2009). Instructed foreign language acquisition as meaning-making: A systemic-functional approach [Special issue]. *Linguistics and Education, 20*(1), 1–79.

Carreiras, M., Seghier, M. L., Baquero, S., Estévez, A., Lozano, A., Devlin, J. T., & Price, C. J. (2009). An anatomical signature for literacy. *Nature, 461*(7266), 983–986.

Cenoz, J., & Gorter, D. (Eds.). (2011). Toward a multilingual approach in the study of multilingualism in school contexts [Special issue]. *The Modern Language Journal, 95*, 339–478.

Chomsky, N. (2011). Language and other cognitive systems. What is special about language? *Language Learning and Development, 7*, 263–278.

Clyne, M. (2008). The monolingual mindset as an impediment to the development of plurilingual potential in Australia. *Sociolinguistic Studies, 2*, 347–366.

Collins, L., & Ellis, N. C. (Eds.). (2009). Input and second language construction learning: Frequency, form, and function [Special issue]. *The Modern Language Journal, 93*, 329–429.

Collins, L., Trofimovich, P., White, J., & Horst, M. (2009). Some input on the easy/difficult grammar question: An empirical study. *The Modern Language Journal, 93*, 336–353.

Cook, V. (1992). Evidence for multicompetence. *Language Learning, 42*, 557–591.

Cook, V. (Ed.). (2002). *Portraits of the L2 user.* Clevedon, UK: Multilingual Matters.

Cook, V. (Ed.). (2003). *Effects of the second language on the first.* Clevedon, UK: Multilingual Matters.

Croft, W. (2010). The origins of grammaticalization in the verbalization of experience. *Linguistics, 48*, 1–48.

Cruz-Ferreira, M. (Ed.). (2010). *Multilingual norms.* Frankfurt, Germany: Peter Lang.

Cummins, J. (2007). Rethinking monolingual instructional strategies in multilingual classrooms. *Canadian Journal of Applied Linguistics, 10*, 221–241.

De Houwer, A. (2009). *Bilingual first language acquisition.* Bristol, UK: Multilingual Matters.

De Houwer, A. (2011). Language input environments and language development in bilingual acquisition. *Applied Linguistics Review, 2*, 221–240.

Diessel, H. (2007). Frequency effects in language acquisition, language use, and diachronic change. *New Ideas in Psychology, 25*, 108–127.

Edge, J. (2010). Elaborating the monolingual deficit. In D. Nunan & J. Choi (Eds.), *Language and culture: Reflective narratives and the emergence of identity* (pp. 89–96). London, UK: Routledge.

Ellis, E. M. (2008). Monolingualism. *Sociolinguistic Studies, 2*, 311–330.

Ellis, N. C. (2011a). The emergence of language as a complex adaptive system. In J. Simpson (Ed.), *Handbook of applied linguistics* (pp. 666–679). London, UK: Routledge.

Ellis, N. C. (2011b). Frequency-based accounts of SLA. In S. M. Gass & A. Mackey (Eds.), *Handbook of second language acquisition* (pp. 193–210). London, UK: Routledge.

Elman, J. L., Bates, E. A., Johnsons, M. H., Karmiloff-Smith, A., Parisi, D., & Plunkett, K. (1996). *Rethinking innateness: A connectionist perspective on development.* Cambridge, MA: The MIT Press, Bradford Books.

Eskildsen, S. (2012). L2 negation constructions at work. *Language Learning, 62*, 335–372. doi:10.1111/j.1467–9922.2012.00698.x

Eskildsen, S. W., & Cadierno, T. (2007). Are recurring multi-word expressions really syntactic freezes? Second language acquisition from the perspective of usage-based linguistics. In M. Nenonen & S. Niemi (Eds.), *Collocations and idioms 1: Papers from the First Nordic Conference on Syntactic Freezes, Joensuu, May 19–20, 2007* (pp. 86–99). Joensuu, Finland: Joensuu University Press.

Firth, A., & Wagner, J. (1997). On discourse, communication, and (some) fundamental concepts in SLA research. *The Modern Language Journal, 81*, 285–300.

Flege, J. E. (2009). Give input a chance! In T. Piske & M. Young-Scholten (Eds.), *Input matters in SLA* (pp. 175–190). Clevedon, UK: Multilingual Matters.

Gal, S., & Irvine, J. T. (1995). The boundaries of languages and disciplines: How ideologies construct difference. *Social Research, 62*, 966–1001.

García, O. (2009). *Bilingual education in the 21st century: A global perspective.* Malden, MA: Wiley-Blackwell.

Gathercole, V. C. M. (2010). Interactive influences in bilingual processing and development. *International Journal of Bilingual Education and Bilingualism, 13*, 481–485.

Gathercole, V. C. M., & Thomas, E. M. (2009). Bilingual first language development: Dominant language takeover, threatened minority language take-up. *Bilingualism: Language and Cognition, 12*, 213–237.

Gogolin, I. (1994). *Der monolinguale Habitus der multilingualen Schule*. Münster, Germany / New York, NY: Waxmann Verlag.

Goldberg, A. E. (2006). *Constructions at work: The nature of argument structure generalizations*. New York, NY: Oxford University Press.

Hall, J. K., Cheng, A., & Carlson, M. T. (2006). Reconceptualizing multicompetence as a theory of language knowledge. *Applied Linguistics*, *27*, 220–240.

Higgins, C., Nettell, R., Furukawa, G., & Sakoda, K. (2012). Beyond contrastive analysis and codeswitching: Student documentary filmmaking as a challenge to linguicism in Hawai'i. *Linguistics and Education*, *23*, 49–61.

Hill, J. H. (2008). *The everyday language of white racism*. Malden, MA: Wiley-Blackwell.

Hoff, E., Core, C., Place, S., Rumiche, R., Señor, M., & Parra, M. (2012). Dual language exposure and early bilingual development. *Journal of Child Language*, *39*, 1–27. doi:10.1017/S0305000910000759

Holliday, A., & Aboshiha, P. (2009). The denial of ideology in perceptions of 'nonnative speaker' teachers. *TESOL Quarterly*, *43*, 669–689.

Hopper, P. J. (2007). Linguistics and micro-rhetoric: A twenty-first century encounter. *Journal of English Linguistics*, *35*, 236–252. doi:10.1177/0075424207305307

Irvine, J. T., & Gal, S. (2000). Language ideology and linguistic differentiation. In P. Kroskrity (Ed.), *Regimes of language: Ideologies, polities, and identities* (pp. 35–84). Santa Fe, NM: School of American Research Press.

Jenkins, J. (2006). Points of view and blind spots: ELF and SLA. *International Journal of Applied Linguistics*, *16*, 137–162.

Jia, G., & Aaronson, D. (2003). A longitudinal study of Chinese children and adolescents learning English in the United States. *Applied Psycholinguistics*, *24*, 131–161.

Kasper, G. (2009). Locating cognition in second language interaction and learning: Inside the skull or in public view? *International Review of Applied Linguistics*, *47*, 11–36.

Keck, C., & Ortega, L. (2011, March). *An empirical appraisal of the construction of nonnativeness as deficit in applied linguistic discourses*. Paper presented at the American Association for Applied Linguistics Conference, Chicago, IL.

Kinginger, C. (2004). Alice doesn't live here anymore: Foreign language learning and identity reconstruction. In A. Pavlenko & A. Blackledge (Eds.), *Negotiation of identities in multilingual contexts* (pp. 219–242). Clevedon, UK: Multilingual Matters.

Klein, W. (1998). The contribution of second language acquisition research. *Language Learning*, *48*, 527–550.

Kramsch, C. (2010). *The multilingual subject*. Oxford, UK: Oxford University Press.

Kroll, J., & De Groot, A. M. B. (Eds.). (2005). *Handbook of bilingualism: Psycholinguistic approaches*. New York, NY: Oxford University Press.

Kroskrity, P. V. (2004). Language ideologies. In A. Duranti (Ed.), *A companion to linguistic anthropology* (pp. 496–517). Malden, MA: Blackwell.

Langacker, R. (2009). A dynamic view of usage and language acquisition. *Cognitive Linguistics*, *20*, 267–640.

Lantolf, J. P., & Thorne, S. L. (2006). *Sociocultural theory and the genesis of second language development*. New York, NY: Oxford University Press.

Larsen-Freeman, D. (2005). Second language acquisition and fossilization: There is no end, and there is no state. In Z.-H. Han & T. Odlin (Eds.), *Studies of fossilization in second language acquisition* (pp. 189–200). Clevedon, UK: Multilingual Matters.

Larsen-Freeman, D. (2012). Complex, dynamic systems: A new transdisciplinary theme for applied linguistics? *Language Teaching*, *45*, 202–214. doi:10.1017/S0261444811000061

Liddicoat, A. J., & Crichton, J. (2008). The monolingual framing of international education in Australia. *Sociolinguistic Studies*, *2*, 367–384.

MacWhinney, B. (Ed.). (1998). *The emergence of language.* Hillsdale, NJ: Lawrence Erlbaum.

Makoni, S., & Pennycook, A. (Eds.). (2007). *Disinventing and reconstituting languages.* Clevedon, UK: Multilingual Matters.

Mantero, M., & Herpe, E. (2007). The three languages and one voice of a multilingual child: Educational implications for monolingual bias in the United States. *Radical Pedagogy, 9*(1), 33–43.

May, S. (2011). The disciplinary constraints of SLA and TESOL: Additive bilingualism and second language acquisition, teaching and learning. *Linguistics and Education, 22*(3), 233–247.

Morita, N. (2004). Negotiating participation and identity in second language academic communities. *TESOL Quarterly, 38*, 573–603.

Muñoz, C. (2011). Input and long-term effects of starting age in foreign language learning. *International Review of Applied Linguistics, 49*, 113–133. doi:10.1515/iral.2011.006

Muñoz, C., & Singleton, D. (2011). A critical review of age-related research on L2 ultimate attainment. *Language Teaching, 44*, 1–35. doi:10.1017/S0261444810000327

Norton Peirce, B. (1995). Social identity, investment, and language learning. *TESOL Quarterly, 29*, 9–31.

Ortega, L. (2005). For what and for whom is our research? The ethical as transformative lens in instructed SLA. *The Modern Language Journal, 89*, 427–443.

Ortega, L. (2009). *Understanding second language acquisition.* London, UK: Hodder.

Ortega, L. (2010, March). *The bilingual turn in SLA.* Plenary speech delivered at the American Association for Applied Linguistics Conference, Atlanta, GA.

Ortega, L. (2011). SLA after the social turn: Where cognitivism and its alternatives stand. In D. Atkinson (Ed.), *Alternative approaches in second language acquisition* (pp. 167–180). New York, NY: Routledge.

Ortega, L. (2012). Epistemological diversity and moral ends of research in instructed SLA. *Language Teaching Research, 16*, 206–226.

Paradis, J., Nicoladis, E., Crago, M., & Genesee, F. (2011). Bilingual children's acquisition of the past tense: A usage-based approach. *Journal of Child Language, 38*, 554–578.

Philips, S. U. (2004). The organization of ideological diversity in discourse: Modern and neotraditional visions of the Tongan state. *American Ethnologist, 31*, 231–250.

Phillipson, R., & Skutnabb-Kangas, T. (Eds.). (1986). *Linguicism rules in education.* Roskilde, Denmark: Roskilde University Centre Institute VI.

Quay, S. (Ed.). (2011). Data-driven insights from trilingual children in the making [Special issue]. *International Journal of Multilingualism, 8*(1), 1–79.

Rampton, M. B. H. (1990). Displacing the "native speaker": Expertise, affiliation, and inheritance. *English Language Teaching Journal, 44*, 97–101.

Robinson, P., & Ellis, N. C. (Eds.). (2008). *Handbook of cognitive linguistics and second language acquisition.* London, UK: Routledge.

Seidlhofer, B. (2001). Closing a conceptual gap: The case for a description of English as a lingua franca. *International Journal of Applied Linguistics, 1*, 133–158.

Shohamy, E. (2006). Rethinking assessment for advanced language proficiency. In H. Byrnes, H. D. Weger-Guntharp, & K. Sprang (Eds.), *Educating for advanced foreign language capacities: Constructs, curriculum, instruction, assessment* (pp. 188–208). Washington, DC: Georgetown University Press.

Singleton, D. (2003). Critical period or general age factor(s)? In M. P. García Mayo & M. L. García Lecumberri (Eds.), *Age and the acquisition of English as a foreign language* (pp. 3–22). Clevedon, UK: Multilingual Matters.

Spivak, G. (1993). *Outside in the teaching machine.* New York, NY: Routledge & Kegan Paul.

Sridhar, S. N. (1994). A reality check for SLA theories. *TESOL Quarterly, 28*, 800–805.

Street, J., & Dąbrowska, E. (2010). More individual differences in language attainment: How much do adult native speakers of English know about passives and quantifiers? *Lingua, 120*, 2080–2094. doi:10.1016/j.lingua.2010.01.004

Swain, M., Kinnear, P., & Steinman, L. (2010). *Sociocultural theory in second language education: An introduction through narratives.* Clevedon, UK: Multilingual Matters.

Thomas, M. (2002). Development of the concept of "the poverty of the stimulus". *Linguistic Review, 19*(1–2), 51–71.

Thomas, M. (2004). *Universal grammar in second language acquisition: A history.* New York, NY: Routledge.

Tomasello, M. (2000). The item-based nature of children's early syntactic development. *Trends in Cognitive Sciences, 4*, 156–163.

Tomasello, M. (2003). *Constructing a language: A usage-based theory of language acquisition.* Harvard, MA: Harvard University Press.

Toohey, K. (2001). Disputes in child L2 learning. *TESOL Quarterly, 35*, 257–278.

Tyler, A. (2010). Usage-based approaches to language and their applications to second language learning. *Annual Review of Applied Linguistics, 30*, 270–291.

Tyler, A. (2012). *Cognitive linguistics and second language learning.* New York, NY: Routledge.

Valdés, G., & Figueroa, R. A. (1994). *Bilingualism and testing: A special case of bias.* Norwood, NJ: Ablex.

Verspoor, M. H., de Bot, K., & Lowie, W. (Eds.). (2011). *A dynamic approach to second language development: Methods and techniques.* Amsterdam, The Netherlands: John Benjamins.

Wells, J. B., Christiansen, M. H., Race, D. S., Acheson, D., & MacDonald, M. C. (2009). Experience and sentence processing: Statistical learning and relative clause comprehension. *Cognitive Psychology, 58*, 250–271.

Werker, J. F., & Byers-Heinlein, K. (2008). Bilingualism in infancy: First steps in perception and comprehension. *Trends in Cognitive Sciences, 12*, 144–151. doi:10.1016/j.tics.2008.01.008

Woolard, K. A. (2004). Codeswitching. In A. Duranti (Ed.), *A companion to linguistic anthropology* (pp. 73–94). Malden, MA: Blackwell.

Zyzik, E. (2009). The role of input revisited: Nativist and usage-based models. *L2 Journal, 1*, 42–61.

3

MOVING BEYOND "LINGUALISM": MULTILINGUAL EMBODIMENT AND MULTIMODALITY IN SLA

David Block

A decade ago, I wrote about the monolingual bias in second language acquisition (SLA) research as follows:

> There is a monolingual bias inherent in use of the word "second" in SLA, as "second" implies a unitary and singular "first" as a predecessor. However, as has often been pointed out by sociolinguists such as Edwards (1994) and Romaine (1995), monolingualism is certainly not the norm in the world—bi and multilingualism are—and in countries which tradition-ally have "monolingualised" immigrants (e.g. the US and Britain), recent changes in the nature of immigration (e.g. communities which retain a large proportion of their home culture such as Mexican Americans and British Sikhs) have meant that in schools in many urban areas, a high pro-portion of students are multilingual, often having variable competence in two, three or four languages, as they take up the formal study of secondary school French or Japanese. In addition, even in contexts that are identified as monolingual, either without or before any exposure to another language via formal education or migration, it is quite likely that these individuals are, in any case, multi-dialectal. By multi-dialectal, I mean that they will have a command of two or more variants of the language of which they are said to be monolingual speakers. Thus . . . in my early years, I would have been classified as a monolingual speaker of Standard American English, despite the fact that I had at least one other code as part of my repertoire, African American Vernacular English. (Block, 2003, pp. 34–35)

I went on from this opening comment to argue that the monolingual first-language (L1) speaker posited in much SLA research is assumed to be on a developmental path that ends with an interlanguage in the second language (L2) that is separate from the L1, and in some cases this individual will achieve the status of a dual monolingual (i.e., with a command of two languages held separately in the mind). By contrast, I examined Vivian Cook's (1996) notion of "multicompetence," which, instead of focusing on how most adult L2 learners never reach what might be considered complete L2 competence, emphasizes the fact that adult L2 learners nonetheless develop "the knowledge of more than one language in the same mind" (Cook, 1996, p. 65; cf. Ortega, this volume). However, this knowledge is not divided up neatly into separate packages corresponding to each language with which the individual has had contact. Thus, at any given point in time during the L2 learning process, the entirety of an L2 learner's linguistic competence "is not just the sum of her/his complete linguistic competence in the L1 and her/his incomplete competence in the L2; rather it is a system that contains both the L1 and the L2" (Block, 2003, pp. 36–37). And, of course, what goes for L1 and L2 goes for L1 and L2 and L3 and so on. Over the years, Cook has shown how grammatical knowledge— syntax, morphology, and lexis—is stored as a unified though ever-evolving linguistic resource rather than as separate languages. However, he has not limited himself to these areas, as he has also shown that pragmatic knowledge, conceptual knowledge, and pronunciation may be held as multicompetence (Cook, 2007). He has thus developed a theory of competence, which while language based, encompasses far more than language. I will come back to this notion later in this chapter.

In my earlier critique of the monolingual bias in SLA (Block, 2003), I also focused on sociolinguistic research focusing on multidialecticism (e.g., Bailey, 2000; Harris, Leung, & Rampton, 2001; see also Blackledge, Creese, & Takhi, this volume). Bailey (2000), for example, examines the language practices of secondary school students from Dominican Republic in Providence, Rhode Island. He notes how these adolescents negotiate different subject positions in a range of communicative contexts through their selective and often discrete uses of different varieties of American English and Spanish. In the case of one student, Wilson, Bailey found uses of some six identifiable varieties on a day-to-day and moment-to-moment basis. These varieties were Spanish (an idealized standard general Spanish), distinctively Dominican Spanish, African American Vernacular English, Dominican English, American English (Providence sociolect), and Hispanicized English (the English spoken by recent immigrants to the United States). Meanwhile, Harris et al. (2001) note how students in London schools generally draw on a wide range of linguistic repertoires when communicating. They often have access to heritage languages at home while they work between more formal and vernacular forms of English in their day-to-day curricular and extracurricular activities.

I was not alone in making these kinds of points about SLA at this time, as the field had reached a point where many prominent researchers (e.g., Meryl Swain), working within what Lourdes Ortega (this volume) calls "linguistic–cognitive SLA," were starting to question its asocial tendencies and its lack of engagement with work in sociolinguistics and multilingualism research. Still, the very existence of this current volume, some ten years later, attests to the fact that not very much progress has been made as regards taking on board the multilingualism and multidialectalism of second language learners in mainstream SLA research (cf. May, this volume). And so I am on the task again, aligning myself with like-minded applied linguists who would (still) like to see an opening up of SLA, in particular, a broadening of horizons. This broadening of horizons would not over-turn linguistic–cognitive SLA. Rather, it would serve to offer up complementary strands of thinking that could only enrich the field.

However, I come to the task of contributing to a book about multilingual-ism and SLA with a slightly different mindset than ten years ago. In the interim period, I have become interested in what I see as an overly narrow view of lan-guage and communication that no doubt permeates SLA to the core but that also is characteristic of much thinking in areas such as Language Policy, World Eng-lishes, and, of relevance here, multilingualism. I refer here to what I will call the *lingual bias*, by which I mean the tendency to conceive of communicative prac-tices exclusively in terms of the linguistic (morphology, syntax, phonology, lexis), although the linguistic is often complemented with a consideration of pragmatics, interculturalism, and learning strategies. Missing in far too many discussions is an active engagement with embodiment and multimodality as a broadened semi-otically based way of looking at what people do when they interact. Of course, some researchers in sociolinguistics have moved to such an engagement with multimodality in their recent work on superdiversity and language practices (see, e.g., Blommaert & Rampton, 2011; cf. Blackledge et al., this volume). However, the general tonic in mainstream multilingualism research is still very much as Pia Lane (2009) describes matters in her discussion of research on bilingual identity:

> In research on bilingual identity, the most prominent focus has been on linguistic aspects such as codeswitching. Bilinguals have other means than codeswitching for identity construction, though in research on bilingual-ism other semiotic tools are often overlooked and language is analysed as an isolated object. However, language is a part of our social semiotic system, and should not be analysed in isolation from other semiotic means. (Lane, 2009, p. 452)

What Lane (2009) argues here applies in general to this volume as well. In it, we see how code-switching may have given way to translanguaging and multilin-gual heteroglossic practices (Blackledge et al. this volume; Canagarajah; García, & Flores, this volume; Li Wei, this volume); how literacies in multilingual settings are framed as complex, as opposed to multidimensional (Leung, this volume; Norton, this volume); and how it is probably not a good idea by now to frame second language learners as deficient second language users (Ortega, this volume); How-ever, the center of what is being discussed is primarily language as linguistic and it therefore still betrays a certain lingual bias.

My starting point in this chapter is a basic acceptance of one of the key arguments driving this volume, namely, that SLA researchers would benefit from interacting with researchers working on multilingualism and multidialectal practices. What I would like to add to this argument is that SLA and multilingualism research need to be framed in terms of embodiment, on the one hand, and multimodality on the other, far more than they are at present. Thus I wish to add to the call for a move from a monolingual approach to SLA to a multilingual approach, a call for an additional perspective, one that takes on board embodiment and multimodality.

The structure of this chapter is simple, consisting as it does of three main sections. I discuss, in order, embodiment, multimodality, and then embodiment and multimodality in SLA research. I then close with some suggestions for future research.

Embodiment

One way to approach the notion of embodiment in social activity, including language practices, is through the work of Pierre Bourdieu and his key constructs, *habitus* and *body hexis*. Habitus was defined in Bourdieu's (1977) earlier work as "systems of durable, transposable dispositions, structured structures predisposed to function as structuring structures . . . as principles of the generation and structuring of practices" (Bourdieu, 1977, p. 72). One point that Bourdieu (1990) has made with regard to habitus is that it is "embodied, turned into a permanent disposition, a durable way of standing, speaking, walking and thereby of feeling and thinking" (Bourdieu, 1990, pp. 69–70) in what is known as body hexis (*hexis corporel* in French). It is also about what Bourdieu (1991) calls a "sense of acceptability," that is, a developed feel for what constitutes appropriate and legitimate behavior in different social contexts. As regards this sense of acceptability applied to linguistic practices (understood to be embodied), Bourdieu writes:

> The sense of acceptability which orients linguistic practices is inscribed in the most deep-rooted of bodily dispositions: it is the whole body which responds by its posture, but also by its inner reactions, or more specifically, the articulatory ones, to the tension of the market. Language is body technique, and specifically linguistic, especially phonetic, competence is a dimension of bodily hexis in which one's whole relation to the social world, and one's whole socially informed relation to the world, are expressed. (Bourdieu, 1991, p. 86)

Body hexis as "deep-rooted" is acquired over time in a subtle, and even subconscious, manner as the individual moves in and out of different fields, understood as:

> spaces of social activity with evolving legitimate ways of thinking and acting, in which individuals occupy positions of inferiority, equality and superiority, which are, in turn dependent on the individual's economic, cultural and social capital in relation to other participants in the social activity. (Block, 2012, p. 79)

However, one must consider the extent to which agents may self-consciously adopt particular ways of standing, speaking, walking, feeling, and thinking. In some of his writing, Bourdieu (1977) makes the case for a body hexis formed in childhood, as the following excerpt illustrates:

> The child imitates not "models" but other people's actions. Body hexis speaks directly to the motor function, in the form of a pattern of postures that is both individual and systematic, because linked to a whole system of techniques involving the body and tools, and charged with a host of social meanings and values: in all societies, children are particularly attentive to gestures and postures which, in their eyes, express everything that goes to make an accomplished adult—a way of walking, a tilt of the head, facial expressions, ways of sitting and of using implements, always associated with a tone of voice, a style of speech, and . . . a certain subjective experience. (Bourdieu, 1977, p. 87)

Notwithstanding the obvious force of primary socialization processes, body hexis might better be seen as ever evolving, flexible, and linked more directly to the life trajectories of individuals. Thus, adolescent and adult migrants who cross borders—both geographical and psychological—may find the social physicality of their existence changes (e.g., space is organized in a different way), but they also find the psychologically based physicality of their lives (e.g., how they move their bodies) may begin to change as they move to fit into their new surroundings. In this sense, posture, bearing, and how one carries oneself in general become important, as I will explain later.

Conceptualizing embodiment in a manner similar to Bourdieu's, William Hanks (1996) draws on Maurice Merleau-Ponty's (2002) concept of "schema corporel" as the "body in motion," where "corporeality is emergent in activity, not prepackaged in cultural categories [and] . . . is constantly under revision, distributed over time" (Hanks, 1996, p. 244). According to this view, there is a *prise de conscience,* as the agent is aware of his/her posture and movement in the present and is able to work reflexively, adapting to new circumstances. As Hanks explains, "body as an experiential field is distributed over physical, physiological, conceptual, affective, aesthetic, and other modes of engagement in the world" (Hanks, 1996, p. 254).

An example of how habitus may change over time, and how an individual has an awareness of such changes, can be found in Holland, Lachicotte, Skinner, and Cain (1998). The authors reproduce a vignette taken from Dorinne Kondo's (1990) *Crafting Selves: Power, Gender and Discourses of Identity in a Japanese Workplace,* a critique of 1980s Japanese society. Kondo is a Japanese American scholar who did extended fieldwork in Japan. In the course of narrating her experiences as a researcher immersed in her context, she describes how shocked she was one day when, upon seeing her image reflected in a butcher's shop window, she realized that she had acquired a local body hexis: "I noticed someone who looked terribly familiar: a typical young housewife, clad in slip-on sandals and the loose, cotton shift called 'home wear', a woman walking in a characteristically Japanese bend to her knees and sliding of feet" (Kondo, 1990, pp. 16–17).

This episode, classified by Kondo as an example of a "collapse of identity," led her to reexamine her role as an ethnographer and it ultimately caused her to self-consciously distance herself from the Japanese people she was in Japan to research. Kondo of course realized the futility of extricating herself from the research context and preventing any kind of drift towards future or further collapse of identity, an intrapersonal phenomenon that she could not avoid. However, she reacted against changes in her body hexis as somehow invasions of a way of being she had acquired earlier in her life.

Elsewhere, scholars interested in metaphor have taken a similar experiential view of embodiment, in particular how early first-language acquisition is embodied and how this embodiment leads to the development of a metaphorical competence underlying linguistic competence. One of the key proponents of this view, Mark Johnson (1987), many years ago discussed experience in the following way:

> "Experience", then, is to be understood in a very rich, broad sense as including basic perceptual, motor-program, emotional, historical, social, and linguistic dimensions. I am rejecting the classical empiricist notion of experience as reducible to passively received sense expressions, which are combined to form atomic experiences. By contrast, experience involves everything that makes us human—our bodily, social, linguistic and intellectual being in complex interactions that make up our understanding of our world. (Johnson, 1987, p. xvi)

Johnson's idea here is experience as embodied and he further argues for experience-derived mental models (and metaphor) as foundational to, and generative of, meaning making. This view articulates well with work done elsewhere in neurobiology by scholars such as Antonio Damasio (1994) who have written about the embodied nature of emotions. Adapting this work to an interest in second language learning, John Schumann made links between neurobiology and affect and language learning many years ago (Schumann, 1997). More recently, Schumann and Wood (2004) have further developed what they call the "biological notion of value," defined as follows:

> a bias that leads an organism to certain preferences and enables it to choose among alternatives . . . Some aspects of value are so important that evolution has selected for them and they have become innate. Value is the basis for all activity; we perceive, move, cognize, and feel on the basis of value. (Schumann & Wood, 2004, p. 24)

The value system mentioned here is dependent on the development of three fundamental motivational systems, that is, systems that impel individuals to act in particular ways. The homeostatic system regulates the human organism, maintaining the stable and consistent fulfillment of basic biological functions such as breathing, eating, keeping warm or cool, maintaining the heart rate, procreating, and caring for kin. The sociostatic system motivates human beings to associate with fellow human beings in their quest for feelings of attachment and group affiliation. The third system, the somatic system, acts as an appraisal system for stimuli encountered as life unfolds.

This appraisal system, according to Klaus Scherer (1988, 2007), consists of a series of dimensions that may be brought to bear on any situation encountered by the individual. Among other things, there is a consideration of whether or not the stimulus event contains novel or unexpected patterns; whether it is pleasant or unpleasant; whether it is relevant to the individual's needs and goals; how urgently a response is required; how much the individual can control the stimulus event or its consequences; how the stimulus event conforms to external socially determined cultural norms and the expectations of others; how the stimulus event conforms internally with cultural norms and expectations; and so on.

What all of the authors cited thus far point to is the development over time—in childhood but also as part of secondary socialization processes—of a relatively stable (though ever-evolving) set of dispositions that guide individuals through their day-to-day activities, both those that are routine and those that are novel. So whether we think of habitus and body hexis (Bourdieu, 1977) or an experience-based network of schemata (Johnson, 1987) or a somatic appraisal system (Scherer, 1988, 2007; Schumann, 1997), we are in the realm of embodied systems, which are inextricably interrelated with, and arise from, interactions with the social world, and which are, as Bourdieu (1977) puts it, "durable, transposable . . . , structured structures predisposed to function as structuring structures" (Bourdieu, 1977, p. 72).

The relevance of this discussion of embodiment to the multilingual turn in SLA is as follows. Everything that has been discussed here about acquired dispositions becomes more complex when we conceptualize individuals as language users or learners in terms of the different repertoires that they develop during their lifetimes. As I argue elsewhere (Block, 2003), even a person identified as a monolingual speaker will have access to multiple linguistic repertoires, all of which will be embodied, as has been discussed in this section, and all of which are linked to body hexis, experience-based schemata, and somatic appraisal systems. This means that the putative monolingual will be able to switch between registers and styles, adopting appropriate body hexis/experience-based schemata/somatic appraisal systems as this is done. An example of this phenomenon can be found in Rampton's (2006) detailed account of "posh" and Cockney English used by adolescents in London schools (see also Blackledge et al., this volume). Although he does not discuss body hexis in his work (nor experience-based schemata and somatic appraisal systems, for that matter), Rampton does make reference to habitus. And I would argue that he does address the multiplicity of embodiment in differentiable language practices when he concludes that "[r]ather than simply being phonological or linguistic entities, the posh–Cockney nexus comprised distinctive clusterings of dialect, mode of speech, preoccupation, and interpersonal and physical demeanor—stylings, in other words, that 'crosscut . . . communicative and behavioural modalities and integrate[d] . . . them thematically' (Irvine 2001: 23 . . .)" (Rampton, 2006, p. 350).

On the other hand, for multilinguals like Kondo (1990), there may be even greater complexity in the language/embodiment nexus. As we observed above, Kondo found that as she became more immersed in her surroundings while doing fieldwork in Japan, she evolved a more prototypical Japanese female body hexis. It would be interesting to examine and compare and contrast Kondo's previous body hexis in Japanese (i.e., the Japanese that she spoke while growing up in the United States) with her later-acquired Japan-based hexis. This, in addition to the obvious contrast with her body hexis as an American English speaker. In any case, and as we observed in the vivid quote above from Kondo (1990), embodiment may be linked to language, but it is also linked to a range of semiotic resources that people draw on to communicate and make their way in the world. In the next section, I move to this key element in communication, which is multimodality.

Multimodality

James Gee (2011) has recently glossed his well-known and oft-cited construct "big D Discourse," which he first put forward over 20 years ago, as follows:

> [P]eople enact identities and activities not just through language, but also by using language together with other "stuff" that isn't language. I use the term "Discourse" with a capital "D," for ways of combining and integrating language actions, interactions, ways of thinking, believing, valuing, and using various symbols, tools, and objects to enact a particular sort of socially recognizable identity. If you want to get recognized as a street-gang member of a certain sort you have to speak in the "right" way, but you also have to act and dress in the "right" way, as well. You also have to engage (or, at least, behave as if you are engaging) in characteristic ways of thinking, acting, interacting, valuing, feeling, and believing. You also have to use or be able to use various sorts of symbols (e.g. graffiti), tools (e.g. a weapon), and objects (e.g. street corners) in the "right" places and at the "right" times. You can't just "talk the talk," you have to "walk the walk" as well. (Gee, 2011, p. 201)

This view of discourse, in a sense as the totality of what comprises communication, has been important in what has come to be known as "new literacies" studies (see Street, 1985 for an early formulation of this development), as it has allowed researchers to escape from a linguistic and print bias to take on board advances in technology and the notion that individuals are literate across a range of modes, of which language is just one. Discourse has also been a useful construct for those focusing on identity, in particular, the poststructuralist take on identity that has become pervasive in applied linguistics in recent years (Block, 2007; Norton & Toohey, 2011). Thus, identity is seen as emergent in the use of a range of semiotic resources in interactions with others. Of particular interest here is Gee's reference to "stuff that isn't language" and how taking this "stuff" on board in the study of identity means going beyond just "talking the talk" to "walking the walk" as well.

If big D Discourse is ultimately about communication writ large, it is also about communication framed multimodally (Jewitt, 2009b; Kress, 2009; O'Halloran & Smith, 2011). Carey Jewitt (2009a) describes multimodality as "approaches that understand communication and representation to be more than about language, and in which language is seen as one form of communication . . . among other modes such as image, gesture, gaze, posture, and so on" (Jewitt, 2009a, p. 14). On where multimodality, or social semiotics, sits vis-à-vis linguistics and pragmatics for many the exclusive staples of an understanding of communication, Gunther Kress (2009) writes the following:

> *linguistics* provides a *description of forms,* of *their occurrence* and of the *relations between them. Pragmatics* – and many forms of sociolinguistics – tells us about *social circumstances,* about *participants* and the *environments of use* and *likely effects. Social semiotics* and the *multimodal* dimension of the theory, tells us about *interest* and *agency;* about *meaning (-making)*; about *processes of sign-making* in social environments; about the *resources* for making meaning and their respective *potentials* as *signifiers* in the making of *signs-as-metaphors;* about the *meaning potentials* of *cultural semiotic forms.* (Kress, 2009, p. 59)

As I suggested in the introduction to this chapter, there has been, to date, a noteworthy lack of attention to multimodality in understandings of communication and meaning making in applied linguistics, in short, a lingual bias. I would add here that this lingual bias is somewhat surprising when one considers that many years ago two scholars often cited in applied linguistics, Dell Hymes and Erving Goffman, showed a deep understanding of multimodality in their work on the ethnography of communication and interaction analysis, respectively. For example, Hymes (1974) argued that, apart from addressing instances of communication as events with various kinds of participants, communication genres, contexts and so on, ethnographers needed to examine "[n]ot codes alone, but whole systems of communication, involving particular . . . alternative modalities" (Hymes, 1974, p. 27). For Hymes, this meant being attentive to:

> the various available *channels,* and their modes of use, speaking, writing, printing, drumming, blowing, whistling, singing, face and body motion

as visually perceived, smelling, tasting, and tactile sensation . . . [and] the various *codes* shared by various participants, linguistic, paralinguistic, kinesic, musical, interpretive, interactional, and other. (Hymes 1974, p. 10)

In making this point, Hymes (1974) was, in some sense pointing to what Kress (2009) would later call "ensembles," that is, temporary arrangements of multiple modes, brought together (or "orchestrated") by an individual in the making of meaning (Kress, 2009).

Elsewhere, Erving Goffman (1981) showed an interest in the multimodality via his analyses of face-to-face interaction:

Everyone knows that when individuals in the presence of others respond to events their glances, looks, and postural shifts carry all kinds of implication and meaning. When in these settings words are spoken, then tone of voice, manner of uptake, restarts, and the variously positioned pauses similarly qualify. As does manner of listening. Every adult is wonderfully accomplished in producing all of these effects, and wonderfully perceptive in catching their significance when performed by accessible others. (Goffman, 1981, pp. 1–2)

And when discussing what speakers and hearers actually do when engaged in face-to-face interaction, he added more layers of multimodality:

the terms "speaker" and "hearer" imply that sound alone is at issue, when, in fact, it is obvious that sight is organizationally very significant too, sometimes even touch. In the management of turn-taking, in the assessment of reception through visual back-channel cues, in paralinguistic function of gesticulation, in the synchrony of gaze shift, in provision of evidence of attention (as in middle-distance look), in the assessment of engrossment through evidence of side-involvements and facial expression—in all of these ways it is apparent that sight is crucial, both for the speaker, and for the hearer. For the effective conduct of talk, speaker and hearer had best be in a position to *watch* each other. (Goffman, 1981, pp. 129–130)

More recently, Sigrid Norris (2004) helpfully breaks down and describes in detail the most common modes drawn on in day-to-day communication in a range of contexts. Norris begins her discussion of modes with spoken language, which she sees as the most researched mode, thus concurring with Jewitt (2009b) and Kress (2009) who, as we observed above, have lamented that communication has for too long been framed according to a linguistic bias. In her examination of spoken language, Norris is interested not only in words as uttered but also in how words are uttered. In other words what kinds of inflections are put on words? Intonation emerges as the chief way in which words are inflected to convey different meanings, although Norris is sensitive to interruptions, pauses, and silence, which also carry meanings.

Moving beyond a focus on the spoken language, Norris (2004) discusses other modes. One of these is proxemics, understood as "[t]he distance that individuals take up with respect to others and relevant objects" (Norris, 2004, p. 19). Importantly (and perhaps obviously), the physical distance maintained between interlocutors during an interaction carries meaning. Thus, in some cultural contexts, such as the German- and English-mediated ones that Norris is most familiar with, if two interlocutors stand very close to one another while speaking, this may convey intimacy and that the two individuals like each other. The opposite might be the case if the distance is relatively great. There is also the issue of what the speech event is about. In some cases, closer proximity may be appropriate, as when someone is trying to give directions while pointing at a map. On the other hand, if the event were a lecture, a few meters' worth of separation between the speaker and audience would seem to be appropriate, given the particular cultural context.

A second important mode to consider in communication is what Norris (2004) calls "posture" or "the ways that participants position their bodies in a given interaction" (Norris, 2004, p. 24). Adopting an open or closed posture can be a significant way of communicating. Again within the cultural settings familiar to Norris, if one turns away from one's face-to-face interlocutor to take a phone call from another, this act of turning is meaningful, conveying that the person receiving the call does not wish to be disturbed during the duration of the call. There is also what Norris calls "general postural behavior"" (Norris, 2004, p. 25), which is about the way that an individual carries him/herself while going about day-to-day activities, what I would call one's bearing. For Norris, the general posture is historically and culturally embedded, a part of the primary socialization process.

An example of how posture and general postural behavior communicate a great deal comes from Hanako Okada's research on international school students in Japan. Okada (2009, 2012) found that *nori,* which she translates as "vibes" (but which also might refer to atmosphere, mood, mode, character, or behavior), was a term used by the students whom she interviewed to describe what they had in common with other international students. Nori symbolizes an affinity that they felt towards one another that they did not feel for Japanese people of their age in general (i.e., the vast majority of Japanese adolescents who do not go to international schools). This affinity was manifested most obviously through the frequent Japanese–English code-switching that students engaged in. But it was also about general postural behavior, the subtle ways that these international students carried themselves, which differentiated them from other Japanese students. Interestingly, one informant, Kenji, extended the notion of shared nori to beyond the Japanese context, claiming that when he studied at a Canadian university, he found that he had a great deal in common with fellow international school graduates from a range of different countries, including France, Netherlands, South Africa, and Thailand.

A third mode, and one that has received a good deal of attention in communication studies, is gesture. Key work on gesture over the past several decades (Efron, 1941; Kendon, 2004; McNeill, 1992) makes the case for the significance of hand and arm movements that accompany speech. Four key gesture types have been identified by McNeill (1992, 2005): (1) iconic, or movements that mimic what the individual is saying, such as lifting one's hands upward while explaining the act of lifting a heavy object; (2) metaphoric, or movements conveying abstract notions, such as a rubbing one's thumb against the index and middle fingers to indicate that something is expensive; (3) deictic, or the movement of pointing at/to objects, people, or events; and (4) beat, or using the fingers, hands, or arms to effect up and down or back and forth movements, such as tapping one's leg while thinking of something to say.

However, gestures do not just stand alone and they are often linked to verbal expressions quite intimately. Indeed, McNeill (1992, 2005) sees language and gestures as constitutive of a single communication system, even if he notes that they can exist separately:

> When co-expressive speech and gesture synchronize, we can see something that is simultaneous and sequential ... There is a combination of two semantic frameworks for the same underlying idea, each with its own expressive potential. Speech and gesture are co-expressive but nonredundant in that each has its own means of packaging meanings. (McNeill, 2005, p. 91)

An example of synchronized speech and gesture can be found in a common expression in Catalan, *Déu n'hi do,* that I first encountered naturalistically when I moved to Barcelona in late 1978. When used in conversation, this expression can convey either excess or agreement with someone who has mentioned excess. When expressing agreement, it is translatable into English as something along the lines of "I'll say" in general American English and perhaps something akin to "quite" in British English, or even the recently ubiquitous "absolutely." An example of how it might be used with this meaning follows:

A: *Quin fred que fa!*   It's so cold!

B: *Déu n'hi do!*   I'll say!

When expressing excess, the expression is embedded in a longer utterance, and in such cases it resembles the adverb "really" (where the first syllable is stressed and elongated) which serves as an augmenter in phrases like "He's really good" or "It's really raining outside." Another expression, "too much," is often used to communicate the basic meaning of *Déu n'hi do.* Two examples of embedded uses follow:

Déu n'hi do com plou!   It's really raining hard!

Porta una camisa que déu n'hi do! He/she's wearing a shirt that is too much!

Translated literally, the expression is a grammaticalization of "May God give it to him/her" (Mayol, 2007). In my experience, the expression is often accompanied by body movement, most commonly a hand-based gesture that involves lifting the forearm slightly and then wagging one's hand in a snapping manner as one simultaneously pronounces the words. In this case, the speaker seems to throw out the words physically with the hand movement in parallel with the enunciation of *Déu n'hi do.* These words are thus embodied in gesture and voice inflection and delivered bodily, exemplifying well what Bourdieu means when he writes that "language is body technique" (Bourdieu, 1991, p. 86). However, it should be noted that the gesture described here can and does exist both on its own at times and in combination with other verbalized expressions, always expressing the basic notion of excess. In this sense, the gesture supports McNeill's (2005) contention that while co-expressive, speech and gesture are not inseparable and that they have their "own means of packaging meanings" (McNeill, 2005, p. 91).

Other modes that can communicate a great deal of information have to do with body movements involving the head, such as head positioning (e.g., nodding), facial expressions (e.g., grimaces, winks), and gaze (how one looks, at whom, or where one looks and how intensely one looks). As Goffman (1981; see above) noted in his work, head positioning, how one holds and moves one's head during conversation, can be important, as nodding up and down and shaking one's head from side to side can convey meaning. A good example of how head movement and gaze work together in communication is to be found in live morning news programs on television channels such as BBC 1 in Britain, where there are normally two presenters, a man and woman, who often appear on the screen at the same time. The interesting issue that arises in such broadcasts is what one presenter does while the other is speaking. I have observed over the years that there are generally three different positions adopted. One is to look directly at the person speaking, showing interest in what they are saying through positive head nodding. A second position is to look directly at the camera, again showing interest in what is being said by alternating between positive head nodding and the adoption of facial expressions that express interest or even show gravity (presumably to support the seriousness of what is being said). A third position is to look off into space or nowhere in particular. However, when the presenters engage in a conversation, then they turn sideways toward one another and conduct themes, as most people would in face-to-face encounters.

However, as has been argued in early work on culture and nonverbal behavior (e.g., Argyle & Cook, 1976; Watson, 1970), such head movement and gaze work is culturally based and therefore the universality of the British news presenters' behavior is in question. For example, Caroline Nash (2008) compared the aversion of gaze (i.e., looking away from one's interlocutor) in conversations involving American, French, and Japanese informants. She found differences across the three groups, although more similar behavior in the American and French groups when compared to the Japanese group. Thus while gaze aversion in conversations involving Americans generally occurred when a speaker disagreed with his/her interlocutor (in effect, as part of a regrouping strategy before returning the gaze and delivering a counterargument), in Japanese conversations it seemed to be part of a general tendency, in that low mutual gaze is the norm in face-to-face interaction involving Japanese speakers. The upshot of such findings is that gaze is yet another mode that needs to be taken into account in research on intercultural and multilingual communication.

Finally, I close this section with a mode which does not emanate from the body, as has been the case with all modes discussed thus far. I refer here to the myriad clothing and accessories with which one can cover one's body and through which one can communicate a wide range of meanings. Indeed, objects of clothing and accessories like glasses, jewelry, and wigs, index, or point to, any number of recognizable and recognized subject positions, an idea developed some time ago by the authors of early publications on subcultures in Britain (e.g., Hall, Clarke, Jefferson, & Roberts, 1976; Hebdige, 1979). A vivid example of how this works comes from a novel that I read some two decades ago, Juan Marsé's (1990) *El Amante Bilingüe* (*The Bilingual Lover*). Marsé's novel is an, at times, surreal narrative that chronicles the multimodal transformation of the protagonist, Joan/Juan Marés.[1] In 1980s Barcelona, Marés struggles with his divorce from his wife—the elegant and upper-class Norma Valentí—and his subsequent fall from middle-class Catalan respectability to his current life as an alcoholic street musician. Significantly, the cause of the divorce was Norma's infidelity with *charnegos,* that is, men who had migrated to Barcelona from the poorer parts of southern Spain, such as Murcia (although it should be noted *charnego* is a derogatory and racist term, which is reclaimed and celebrated by Marsé in his novels).

In an attempt to get closer to his ex-wife, he physically transforms himself from Joan Marés to the stereotypically folkloric *charnego* Juan Faneca, who alternates between being a street musician and working as a shoe shiner. In this transformation, Faneca speaks Spanish with an exaggerated accent from Murcia in the south of Spain. He hardly speaks any Catalan and when he does try to utter a few words in this language, everything comes out inflected with his strong Murcian accent. Marés as Faneca also begins to move his body in a different manner, although the most noteworthy aspect of his transformation is to be found in how he dresses and accessorizes himself. In the following excerpt, we observe how Marés is multimodally transformed into Faneca for the first time:

> He put on the curly wig, the black patch on his [left] eye and he fitted the [green] contact lens in the other, and besides that he resorted to a trick that he remembered having seen done by his mother's caricaturist friends when he was a child: cotton fillings in his nose and mouth. With the black eye-pencil he painted his eyebrows very thin and high, which made his expression of sardonic adequacy more pronounced. The patch on his eye rested on his now elongated face which bore the novelty of an intelligent grin. He chose

his old-fashioned brown striped suit, the one with a double breasted jacket, a rose-coloured silk shirt—the one he was wearing the day that Norma left him, and which he had not worn since—and a claret-coloured tie.

Se puso la peluca rizada, el parche negro en el ojo y ajustó la lentilla en el otro, y además echó mano de un truco que recordaba haber visto hacer a los caricatos amigos de su madre cuando él era un niño: rellenos de algodón en la nariz y en la boca. Con la lápiz negro se pintó las cejas muy finas y altas, con lo que su expresión de suficiencia socarrona se acentuó. El parche en el ojo gravitaba en una cara ahora muy alargada cuya novedad era un rictus de inteligencia. Escogió el anticuado traje marrón a rayas, de americana cruzada, una camisa de seda rosa – la que llevaba el día que Norma lo abandonó, y que no había vuelto a ponerse – y una corbata granate. (Marsé, 1990, p. 63; translation by David Block)

Marsé's (1990) description is from a novel, obviously a work of fiction. However, his portrayal of Marés's transformation resonates with the day-to-day indexicality of clothing and accessories that we come to take for granted. Marés becomes Faneca by changing his spoken language, by changing his general postural behavior, and by dressing and accessorizing himself in a particular way. There is no better example of how different, but interrelated, modes come together than this. Nevertheless, the reader may well wonder at this point what all of this has to do with the multilingual turn in SLA and my stated intention to combat the lingual bias in SLA research. I therefore now move to a consideration of SLA as an embodied and multimodal phenomenon.

Embodiment and Multimodality in SLA

In general communication studies, and specifically, under the auspices of the International Society for Gesture Studies (see http://www.gesturestudies.com/publications.php), there has been a good number of publications recently on the importance of gestures, and some of these contain findings of interest to SLA researchers. Recent examples include Gullberg and de Bot (2010) on gestures and first-language acquisition; Calbris (2011) on the relationship between gesture, speech, and thought; and Stam and Ishino (2011), an edited collection that includes chapters on gesture and first and second language acquisition and use. Directly integrating the study of gestures into SLA, Gullberg's (2006) special issue of *IRAL*, Gullberg and McCafferty's (2008) special issue of *Studies in Second Language Acquisition*, and McCafferty and Stam's (2008) edited collection, entitled *Gesture: Second Language Acquisition and Classroom Research,* stand out. All three showcase a good range of research by many of the same researchers (all the authors in Gullberg's special issue are in McCafferty and Stam's collection), and most of the published pieces adopt a sociocultural perspective on SLA (Lantolf & Thorne, 2006). In a sense, they stand in opposition to cognitive–linguistic SLA, where there appears to be no such interest in gesture or indeed anything to do with embodiment, with the possible exception of usage-based linguistics (see Ortega, this volume).

Interestingly, the authors in these three collections do not refer to multimodality; rather, they frame their work in terms of "non-verbal communication," and, specifically, gesture. In a survey piece in McCafferty and Stam (2008), Carla Chamberlin-Quinlisk (2008) makes a case not only for the study of gesture and SLA, but also for a focus on nonverbal behavior (NVB) in general:

> successful language learning is not simply the memorization of vocabulary and grammatical rules but involves knowledge of how language is used appropriately and strategically to convey intended meaning in diverse contexts. Successful language learners are able to negotiate their social positions and participate in target language communities (Lave and Wenger 1991; Norton and Toohey, 2001), yet language can only partially determine how a learner builds relationships, creates a sense of identity, and participates in social activity. Nonverbal communication also plays a significant role in how people move in and out of conversations, groups and social, academic, and professional settings. (Chamberlin-Quinlisk, 2008, p. 25)

However, in his contribution to the special issue of *Studies in Second Language Acquisition,* McCafferty (2008a) writes the following, using terminology very similar to that used by Jewitt, Kress, Norris, and others cited above:

> People are used to interacting in face-to-face situations through nonverbal forms of communication such as facial expressions, gaze, gestures, and proxemics. We also recognize that extrapersonal forms of expression such as dress, makeup, hairstyle, scent, and jewelry play a part in how we communicate with others. Indeed, some linguists have called for language to be studied in a way that does not isolate it from the entirety of the communicative contexts in which it is used, including aspects of the local environment. (McCafferty, 2008a, pp. 147–148)

The question to consider, then, is how embodied and multimodal has research under the general heading of gesture and SLA been. Space does not allow a thorough review of this growing area of research.[2] However, I list below some of the key general findings from this work.

> In language classrooms, teachers may effectively use gestures to accompany their verbal attempts to manage, explain and provide input to students (Faraco & Kida, 2008; Sime, 2006, 2008; Tabensky, 2008).
> In language classrooms, there is a significant amount of observed bodily movement, above all gestures, but also the use of gaze and posture, which

help learners achieve established goals in carrying out tasks (Olsher, 2008; Platt & Brooks, 2008).

The link between the use of gesture in inner speech and the internalization of language knowledge means that bodily movements can mediate cognition and ultimately language learning (Lee, 2008; McCafferty, 2006, 2008b).

In storytelling and explanations of process in face-to-face interaction, there is a great deal of iconic and deictic gesturing going on that helps the story-teller elaborate a narrative structure and that guides the interlocutor to an understanding (Kida, 2008; Negueruela & Lantolf, 2008; Stam, 2006, 2008, 2010; Yoshioka, 2008; Yoshioka & Kellerman, 2006).

There is a good deal of transfer, both in the terms of what gestures are used and how they are used, in second language learning contexts (Brown & Gullberg, 2008; Choi & Lantolf, 2008; Gullberg, 2008, 2011a, 2011b; Jung-heim, 2006, 2008; Stam, 2008).

All of these findings are of interest in that they capture the importance of embodiment and multimodality in SLA. However, they suffer from several short-comings. First, there is a certain narrowness of focus as just one mode, gesture, receives most of the attention of researchers. Notwithstanding McCafferty's (2008a) statement above, which includes a wide range of modes, other forms of embodiment, from posture and gaze to dress and hairstyle, remain periph-eral. Surely researchers need to take on board this wide range of modes more explicitly and more completely, examining how they form ensembles to commu-nicate meanings in different contexts? Thus SLA is not just about the linguistic + gesture; it is about all of the possible semiotic forms that communicate mean-ing. However, there is one important issue that arises if we take this multimodal approach to SLA, and it is one that impacts on how classroom-based SLA is both researched and understood.

In the formal SLA context there is generally little opportunity to take on integral aspects of communication that, by their very nature, are emergent in ongoing inter-actions taking place far away from the classroom. This means that while students can practice a service exchange in Spanish, they are missing the visual backdrop, the smells, the sounds, and so on that accompany the mere use of words, as they utter to their partner: "*¿Cuanto vale un kilo de patatas?*" ("How much is a kilo of pota-toes?"). To be sure, classrooms, and indeed all settings, are constant sites of emergent multimodal ensembles, something well documented in studies like Olsher (2008) and Platt and Brooks (2008), cited above. However, these ensembles will always be specifically about the here and now of these contexts and are likely quite different from what students of languages imagine as their future uses of language. Elsewhere (Block, 2007), I make a similar point about the paucity of target-language-mediated identity work in many foreign-language classrooms around the world.

One way to take a multimodal approach to classroom language learning is found in the recent work by Dwight Atkinson et al. (e.g., Atkinson, 2010, 2011;

Atkinson, Churchill, Nishino, & Okada, 2007; Churchill, Okada, Nishino, & Atkinson, 2010). Atkinson et al. draw directly on the work of Charles Goodwin and Marjorie Goodwin (Goodwin, 2007; Goodwin & Goodwin, 2004), who have examined "embodied participation frameworks," in which stance, gaze, deictic gestures, and other modes come together in interactions, such as when a father helps his daughter with her maths homework (Goodwin, 2007). In Atkinson et al.'s work, there is detailed exploration of interaction in EFL (English as a foreign language) classrooms in Japan, with a focus on phenomena like "alignment," understood as "the complex processes through which human beings effect coordinated interaction, both with other human beings and (usually human-engineered) environments, situations, tools, and affordances" (Atkinson et al., 2007, p. 169). This is a more holistic and ecological approach to classroom interaction and SLA and it is one that promises a great deal. I say this especially because it is moves beyond the examination of gesture in SLA to take on board many of the modes described earlier in this chapter, such as posture and gaze. In this sense, it articulates well with research by Jewitt, Kress, and other multimodal specialists (e.g., Jewitt, 2011; Kress et al., 2005), who have examined how subject English is taught in London secondary school classrooms, focusing on "how modes and semiotic resources feature and are orchestrated in the production of school knowledge" (Jewitt, 2011, p. 185).

An additional problem with the focus on gesture in SLA studies is the ways in which there is little or no acknowledgment of study participants' statuses as sophisticated knowers and users of language, as multidialectal and multilingual. There is, therefore, little or no overt attention to the fact that, as multicompetent learners (Cook, 1996), these individuals are likely to have been exposed and to have acquired not only linguistic knowledge of more than one language during their lifetimes but also more than one assembly of semantic resources. And so an opportunity is missed here to frame learners as multilinguals and as multi-multimodal, that is, as individuals who have an accumulated and combined knowledge of two or more languages and the semiotic resources that accompany uses of these languages (including not only gesture but also gaze and stance).

In this sense, we are once again back to the purpose of this volume, which is to address and critique the lack of complex portrayals of second language learners as linguistically complex individuals in SLA research. However, it adds to this assessment a critique of how many of those who take linguistic–cognitive SLA to task for having a monolingual bias themselves manifest a certain lingual bias. They do not take on board sufficiently that, in communication, the linguistic realm is but one of many realms. And although it may well be the most important mode of communication, it seldom if ever stands alone. It is, therefore, important to consider any number of other semiotic modes—from gesture to gaze and from accessories to clothes—that come together to make communication happen in all its complexity. This means that what is needed in SLA is a multilingual turn in the form of an exploration of the myriad associations between the multiple varieties in the individual's linguistic repertoire—defined in terms of dialects, languages, and both. But there is also a need for a multimodal turn, which means simultaneously taking on board the multiplicity of embodied and multimodal forms associated with any given linguistic repertoire.

Finally, I end this discussion with a consideration of another phenomenon that I think needs to be explored in more detail in future SLA research. It is based on Cook's (1996) groundbreaking work on multicompetence discussed above (cf. Ortega, this volume), the idea that one's competence in an L2, L3, L4, and so on, can impact on one's L1 competence, or better said, becomes intermeshed with one's L1 competence. In Cook's work, multilinguals responded very differently from monolinguals to grammaticality judgments in their L1, manifesting more complex and multiple, although more unstable, overall linguistic competence. In the context of this chapter, there is an issue of embodiment and multimodality being seen as multi-embodiment and multi-multimodality and as the differentiable embodiments and multimodalities associated with the different languages in one's multilingual repertoire that impact on one another. Just to show how complicated matters can become in the bi/multilingual universe, I return to my *Deu n'hi do* example above, as there is a kind of epilogue to the story that shows how multiplicity works in terms of embodiment and multimodality. A few years after I moved to Barcelona, sometime in the mid-1980s, I was visiting a friend in the United States. During the course of a conversation I referred to something that I thought was excessive—probably saying something along the lines of: "It's really too much!" As I produced this utterance, I simultaneously produced a gesture with my right hand that involved lifting my forearm slightly and then wagging my hand in a snapping manner. I continued to make this gesture a few seconds after completing the verbal part of my message. I had, it seemed, fallen into a body-hexis–linguistic disjuncture, as my words were in English but my body movements were based in a relatively recently acquired Catalan-based body hexis. All of this prompted my friend, by most estimates a monolingual English speaker, to ask me what was wrong with my hand and why I was shaking it in this manner. I did not then have the wherewithal or the terminology to explain what was happening as I would today, but I no doubt was living the kind of multilingual embodiment and multimodality experience that escapes the radar of most SLA research.

Conclusion

We see human beings in the social world as bundles of histories—of language, of discourses, and experiences, of social and political performances, as juggling multiple social roles and performances, largely unconsciously, and as being physical bodies which carry and express genetic, social, and momentary dispositions which are never possible to fully occlude behind those socially constructed performances. (Scollon & Scollon, 2003, pp. 15–16)

In this way, Ron Scollon and Suzie Wong Scollon (2003) provide a succinct statement of the complexity and ever presence of embodiment and multimodality in our lives. In this chapter, I hope to have made the point that embodiment and multimodality are essential to any understanding of communication and that, as communication is at the heart of SLA, they are essential to any understanding of the kinds of processes studied by SLA researchers. In addition, the multidialectalism and multimodality of second language learners not only needs to be taken into account but it needs to be combined with this acknowledgement of the importance of the embodied and multimodal nature of communication. Too much is at stake in maintaining a line of research that has evolved, but that has done so only within the confines of what the linguistic–cognitive approach allows. And in the case of this chapter, the task would be double, for there are not only the "multis" of multidialectalism and multilingualism to contend with but also the "multis" of embodiment and multimodality. And this is all perhaps too much to take on board in one go. *Deu n'hi do!*

Notes

Some of the ideas expressed in this chapter appear in two earlier publications, Block (2010a, 2010b), and were presented as part of the colloquium "Addressing the Multilingual Turn: Implications for SLA, TESOL and Bilingual Education" organized by Stephen May at the American Association of Applied Linguistics conference in Boston, Massachusetts, in 2012. I thank Stephen for inviting me to be on this panel as well as for providing helpful feedback on earlier drafts of this chapter, along with John Gray and Hanako Okada.

1. The similarity between the author's name and the protagonist's name is deliberate and significant, as is the fact that Juan Marsé was born Juan Faneca, although after his mother died during childbirth he was adopted by a family with the surname Marsé. The ambiguity and duality parallels the way that Marsé has always positioned himself as a Catalan but also as someone outside mainstream middle-class Catalan culture. His roots are working class, and he has always written characters from the south of Spain into his narratives. And although he is perfectly proficient and literate in Catalan, Marsé has always written his novels in Castilian, a practice that has not always been well received among the officialdom of Catalan culture.
2. I refer the interested reader to introductions to the edited volumes cited previously and to Gullberg (2012).

References

Argyle, M., & Cook, M. (1976). *Gaze and mutual gaze*. New York, NY: Cambridge University Press.

Atkinson, D. (2010). Extended, embodied cognition and second language acquisition. *Applied Linguistics*, *31*(4), 599–622.

Atkinson, D. (2011). A sociocognitive approach to second language acquisition: How mind, body, and world work together in learning additional languages. In D. Atkinson (Ed.), *Alternative approaches to second language acquisition* (pp. 143–166). London, UK: Routledge.

Atkinson, D., Churchill, E., Nishino, T., & Okada, H. (2007). Alignment and interaction in a sociocognitive approach to second language acquisition. *The Modern Language Journal*, *91*(2), 169–188.

Bailey, B. (2000). Language and negotiation of ethnic/racial identity among Dominican Americans. *Language in Society*, *29*(4), 555–582.

Block, D. (2003). *The social turn in second language acquisition*. Edinburgh, UK: Edinburgh University Press.

Block, D. (2007). *Second language identities.* London, UK: Continuum.

Block, D. (2010a). La compétence de communication revisitée: Multimodalité et incorporation [Communicative competence reoriented: Multimodality and embodiment]. *Le français dans le monde, Recherches et applications, Interrogations épistémologiques en didactique des langues*, *48*, 150–163.

Block, D. (2010b). Engaging with human sociality: Thoughts on communication and embodiment. *Applied Linguistics Review*, *1*(1), 45–56.

Block, D. (2012). Economising globalisation and identity in applied linguistics in neoliberal times. In D. Block, J. Gray, & M. Holborow (Eds.), *Neoliberalism and applied linguistics* (pp. 56–85). London, UK: Routledge.

Blommaert, J., & Rampton, B. (2011). *Language and superdiversity: A position paper* (Paper 70). Retrieved from Working Papers in Urban Language and Literacies website: http://www.kcl.ac.uk/innovation/groups/ldc/publications/workingpapers/70.pdf

Bourdieu, P. (1977). *Outline of a theory of practice*. Cambridge, UK: Cambridge University Press.

Bourdieu, P. (1990). *The logic of practice*. Cambridge, UK: Polity.

Bourdieu, P. (1991). *Language and symbolic power.* Cambridge, UK: Polity.

Brown, A., & Gullberg, M. (2008). Bidirectional crosslinguistic influence in L1-L2 encoding of manner in speech and gesture: A study of Japanese speakers of English. *Studies in Second Language Acquisition*, *30*(2), 225–251.

Calbris, G. (2011). *Elements of meaning in gesture*. Amsterdam, The Netherlands: Benjamins.

Chamberlin-Quinlisk, C. R. (2008). Nonverbal communication, gesture, and second language classrooms: A review. In S. McCafferty & G. Stam (Eds.), *Gesture: Second language acquisition and classroom research* (pp. 25–44). London, UK: Routledge.

Choi, S., & Lantolf, J. P. (2008). Representation and embodiment of meaning in L2 communication: Motion events in the speech and gesture of advanced L2 Korean and L2 English speakers. *Studies in Second Language Acquisition,* *30*(2), 191–224.

Churchill, E., Okada, H., Nishino, T., & Atkinson, D. (2010). Symbiotic gesture and the sociocognitive visibility of grammar in second language acquisition. *The Modern Language Journal*, *94*(2), 234–253.

Cook, V. (1996). Competence and multi-competence. In G. Brown, K. Malmkjaer, & J. Williams (Eds.), *Performance and competence in second language acquisition* (pp. 57–69). Cambridge, UK: Cambridge University Press.

Cook, V. J. (2007). Multi-competence: Black-hole or worm-hole for second language acquisition research. In Z. Han (Ed.), *Understanding second language process* (pp. 16–26). Clevedon, UK: Multilingual Matters.

Damasio, A. (1994). *Descartes' error: Emotion, reason, and the human brain*. New York, NY: G. P. Putnam's Sons.

Efron, D. (1941). *Gesture and environment*. Morningside Heights, NY: King's Crown Press.

Faraco, M., & Kida, T. (2008). Gesture and the negotiation of meaning in a second language classroom. In S. McCafferty & G. Stam (Eds.), *Gesture: Second language acquisition and classroom research* (pp. 280–297). London, UK: Routledge.

Gee, J. P. (2011). *An introduction to discourse analysis* (3rd ed.). London, UK: Routledge.

Goffman, E. (1981). *Forms of talk*. Oxford, UK: Blackwell.

Goodwin, C. (2007). Participation, stance and affect in the organization of activities. *Discourse and Society, 18*(1), 53–73.

Goodwin, C., & Goodwin, M. (2004). Participation. In A. Duranti (Ed.), *A companion to linguistic anthropology* (pp. 222–244). Oxford, UK: Blackwell.

Gullberg, M. (Ed.). (2006). Gestures and second language acquisition [Special issue]. *International Review of Applied Linguistics, 44*(2).

Gullberg, M. (2008). A helping hand? Gestures, L2 learners, and grammar. In S. McCafferty & G. Stam (Eds.), *Gesture: Second language acquisition and classroom research* (pp. 185–210). London, UK: Routledge.

Gullberg, M. (2011a). Thinking, speaking, and gesturing about motion in more than one language. In A. Pavelnko (Ed.), *Thinking and speaking in two languages* (pp. 143–169). Clevedon, UK: Multilingual Matters.

Gullberg, M. (2011b). Multilingual multimodality: Communicative difficulties and their solutions in second language use. In J. Streeck, C. Goodwin, & C. LeBaron (Eds.), *Embodied interaction: Language and body in the material world* (pp. 137–151). Cambridge, UK: Cambridge University Press.

Gullberg, M. (2012). *Gestures in second language acquisition.* London, UK: Routledge.

Gullberg, M., & de Bot, K. (Eds.). (2010). *Gestures in language development.* Amsterdam, The Netherlands: Benjamins.

Gullberg, M. & McCafferty, S. G. (Eds.) (2008). Gesture and SLA: Toward an integrated approach [Special issue]. *Studies in second language acquisition, 30*(2).

Hall, S., Clarke, J., Jefferson, T., & Roberts, B. (Eds.). (1976). *Resistance through rituals.* London, UK: Hutchinson.

Hanks, W. (1996). *Language and communicative practices.* Boulder, CO: Westview Press.

Harris, R., Leung, C., & Rampton, B. (2001). Globalization, diaspora and language education in England. In D. Block & D. Cameron (Eds.), *Globalization and language teaching* (pp. 29–46). London, UK: Routledge.

Hebdige, D. (1979). *Subculture: The meaning of style.* London, UK: Methuen.

Holland, D., Lachicotte, W., Skinner, D., & Cain, C. (1998). *Identity and agency in cultural worlds.* Cambridge, MA: Harvard University Press.

Hymes, D. (1974). *Foundations in sociolinguistics: An ethnographic approach.* Philadelphia, PA: University of Pennsylvania Press.

Jewitt, C. (Ed.). (2009a). An introduction to multimodality. In C. Jewitt (Ed.), *Handbook of multimodal analysis* (pp. 14–27). London, UK: Routledge.

Jewitt, C. (Ed.). (2009b). *Handbook of multimodal analysis.* London, UK: Routledge.

Jewitt, C. (2011). The changing pedagogic landscape of subject English. In K. O'Halloran & B. A. Smith (Eds.), *Multimodal studies: Exploring issues and domains* (pp. 184–201). London, UK: Routledge.

Johnson, M. (1987). *The body in the mind.* Chicago, IL: Chicago University Press.

Jungheim, N. O. (2006). Learner and native speaker perspectives on a culturally-specific Japanese refusal gesture. *International Review of Applied Linguistics, 44*(2), 125–144.

Jungheim, N. O. (2008). Language learner and native speaker perceptions of Japanese refusal gestures portrayed in video. In S. McCafferty & G. Stam (Eds.), *Gesture: Second language acquisition and classroom research* (pp. 157–182). London, UK: Routledge.

Kendon, A. (2004). *Gesture: Visible action as utterance.* Cambridge, UK: Cambridge University Press.

Kida, T. (2008). Does gesture aid discourse comprehension in the L2? In S. McCafferty and G. Stam (Eds.), *Gesture: Second language acquisition and classroom research* (pp. 131–156). London, UK: Routledge.

Kondo, D. (1990). *Crafting selves: Power, gender and discourses of identity in a Japanese workplace.* Chicago, IL: Chicago University Press.

Kress, G. (2009). *Multimodality: A social semiotic approach to contemporary communication.* London, UK: Routledge.

Kress, G., Jewitt, C., Bourne, J., Franks, A., Hardcastle, J., Jones, K., & Reid, E. (2005). *English urban classrooms: A multimodal perspective on teaching and learning.* London, UK: Routledge.

Lane, P. (2009). Identities in action: A nexus analysis of identity construction and language shift. *Visual Communication, 8*(4), 450–468.

Lantolf, J. P., & Thorne, S. L. (2006). *Sociocultural theory and the genesis of second language development.* Oxford, UK: Oxford University Press.

Lee, G. (2008). Gesture and private speech in second language acquisition. *Studies in Second Language Acquisition, 30*(2), 169–190.

Marsé, J. (1990). *El amante bilingüe* [The Bilingual Lover]. Barcelona, Spain: Random House Mondadori.

Mayol, L. (2007). Catalan "De ´u n'hi do" and levels of meaning in exclamatives. In C. B. Chang & H. J. Haynie (Eds.), *Proceedings of the 26th West Coast Conference on Formal Linguistics* (pp. 375–383). Somerville, MA: Cascadilla Proceedings Project.

McCafferty, S. G. (2006). Gesture and the materialization of second language prosody. *International Review of Applied Linguistics, 44*(2), 197–209.

McCafferty, S. G. (2008a). Mimesis and second language acquisition: A sociocultural perspective. *Studies in second language acquisition, 30*(2), 147–167.

McCafferty, S. G. (2008b). Material foundations for second language acquisition: Gesture, metaphor, and internalization. In S. McCafferty & G. Stam (Eds.), *Gesture: Second language acquisition and classroom research* (pp. 47–65). London, UK: Routledge.

McCafferty, S. & Stam, G. (Eds.). (2008). *Gesture: Second language acquisition and classroom research.* London, UK: Routledge.

McNeill, D. (1992). *Hand and mind.* Chicago, IL: Chicago University Press.

McNeill, D. (2005). *Gesture and thought.* Chicago, IL: Chicago University Press.

Merleau-Ponty, M. (2002). *Phenomenology of perception.* London, UK: Routledge. (Reprinted from *Phénomènologie de la perception,* by M. Merleau-Ponty, 1945, Paris: Gallimard)

Nash, C. E. (2008). The role of nonverbal expressions as precursors to argumentative discourse in French, Japanese and American English conversation. *L'Analisi Linguistica e Letteraria, 16,* 385–399.

Negueruela, E., & Lantolf, J. P. (2008). The dialectics of gesture in the construction of meaning in second language oral narratives. In S. McCafferty & G. Stam (Eds.), *Gesture: Second language acquisition and classroom research* (pp. 88–106). London, UK: Routledge.

Norris, S. (2004). *Analyzing multimodal interaction: A methodological framework.* London, UK: Routledge.

Norton, B., & Toohey, K. (2011). Identity, language learning, social change. *Language Teaching, 44*(4), 412–446.

O'Halloran, K., & Smith, B. A. (Eds.). (2011). *Multimodal studies: Exploring issues and domains.* London, UK: Routledge.

Okada, H. (2009). Somewhere "in between": Languages and identities of three Japanese international school students. *Dissertation Abstracts International, 70*(06).

Okada, H. (2012, March). *Somewhere "in between": The complex languages and identities of Japanese students in international schools in Japan.* Paper presented at the American Association of Applied Linguistics Conference, Boston, MA.

Olsher, D. (2008). Gesturally enhanced repeats in the repair turn: Communication strategy or cognitive language-learning tool? In S. McCafferty & G. Stam (Eds.), *Gesture: Second language acquisition and classroom research* (pp. 109–130). London, UK: Routledge.

Platt, E., & Brooks, F. B. (2008). Embodiment as self-regulation in L2 task performance. In S. McCafferty & G. Stam (Eds.), *Gesture: Second language acquisition and classroom research* (pp. 66–87). London, UK: Routledge.

Rampton, B. (2006). *Language in late modernity.* Cambridge, UK: Cambridge University Press.

Scherer, K. (1988). *Facets of emotion: Recent research.* Mahwah, NJ: Lawrence Erlbaum.

Scherer, K. (2007). Component models of emotion can inform the quest for emotional competence. In G. Matthews, M. Zeidner, & R. D. Roberts (Eds.), *The science of emotional intelligence: Knowns and unknowns* (pp. 101–126). Oxford, UK: Oxford University Press.

Schumann, J. H. (1997). *The neurobiology of affect in language.* Oxford, UK: Blackwell.

Schumann, J. H., & Wood, L. E. (2004). The neurobiology of motivation. In J. H. Schumann, S. E. Crowell, N. E. Jones, & N. Lee (Eds.), *Neurobiology of learning: Perspectives from second language acquisition* (pp. 21–38). Mahwah, NJ: Lawrence Erlbaum.

Scollon, R., & Scollon, S. W. (2003). *Discourses in place: Language in the material world.* London, UK: Routledge.

Sime, D. (2006). What do learners make of teachers' gestures in the language classroom? *International Review of Applied Linguistics, 44*(2), 211–230.

Sime, D. (2008). "Because of her gesture, It's very easy to understand"—Learners' perceptions of teachers' gestures in the foreign language class. In S. McCafferty & G. Stam (Eds.), *Gesture: Second language acquisition and classroom research* (pp. 259–279). London, UK: Routledge.

Stam, G. (2006). Thinking for speaking about motion: L1 and L2 speech and gesture. *International Review of Applied Linguistics, 44*(2), 143–169.

Stam, G. (2008). What gestures reveal about second language acquisition. In S. McCafferty and G. Stam (Eds.), *Gesture: Second language acquisition and classroom research* (pp. 231–255). London, UK: Routledge.

Stam, G. (2010). Can a L2 speaker's patterns of thinking for speaking change? In Z. Han and T. Cadierno (Eds.), *Linguistic relativity in L2 acquisition: Evidence of L1 thinking for speaking* (pp. 59–83). Clevedon, UK: Multilingual Matters.

Stam, G., & Ishino, M. (Eds.) (2011). *Integrating gestures: The interdisciplinary nature of gesture.* Amsterdam, The Netherlands: Benjamins.

Street, B. (1985). *Literacy in theory and practice.* Cambridge, UK: Cambridge University Press.

Tabensky, A. (2008). Expository discourse in a second language classroom: How learners use gesture. In S. McCafferty & G. Stam (Eds.), *Gesture: Second language acquisition and classroom research* (pp. 298–320). London, UK: Routledge.

Watson, O. M. (1970). *Proxemic behavior: A cross-cultural study.* The Hague, The Netherlands: Mouton de Gruyter.

Yoshioka, K. (2008). Linguistic and gestural introduction of ground reference in L1 and L2 narrative. In S. McCafferty & G. Stam (Eds.), *Gesture: Second language acquisition and classroom research* (pp. 211–230). London, UK: Routledge.

Yoshioka, K., & Kellerman, E. (2006). Gestural introduction of ground reference in L2 narrative discourse. *International Review of Applied Linguistics, 44*(2), 173–196.

4

THEORIZING A COMPETENCE FOR TRANSLINGUAL PRACTICE AT THE CONTACT ZONE

Suresh Canagarajah

Mary Louise Pratt (1987) initiated an important line of inquiry in applied linguistics when she called for a shift from "a linguistics of community" to a "linguistics of contact." We are finding this reorientation gaining urgency as we grapple with communication in conditions of late modern globalization, featuring migration, diaspora relationships, superdiverse urban settlements, digital media scapes, and transnational economic and production relationships. We realize now that Pratt's (1991) notion of the "contact zone" is not a secondary space between the more primary "community." All communities are contact zones that involve interactions between diverse languages and cultures. From this perspective, it is attempts to essentialize, territorialize, and circumscribe communities and languages that appear unusual. As we break away from the notion of bounded communities and attend to communication in the liminal spaces of contact, we have new questions confronting communication and competence.

Though there is more work to be done in theorizing competence, some scholars have made headway in addressing communication. Blommaert (2010, p. 43) has called for a shift from treating languages as "immobile" to treating them as "mobile semiotic resources." Looking at language as immobile has involved treating it as territorialized in one place and owned by one community. It has left us with a strong sense of language ownership, treating those who borrow resources from another language as "illegitimate" users. Perceiving languages as made up of semiotic resources involves understanding language as an ideological construct, with an order and identity imposed by people. Languages constitute mobile semiotic resources that can be freely adopted by people for their purposes and interests. The fact that these are semiotic involves seeing language as one of many sign systems that involve different symbolic means of representation working in alignment with diverse modalities, media, and ecologies. How these mobile resources gain meaning is through social practice, as people construct shared indexicalities in situated interactions. I use the term *translingual practice* to capture the notion that people shuttle in and out of languages to borrow resources from different communities to communicate meaningfully at the contact zone through strategic communicative practices.

In some ways, translingual practice shares some similar assumptions motivating other terms like "plurilingual," "translanguaging," and "dynamic bilingualism" (all from García, 2009), "fragmented" or "truncated multilingualism" (Blommaert, 2010), "metrolinguistics" and "ludic Englishes" (Pennycook, 2010), and "poly-lingual languaging" (Jørgenson, 2008; see also Blackledge, Creese, & Takhi, this volume). There are some minor differences in emphases in the way I use my term. Terms like metrolinguistics, fragmented multilingualism, polylingual lan-guaging, and ludic Englishes have been presented as urban and late modern phenomena in the context of recent forms of globalization. However, unlike some of these commentators, I don't treat translingual practice as new or recent. Though we have fascinating new forms of translingual practice in contemporary times, especially in the context of new technology, I think of this orientation as having a long tradition in precolonial and non-Western communities. My data below suggest that the participants have been socialized into these practices in everyday contexts along traditions that are ancient. My approach deviates also from terms such as "translanguaging," "dynamic bilingualism," and "plurilin-gualism" that have hitherto been defined largely in cognitive terms. Scholars in applied linguistics who favor these terms have been more concerned with defin-ing translingual practices as involving a different type of cognitive competence. Working against the Chomskyan model, they have developed the implications of multicompetence (Cook, 1999; cf. Block, this volume; Ortega, this volume) and theorized multilingual competence as qualitatively different from mono-lingualism (Franceschini, 2011). Although this is an important project, it faces the danger of treating translingual practice as a solitary mental activity. I argue that we have to treat meaning making as a social practice that engages holisti-cally with ecological and contextual affordances. Though there are implications for cognition, I define this form of competence in fundamentally social- and practice-based terms. I also have reservations against terms like fragmented or truncated multilingualism (Blommaert, 2010). These terms treat translingual practices as deficient. They assume a purported whole language as the norm, forgetting that wholeness is a social and ideological construction that people provide to their language resources.

The dominance of ideologies of monolingualism and essentialized communi-ties has left us with some conceptual binaries that prevent us from addressing the complexity of communication and competence at the contact zone (see Canag-arajah, 2007, for a detailed critique). Consider familiar constructs such as the following in second language acquisition (SLA):

1. Shared norms	heterogeneous codes
2. Fixed grammars	fluid resources
3. System	openness
4. Homogeneity	diversity
5. Target	interlanguage
6. Native speaker	nonnative speaker
7. User	learner
8. Competence	performance

The first four terms have helped us define the target to be learned in a convenient manner. We treat language as having a fixed system as defined by its "native speakers." Appropriations, variations, and difference of learners from other communities are treated as deviant and wrong. Such divergence is treated as harmful for meaning construction and successful communication. We mark their illegitimacy with the fifth construct above, "interlanguage." Because we have a fixed target to be learned we are not prepared to acknowledge that deviations from the system may still gain new meaning in situated contexts. Speakers in the contact zone can still achieve meaning and intelligibility for non-shared items through their interactions. Sharedness is not given, but achieved. Similarly, the emphasis on a tight and fixed system ignores the ways in which languages are always in contact and influence each other, still allowing people to communicate despite this fluidity in structure. The homogeneous and fixed structuring of the language gives power to the native speakers to define norms in their own terms. However, the idea of "native speakerhood" has also been questioned (see Canagarajah, 1999; Singh, 1998). We all have partial competence in multiple languages, with our presumed nativeness in a language mediated by contact with diverse cultures and communities. Native speakerhood, too, is eventually an ideological position, as it helps define all those who don't belong to that community as nonnative, with their use defined as illegitimate. Closely paralleling this construct in SLA is the next one relating to *users* and *learners.* Nonnatives are positioned in the status of perennial learners, with their functionality in divergent language forms treated as imperfect and even noncommunicative (cf. Ortega, this volume). Their appropriations of the language are supposed to identify them as learners. A practice-based view of language and competence would help us see how forms and grammars that deviate from the "system" as defined by linguists or native speakers are still communicative in socially situated interactions. However, a practice-based perspective is also ruled insignificant by the final binary that treats competence as cognitive, innate, and abstract according to the Chomskyan tradition, treating performance as unsystematic, unruly, and superficial.

In this chapter, I consider how we can retheorize competence for translingual practice at the contact zone. I base my reflections on the narratives and opinions of

African skilled migrants in English-dominant countries (i.e., United States, Britain, Australia, and South Africa). Their experiences were elicited in interviews conducted for the research project *Skilled Migration and Global English: Language, Development, and the African Professional* between February 2010 and 2011.[1] A multidisciplinary group of scholars from the following universities collaborated with me as the Principal Investigator (PI) in obtaining data: Bristol, Cape Town, Leeds, Sydney, York, and the Universities of Wisconsin (Madison) and Washington (Seattle). The informants come from sub-Saharan Africa. "Skilled professionals" are defined as those enjoying a baccalaureate or comparable educational degree and working in a profession that requires credentialed skills. The informants came from a range of professions, especially education, health care, and management. For data-gathering purposes, field workers focused on urban settings close to their universities (i.e., State College and Seattle, United States; Bradford, Bristol, and Sheffield, Britain; and Sydney, Australia). The study involved a total of 65 participants. The objective was to obtain in-depth narratives and opinions on the ways skilled migrants negotiate language differences in intercommunity relations. The data-gathering method involved face-to-face, telephone, and email interviews. All face-to-face and telephone interviews were audio recorded and transcribed. Each interview ran for around 45 to 90 minutes.

Skilled migrants have generated a lot of attention recently in fields such as economics, geography, and sociology on how their trajectories between sending and receiving countries encourage knowledge circulation and how this circulation contributes to development both at home and in receiving countries (Kuznetsov, 2006; Mercer, Page, & Evans, 2008). In addition to their skills, their remittances also help development in their home countries. Though much of the research so far has been conducted on remittances, demography, and diaspora identity/ community formation, the communicative challenges for skilled migrants raise some fascinating questions for applied linguists and require more study. As skilled migrants participate in social and knowledge flows, we have to ask how they handle multilingual life at the contact zone. In many cases, they don't go to school to learn a new language, but develop their competence as they engage in their work. They seem to bring certain dispositions and resources that help them develop competence in new communicative genres and codes in their adult life.

It might be argued that skilled migrants belong to the educated middle class and cannot be treated as comparable to other multilinguals or migrants. It is possible that my informants have access to certain privileged forms of English that unskilled and less educated migrants may not enjoy (see also Blackledge et al., this volume). However, their class and professional background is mediated by other considerations such as ethnicity, race, and language identity that often place them at a relative disadvantage in Western professional contexts. My position is that all multilinguals have to negotiate their conflicting and hybrid subject positions, with the mix of limitations and advantages they enjoy in diverse communicative situations, for voice. What are more important are the negotiation practices and dispositions multilinguals bring to conduct such negotiations in their favor.

Though we need more research on unskilled migrants, my contention is that the practices and dispositions I identify in what follows have an underlying similarity across multilingual and migrant communities, accounting for a different orientation to language competence.

A Note on Terminology

The questioning of the traditional dichotomies in SLA creates a challenge on how we should label speakers and learners without being influenced by similar biases. The terms *native/nonnative* have been critiqued, as I have discussed above, as they are based on birthright in specific autonomous languages. However, I need a way to distinguish those who traditionally claim native ownership over the language and others who claim English as an additional language in their repertoire. I also have the practical need to examine critically how language learners have been discussed in previous scholarship in order to demonstrate the limitations therein and to move the field to a different orientation for both groups. Therefore, I will use the term *native English speaker* for the former and *multilinguals* for the latter, with the caveat that multilinguals often claim ownership over English, and both groups have competence in translingual practices.

I first describe the orientation that my informants bring to language contact in their life and work before characterizing their competence for this type of communication and inquiring how they develop this competence.

Translingual Practice at the Contact Zone

A key question in the interview focused on the way the participants negotiated the dominant varieties of English in the host communities, given the fact that they brought diverse other varieties with them from their postcolonial countries, many of them located in Kachru's (1986) Outer Circle. The question was posed as follows: "Do you experience any tensions between the variety of English you speak and the other varieties spoken in the host community? How do you handle these differences? Would you say that these have any implications for your work and social life?" This is part of a series of 18 questions we posed on their multilingual language background at home, trajectories of migration, and experiences in host communities. The response to the question above on English is informed by our participants' experiences and positions on the other languages in their repertoire. However, the question on English has a special resonance for education and linguistics, as English is touted as the linguistic capital that assures mobility and development (see also Norton, this volume). I find that such pronouncements ignore the diversity and inequality in the varieties spoken by migrants and the controversial implications for language competence, hence the significance of the question.

In retrospect, the question posed appears somewhat biased, as it assumes that the contact with native speaker varieties will be stressful for the participants. I was surprised that a majority of the participants contested the view that communication at the contact zone involved tensions. They conveyed how they viewed language contact differently. Consider GHM below:

> 1. GHM (Uganda, female, school administrator in Bristol): I don't feel any tension about my ability to communicate in English and I think that it is sloppy when people say that they do not understand a person due to accent et cetera, as I speak a little of many different languages and try my best to communicate with everybody and expect all to do likewise.

GHM doesn't experience any tension because she treats communication in these contexts as involving diverse norms. She expects all parties in these contexts to accept this diversity and negotiate their difference. She assumes that people can retain their own accent and different languages and still communicate. From her perspective, these contact zones are multilingual. Note also that she doesn't claim advanced or all-purpose proficiency in English, but a functional repertoire of many codes ("a little of many different languages"), which Blommaert (2010) has labeled "fragmented multilingualism" (p. 9). It is clear that GHM is focusing not on correctness of form but negotiation of difference for communicative success. It is because she is confident that people can still communicate across such repertoires and differences through their creative strategies that GHM resists our imputation of "tension" for such modes of communication.

How then do my informants manage to communicate across such difference? MA explains some of the many strategies adopted:

> 2. MA (Nigeria, male, university administrator at Penn State): Probably by paying more attention, just like they have to pay more attention to me as well. It is a two-way street, because of the combination of my Nigerian and British accent and all sorts of things. People had to listen to me more closely to understand what I said, OK? With the same token, I had to listen more carefully to them in order to understand them, [. . .] It was both ways, so I will, just by paying more attention.

For MA, communication is a "two-way street." Both parties have to co-construct meaning, without assuming that one person's norms can be imposed on the other. There are no predefined norms and meanings in contact zones. Interlocutors have to work with each other to co-construct norms and intelligibility. MA illustrates some of the negotiation strategies involved. The contact zone involves both parties paying more attention and listening more attentively, without relying on their own assumptions of meaning.

What we see is a focus on practices rather than grammar for meaning in contact zones. This doesn't mean that multilinguals remain with their own norms and repertoires after such interactions. They display a strong language awareness, sensitivity to diversity of norms, and adaptability to change. They can even be self-critical as they note their own mistakes or limitations in moving on to higher levels of competence. A professor from Sierra Leone recounts how her Nigerian-born husband theorized the difference between his use of the /i/ sound and that of Americans, as they make relevant adjustments:

> 3. OI (Sierra Leone, female, professor of English at Penn State): But my husband had a much stronger Nigerian accent. I remember one day he said to me "You are so funny, I just realized the other day when you say b-i-l-l you gonna make it like a . . . it's like a b-i-e-l because that's the only way the Americans would know what you were saying," you know what I mean? He suddenly got it you know, that if you have to say "Hi Bill," you know, that you kind of say "Hi Biel," [laughter] which just sounds like, a Nigerian would say for b-i-l-l, you know, but Americans would say they open it up they would say "Hi Biel," you know it's kind of open, you know hidden, that you know it doesn't sound like *bill* you know?

This realization doesn't mean that the couple will adopt this diphthong as the new norm for all communication, but use this awareness to negotiate more effectively with American interlocutors. They may code-switch into this alternative when necessary, and certainly accommodate it into their evolving repertoire. In this sense, contact zone communication involves both using and learning language, as participants meet interlocutors with differing norms all the time.

It also emerged from the interviews that such translingual practice is not new for my informants in migrant settings. They are already socialized into such communicative practices in their own countries. The attitudes and practices they are adopting to different varieties of English, they have already adopted to different languages before migration. Their pre-migration settings are already multilingual contact zones. Listen to DB's articulation of her experience in South Africa, which is confirmed by many other participants in the interviews:

> 4. DB (Zimbabwe, female, researcher in Penn State): We speak that language and may be somebody walks in and speaks Afrikaans, you start speaking Afrikaans and a conversation can continue in three different languages. Somebody speaks Afrikaans and I respond in Zulu and she responds in Tswana and continues talking, nothing unusual there. I understand what he says, she/he understands what I'm saying, I understand what she say and he understands, so we all are engaged in a conversation. And there is nothing abnormal for us.

What we see here is a conversation in three different languages, with each person using a different code. Such a practice has been labeled "polyglot dialogue"

(Posner, 1991). Intelligibility is possible because the interlocutors have "receptive multilingualism" (Braünmuller, 2006). They can understand more languages than they speak. Besides, as mentioned earlier, communication doesn't rely on words alone but alignment of different contextual, environmental, and ecological affordances for meaning making. Words are matched with gestures, objects, setting, and topic, for example, to achieve intelligibility (cf. Block, this volume). In this manner, a dialogue in three languages is quite possible in contact zones.

Defining Performative Competence

What I have described above is that my informants define communication as working differently in contact zones. It involves different assumptions and practices from those theorized by a "linguistics of community." In the contact zone, interactants can communicate through heterogeneous codes and diverse norms because they adopt negotiation strategies to co-construct meaning. They also learn new repertoires as they communicate, engaged as they are in practice-based learning. What is important now is to define the competence my informants bring to such communication. It emerged that what makes such communication possible is not a competence for form but a competence for practice. Adopting Michael Byram's (2008) labels for intercultural competence, I want to describe this competence as a "procedural knowledge, not a propositional knowledge." Based on the narratives and experiences of my informants, I would describe this procedural knowledge as involving the following practices:

- Start from your positionality,
- negotiate on equal terms,
- focus on practices, not form,
- co-construct rules and terms of engagement,
- be responsive to joint accomplishment of goals, and
- reconfigure your norms and expand your repertoire.

To begin with, multilinguals start their communication from the contexts in which they are located and the language resources and values they bring with them. We see this in GHM (#1). She disparages people who ask her for repetitions or clarifications. Such a response is a denial of one's voice. Many other participants expressed a strong preference not to ask for repetitions but to acknowledge one's difference and focus on negotiating for meaning (as we will see below). More strikingly, my informants don't express a desire to move to elite forms of English even in so-called Inner Circle communities. Nor do they strive for a value-free or neutral form of English to make communication easier. ELT (English Language Teaching) pedagogies that assume privileged forms of Inner Circle as desirable for and desired by multilinguals should thus reconsider their position on uniform norms. The attitude of my informants suggests that we need pedagogies that provide spaces for learners to appropriate dominant norms based on their own values and interests. Multilinguals base their interactions on a strong sense of voice and locus of enunciation.

However, one's own resources are only the starting point and a basis for negotiation. What enables my informants to achieve meaning, despite the fact that they all start with their own codes, is their openness to negotiate on equal terms. Though they understand that in certain contexts the norms of certain participants enjoy more status, they expect everyone to be open to co-constructing meaning. We see this preference coming out strongly in MA (#2). He treats communication as a "two-way street." As the forms and norms the parties bring to the interaction may be very diverse, multilinguals don't depend on them as the sole or primary sources of meaning. They depend on practices that are adaptive, reciprocal, and supportive to co-construct meaning. MA suggests some of these strategies in his statements. I call them "negotiation strategies" and develop them elsewhere (see Canagarajah, 2011). They include strategies such as "let-it-pass" and "make it normal," identified by Firth (1996). Other strategies of clarification, repair, and confirmation that lingua franca scholars have observed are also part of these practices (see Kaur, 2009; Pitzl, 2010). A key principle behind all these strategies is the notion of *alignment* (Atkinson, Churchill, Nishino, & Okada, 2007). Interlocutors are able to connect words with other diverse ecological resources for meaning. It is in this way that they don't depend solely on grammar to guarantee meaning. Meaning is something they achieve in relation to the multimodal affordances in the environment (cf. Block, this volume).

All this doesn't mean that my informants don't acknowledge the reality of power. They do, but they treat it as negotiable. They often find themselves in situations where native English speakers make it appear that they are deficient or ignorant. For example, GHM acknowledges that people ask her for repetitions and make her feel ignorant or deficient (#1). However, her expectations are different. My informants employ suitable strategies to persuade their interlocutors to adopt an openness to negotiating difference. Without disregarding locally dominant norms, they engage in constructing new meanings and values in situational terms. To encourage their interlocutors to negotiate on equal terms, an important step in the contact zone encounter, is a suitable *frame* and *footing* for the context of communication (Goffman, 1981). These two processes help define the ground rules and terms of interaction. If the interlocutors are confused or conflicted about the relevant ecological features and contextual conditions informing the interaction, they won't have a suitable context to frame the interaction or shape the meaning of their semiotic resources. The frame and footing have to be mutually established. The contextual cues in their text and/or talk will help interlocutors signal to each other the features they consider relevant for this interaction. South Asian linguist Khubchandani (1997) calls the outcome "mutuality of focus" (Khubchandani, 1997, p. 49). Obviously, my informants will define the footing and frames to favor negotiation and resist ideologies based on a linguistics of community. Though this framing and footing can be subtle (for example, MA would cue his assumptions of two-way street communication to his interlocutors in indirect ways during his talk), it can also be explicit. Some can use metaprag-matic cues for this purpose. Consider the strategy adopted by Tadese when he meets interlocutors who refuse to negotiate:

> 5. Tadese (Ethiopia, male, health professor in Seattle): For most of the time, it is not a problem unless others make an issue of it. Then, it may resort to a little bit of educating—depending on how much time or the need to being polite. Mostly it is situational, and requires just patience and tact, time permitting.

It appears that Tadese would resort to "educating" his interlocutors on the diversity of norms on the contact zones if he had more time and felt comfort-able in being more assertive. On most other occasions, however, he is able to cue interlocutors to adopt such an orientation through patience and tact.

As for the outcomes of the talk, multilinguals don't assume that the pre-constructed meanings and objectives of the communicative interaction will be unconditionally accomplished. They are open to hybrid, qualified, and negotiated outcomes. This orientation makes the interaction very dialogical. In this manner, there is an opportunity for both parties to gain from the contribution of the other. Thus multilinguals are able to connect learning with use in their language inter-actions—constructs that are kept separate in other models of competence—as we saw in the statement of OI (#3). It is this orientation that enables them to add to the repertoires they bring with them. It enables them to sharpen, refine, and add to their negotiation strategies as well. In this sense, their competence doesn't make them remain where they started but moves them to a higher proficiency and awareness. The competence they bring with them is made more advanced. Multilinguals thus develop a more complex language awareness and metalinguis-tic competence through practice. This is especially important as there is no end point or threshold for proficiency in contact zone communication.

Though performative competence is not defined in relation to form, it does have implications for form—as we saw in the way OI and her husband add a new phonological resource to their repertoire (in #3). This competence thus enables multilinguals not to master one language system at a time but to develop an integrated repertoire of codes. Their focus is not mastery but open-ended devel-opment of more semiotic resources. Similarly, multilinguals focus on developing a language awareness or metalinguistic competence that enables them to deal with any grammar they encounter in contact situations. In contexts where norms are always new, diverse, and unpredictable, such metalinguistic competence helps them to decode the interlocutor's norms on the spot as they engage in commu-nication (see House, 2003). In this form of competence, proficiency in languages is not conceptualized individually, with separate competencies developed for each language. What is emphasized is the repertoire—the way the different language resources constitute an integrated and ever widening competence. Furthermore, equal or advanced proficiency is not expected in all the languages. Using different languages for distinct purposes qualifies as competence. Note how GHM describes her competence as "little of many different languages" (#1). One doesn't have to use all the languages involved in one's repertoire as all-purpose languages, as multilinguals use different languages for different purposes.

How is the model of competence we see in contact zones different from those defined in traditional "linguistic–cognitive" SLA models (see May, this volume; Ortega, this volume)? The Chomskyan model of grammatical competence dominates discussions of proficiency, even well-meaning efforts to define multilingual competence as different from that of monolinguals. Competence is treated as grammatical, mentalist, and abstract in the Chomskyan tradition, as knowledge of form, constituted as a system and shared by a homogeneous community, as the basis for successful communication (cf. Ortega, this volume). Multilingual alternatives define competence as an innate capacity for multiple languages (see Cook, 1999; Franceschini, 2011). The cognitive and form-based emphasis is still present in these multilingual models. A few other scholars have given more importance to the negotiation strategies of multilinguals by adding communicative competence to their models (see Kaur, 2009). Performance, which Chomsky defined as having only secondary importance for putting into practice the basic grammatical competence, was given much greater significance by Dell Hymes (1974) in his formulation of "communicative competence." Hymes makes a space for social knowledge without which grammatical knowledge is useless in communication (cf. Block, this volume; Leung, this volume). Though this is a useful clarification, Hymes' communicative competence doesn't come close to addressing the competence displayed by my informants in the contact zone either. The binaries of grammar and practice, and cognition and context, are still preserved in Hymes' model. Communicative competence is defined as a form of knowledge and located in cognition. As I mentioned earlier, what multilinguals bring to contact zones is a form of procedural knowledge, not the propositional knowledge of either grammatical or communicative competence. Their competence doesn't constitute of the what, but rather of the how, of communication. This type of knowledge is developed in and through practice, shaping both cognition and form in terms of one's ongoing experiences. The dynamic and reciprocal strategies multilinguals adopt, based on their knowledge of the how, motivates them to respond strategically to unexpected interlocutors and spaces with diverse norms in contact zones. I label this form of competence *performative competence* in an effort to emphasize its practice-based nature. Though performative competence has a cognitive dimension and implications for grammatical awareness, it treats both as shaped by locally situated performance.

In some ways, performative competence is similar to *strategic competence*, the last of the three components Canale and Swain (1980) identify in an effort to unpack Hymes' (1974) notion of communicative competence (see also Leung, this volume). This kind of competence constitutes strategies that enable inter-locutors to deal with breakdowns and trouble spots in interactions. However, I see this kind of strategic competence as forming the basic component of all communication and shaping the other two components of grammatical or socio-linguistic competence in the model of Canale and Swain. Another term that relates closely to performative competence is *interactional competence* (see Kaur, 2009). It is used largely by scholars in conversation analysis to refer to the ability to conduct conversational interactions, with an awareness of the interpersonal strategies that accompany the use of language. Though it usefully focuses on the practical nature of conducting everyday interactions, I define performative com-petence as going beyond the microstructure of conversational turns to include negotiation of broader social and ecological dimensions.

My orientation to performative competence draws from models theorized in ways different from traditional linguistic–cognitive SLA by many scholars today (see Atkinson, 2011a). For example, sociocultural theory demonstrates how environment mediates language learning in productive ways (see Lantolf, 2011). Sociocognitive theory explores how embedded and extended cognition enables language learners to align mind, body, world relationships in their competence (see Atkinson, 2011b; Block, this volume). Dynamic systems theory accommodates knowledge of a system that is open yet stable, diverse yet patterned (Larsen-Freeman, 2011). Language-socialization models theorize how learners develop their competence in ecologically embedded language resources through everyday social relationships and practice (Duff & Talmy, 2011). All these schools situate the previously dominant constructs such as form, cognition, and the individual in a more socially sensitive, ecologically embedded, environmentally situated, and interactionally open model.

Despite these positive developments, there are also differences from my notion of performative competence. All of these models still assume languages as hav-ing their own independent systems, different from the translingual orientation of languages as mobile resources. Most of them (excluding dynamic systems theory) also assume that learners acquire the system without at the same time changing the system. Though dynamic systems theory treats the language system as diverse and open, it still considers the system as independently patterned and located in order to produce meaning. In treating the system as capable of producing mean-ing by itself, the model is somewhat impersonal. The orientation in this chapter is that it is practices and social negotiations that generate meaning out of fluid and hybrid codes. Performative competence emphasizes human agency and social practices in producing meaning. More importantly, while these models are busy developing alternate learning and cognitive models at a theoretical level, we lack adequate information on the learning strategies and processes that will help us translate these models for pedagogical purposes. We need more information on the interface between competence and learning to develop effective pedagogical approaches.

Cooperative Disposition

How do my informants develop performative competence? This competence seems natural and intuitive to them. It is not only that they feel no "tension" in contact zone interactions, they are also not formally schooled into such a proficiency. The few occasions they were sent for remedial classes by their employers, my informants came back disillusioned. They found the formal language teaching contexts inadequate for their needs. Their norm-based and product-oriented pedagogies went against their orientation to communication as practice based and collaborative. Their answers to the way they developed performative competence points to socialization in everyday contexts. Consider OI's observations on how and why she is different:

> 6. OI (Sierra Leone, female, professor of English at Penn State): One thing I have realized personally for a while is that I always loved, maybe because I grew up in a multilingual society where you always knew there other languages all around you, and so you had a way of opening up of other things. I have a feeling that . . . it is easier for us to translate and become something else and understand. But Americans tend to be so unique, language, so just like one language and sound one way.

It is evident that OI attributes her competence to the multilingual environment in her home community in Sierra Leone, where she shuttled between diverse languages, enabling her to develop the negotiation strategies that help her achieve intelligibility across diverse varieties of English in the United States. She suggests a difference between her multilingual home community and the monolingual U.S. context she works in presently. She considers those in the United States as having a different kind of disposition (i.e., "like one language and sound one way") that doesn't help them negotiate differences but makes them insist on their own norms.

My reading of the narratives and opinions of my informants points to certain dispositions that they bring to contact zone interactions to achieve communicative success and further develop their performative competence. These dispositions are developed through socialization in their multilingual home communities and provide the aptitude for translingual practices. This socialization background explains how my informants don't wait for their performative competence to be developed inside the classroom or by teachers in their migrant work settings. Their dispositions help them negotiate contact zone interactions and practice their performative competence. They also help develop their performative competence further through their interactions.

The attitudes and skills multilinguals bring from their home communities I call the *cooperative disposition*. I borrow the cooperative metaphor from Tomasello (2008), who views cooperation and collaboration as the basic principles behind human biological development of communication and cognition (cf. Ortega, this volume). What do these dispositions consist of? They constitute a set of tastes, values, and skills, similar to the way Bourdieu (1977) defines *habitus*. In relation to language learning, these three components can be defined more specifically as language awareness, social values, and learning/communicative strategies, respectively. Multilinguals bring a set of language assumptions, social orientation, and strategies of negotiation/learning that help them develop performative competence and engage in translingual practices. These dispositions are developed in social contexts through everyday experiences, as in habitus (cf. Block, this volume). However, there is also space for agency and personal development. How similar social experiences in contact zones fail to help some to develop these dispositions, or develop them to a higher degree than others, cannot be explained by social context alone. Therefore, these dispositions are not treated in socially deterministic ways. Since all of us inhabit contact zones, it is possible that some native speakers also enjoy personal investments and agency to develop such dispositions. Therefore, performative competence and cooperative disposition are not defined according to birthright. For such reasons, it is important for dispositions to be defined with a cognitive and affective component that is not socially overdetermined. Though cooperative disposition has a psychological dimension then, I adopt a practice-based orientation toward subjective life, different from the innate and transcendental orientation of traditional Cartesian models. Disposition provides subjective processes a social and material character.

I highlight three key features that emerge from my data for each domain of language awareness, social values, and learning strategies that constitute the dispositions that favor contact zone interactions:

1. Language awareness:
   a. language norms as open to negotiation
   b. languages as mobile semiotic resources
   c. a functional orientation to communication and meaning
2. Social values:
   a. openness to diversity
   b. a sense of voice and locus of enunciation
   c. strong ethic of collaboration
3. Learning strategies:
   a. learning from practice
   b. adaptive skills
   c. use of scaffolding

Let me illustrate.

Language Awareness

Skilled migrants treat language norms as open to negotiation. They don't come with rigid and predefined norms for their own languages or for those of others. They are open to reconstructing meanings and values in context in collaboration with their interlocutors. For instance, in response to the question if he has any tensions among the varieties of Englishes he encounters in his work, ZA mentions:

> 7. ZA (Zambia, male, University professor in South Africa): No, one has to accept the reality that people will have different accents and will have different expressions. I don't know, I don't have to have a problem with it . . . It's a pleasure to hear that actually people are using it. . . . No I don't tend to have a problem.

ZA seems to have a very egalitarian view of language norms. He actually considers the diversity of norms "a pleasure." Similarly, in the excerpt cited above in #4, DB says she doesn't consider it "abnormal" or "unusual" in her community to have interactions that involve diverse codes simultaneously. It is this disposition that helps my informants to engage with the diverse norms belonging to the host community and the different migrant groups interacting with them in professional contact zones. Such an open orientation to language encourages skilled migrants to develop performative competence in their social experiences to renegotiate norms, when others resort to their own norms to define meaning.

The participants also treat languages as mobile semiotic resources. They perceive languages as constituting resources they can mix and mesh in unusual patterns to construct meaning. It is this assumption that enables them to appropriate English for their own purposes without being inhibited by native English speaker norms. They also perceive these resources as not owned by any one community or place, as they are mobile. For instance, the participant below from Sierra Leone mentions how it is natural ("without thinking twice") to mix languages and switch languages in her interactions in her community:

> 8. OI (Sierra Leone, female, professor at Penn State):
>
> I:[2] But there is not that kind of arbitrary distinction, hopefully it will be
>   . . .
> OI: People actually switching, there is a lot of codeswitching easily, so that you can find yourself in and out of English and Krio without even without thinking twice.
> I: When in multilingual community, like all those local languages mixed with English . . .
> OI: And somehow you make sense of it and everybody knows what you are saying.

It is clear that my informants don't display a puristic attitude of keeping their languages unmixed with other people's languages. There is a very relaxed attitude to language ownership. Likewise, the participants treat language as part of a broader set of multimodal semiotic resources. Language combines with other symbol systems, diverse modalities of communication, and environmental resources to create meaning. This disposition too motivates them to develop performative competence in their everyday contexts as they appropriate codes for negotiated and aligned meaning. We see this coming out clearly in the statement below by a physician, ET, on how language has to be connected to the discourses and setting of his profession in considering his communicative success.

I present ET's views in relation to the third disposition in language awareness, that is, skilled migrants adopt a functional orientation to communication and meaning. They focus more on the functions performed through communication through diverse semiotic resources. In this disposition again, skilled migrants adopt a relaxed attitude to norms, as described above. They look beyond correctness of form to the functions performed. They consider form as the servant of meaning. Consider ET's position below:

> 9. ET (Zimbabwe, male, doctor at Sheffield): I have also seen some doctors whose first language isn't English who struggle to speak it but are excellent physicians. I think because it is such a professional job, people are prepared to overlook the language issue. They would rather have an excellent physician who speaks little English than see him go to another country, like [the] US. Besides, I think the patients wouldn't mind whether the physician who treated them, saved their life was speaking broken English or fluent English as long as they are good at what they do, that is all that matters. I think medicine and other technically demanding fields don't really need someone to be fluent in English, as long as they can make a diagnosis that is all that matters. It's more like football, Ronaldo didn't speak a word of English, neither does Messi, but they are technically very good at it. Most teams now are composed of footballers from different countries who all speak different languages but they still deliver. That is what medicine is like.

What is important for ET is the ability to "perform" in English. He feels so strongly about this that he is able to disconnect language proficiency from communicative practice. That is, those who "struggle to speak" English can still be "excellent physicians." This is possible because of the functional orientation he brings to communication. Being an excellent physician presumably involves practices beyond language or practices that accompany language use. For him, "mak[ing] a diagnosis" is not directly tied to being "fluent in English." As he goes on to explain through the ingenious metaphor of football, though the team might be multilingual and speak "broken English,"[3] what is more important is that "they still deliver." He is confident that what even "native English speakers" care about is the ability to deliver, not language correctness. A functional orientation encourages skilled migrants to develop negotiation strategies and communicative practices without focusing on accuracy or correctness.

Social Values

Such language assumptions and ideologies are complemented by certain social values that enable skilled migrants to develop their performative competence. A key social value is their openness to diversity. As South Asian linguist Khubchandani (1997, p. 94) affirms, it is this disposition that motivates multilinguals to treat "deviations as the norm"—whether in language, culture, or social relationships. It is also remarkable how the African skilled migrants consider transnational contact zones as shared by all, wherever they come from. They expect native speakers, traditional "owners" of English, to also assume differences as expected and focus on negotiating them for meaning. Skilled migrants can take this preparedness for diversity to unexpected levels. They can take it to the level of assuming nothing as shared—whether values, norms, or conventions. This disposition would also motivate them to develop performative competence that would help co-construct meaning and achieve temporary states of sharedness, as evident in the excerpt below:

10. DB (Zimbabwe, female, researcher in Penn State):

I: OK, in what language do you communicate with people from your native country as you undertake professional connections or other development efforts?
DB: Well, in any language.
I: Any language?
DB: Any other language or anything goes, and it could be just also a mixture of the communities, for example I was talking to a person in Facebook right now, moving Zulu, English and sometimes Afrikaans but that's how we always operate.

It is remarkable here that for DB what language is used by her interlocutors is not of much concern, because what counts more is the social value that enables her to negotiate all possible differences. There is an openness to diversity. This openness was matched by a strong conversational ethic of not asking people to repeat their statements or clarify themselves. Such interjection is treated as an insult, as we see in NS's statement below:

11. NS (Kenya, female, nurse in Bradford): No, I never ask. *They* ask me to repeat.

I: Yeah, you'd never—
NS: No, I do feel I understand—
I: Sometimes, because if some of them was speaking a heavy regional accent and—
NS: *I'm* the one to ask? No.

Here, the participant vehemently denies that she would ask for repetitions. She considers it a violation of the ethic of diversity to do so.

This ethic was expressed the reverse way also. The participants brought a strong sense of voice and considered it rude when others would ask them for repetitions. We saw this in the statement by GHM in #1 above. She considered it "sloppy when people say that they do not understand a person due to accent, et cetera." This is affirmed by another participant who expressed the need for identity in another interview. In response to a question that sought her opinion on the role of English for the social and economic development of her country, she argued as follows:

> 12. ZS (Zimbabwe, female, nurse in Sheffield): I think together with other languages, it is important. People need to be bilingual, speak English and their own languages, that way they can develop. It's pointless to be able to speak English without being able to speak your own.

ZS sees the need to maintain her own local languages while speaking English. It is evident that she is comfortable with using English in combination with local languages and even having influences of one's own values and identities. What we see then is that skilled migrants have a strong sense of voice and locus of enunciation. They start from their own positionality in their interactions. It is their openness to diversity that makes them comfortable with their own voice and difference. They don't feel that their voice or identity should be suppressed for the sake of power, social harmony, or intelligibility.

However, there is a paradox in insisting on one's difference, acknowledging the interlocutor's difference, and still achieving intelligibility. What enables ZS as well as other skilled migrants to deal with this paradox effectively is their strong ethic of collaboration. This is the third social ethic I found in their disposition. They bring strong skills for collaborating with others to co-construct meaning. This ethic explains the ideology among my informants that they should not ask for repetitions from their interlocutors. To ask for clarifications or corrections is an admission of failure in collaborative strategies. Scholars of lingua franca communication, like Firth (1996), House (2003), and Seidlhofer (2004), also observe this social ethic of collaboration (cf. Leung, this volume). What MA explains in #2 as "two-way street" communication emphasizes this social ethic. The strong ethic of collaboration manifests itself in the many strategies my informants adopt to achieve intelligibility. As we already found in MA in #2, they listen intently. Others stated how they might adopt strategies like "let-it-pass" to collaborate in meaning making. Consider the motivations behind adopting the let-it-pass strategy by the following participant. Asked whether he faced tensions because of differences in English, EV said:

> 13. EV [Zimbabwe, male, social worker in Sheffield]: Maybe not explicit, people don't want to be seen as though they are rude, lest they are accused of racism or harassment. Even on occasions when you have genuinely not

understood what someone has said, you just let it pass, you may follow it up with an email just to be sure. At work, I always follow everything that I have said whether in a meeting or elsewhere with an email to forestall the chances of someone saying that they misunderstood what I was saying or to blame it on my accent.

Note that, though he doesn't ask for repetitions as it is rude, he does follow his communication up with other compensatory strategies, such as email. Through this strategy, he makes sure that he has communicated what he expected. He doesn't leave any room for excuses or misunderstandings.

Learning Strategies

Skilled migrants combine the linguistic and social values discussed above with effective learning strategies to both succeed in translingual practice and develop their performative competence further. An important skill they bring is to learn from practice. Thus they combine language use and learning. As I pointed out earlier, these are not separate processes. Communication in everyday life provides them with opportunities for purposive and meaningful learning. Such learning is challenging and brings its own difficulties. Learning has to take place in ecological contexts where input is embedded and constantly changing with the environment. Skilled migrants bring the disposition to form rules and resources from such holistic input. Consider the everyday learning of language by the participant below:

> 14. AZ (Zambia, female, researcher at Cape Town): My father is British, so I have to remember that I grew up communicating in English in the house I didn't really need any other language really and then I grew . . . and Nyanja because of friends. And school, I grew up and it's like in class I didn't need another language to communicate with formal school work. But it was in informal play and communication that English wasn't enough. That's when I learnt Nyanja. Not because it was one of the subjects at school but because everybody else included both English and Nyanja and Bemba, Tonga and Lozi and what not. But in Lozi all I can say is "kaufela."

It is evident that AZ mastered Nyanja through friends and play situations. In a context where English was valued in school, she had to resort to other means for developing a repertoire for other communicative situations. School and formal pedagogies cannot be relied on for developing a wide repertoire.

More importantly, the contact zone requires that one keeps learning even beyond childhood learning of languages in schools. Especially in contexts of skilled migration, one is compelled to develop proficiency in the new codes for work and social contexts. Below is an elderly priest who keeps on learning the languages of the diverse African communities he ministers to after his migration to the United Kingdom:

> 15. PZ (Zimbabwe, male, Priest in Leeds): I am learning different lan-
> guages at the moment. I am learning Kalanga, Chichewa, Swahili and
> French which will enable me to communicate more with people from
> different countries. I want to reach as many people as possible from Africa
> who are here, . . . I learn the languages by talking to people, I listen when
> they are speaking in their own languages and I learn that way. I also use
> the computer to learn new languages; this is true for Swahili because
> there are translations already done for most of the words that you can buy.
> For the other languages, I sit down with a tutor here and there to learn
> these languages.

It is clear that PZ is learning these languages mostly through practice, that is, through speaking and listening in actual interactions. He also uses various tools at his disposal to learn languages, such as computer and relevant software. Like him, almost all migrants affirmed that they developed their performative competence from communicative practice outside formal pedagogical domains.

What enables skilled migrants to progress in this type of learning in contact zones is their adaptive skill. Consider how MA, a Nigerian migrant we met earlier (#2), has learned to adapt to the differences in Englishes in his work experience that involves international travel:

> 16. MA: (Nigeria, male, university administrator at Penn State): In my cur-
> rent [situation], it doesn't. Like I said before, that will disappear with time. In
> other words, it used to be a barrier, it's no longer a barrier because naturally,
> right now, I can cope with any varieties of English. Because I deal with
> people who speak different accents, because I travel all over the world, and
> when in India, for example, then I'm in China, when I'm in Britain. And
> so now my ear is tuned towards different accents, or what they call accent.

Though he accepts that he used to have difficulties with different accents ear-lier, he has now adapted to even more diverse English varieties through exposure. This adaptive skill is aided strongly by reflective skills, motivated by an openness to learning. Skilled migrants also bring the humility to make mistakes, acknowl-edge their failures or limitations, and engage in self-correction. They can apply lessons learned in one context to a new context. They can infer lessons from past mistakes for improved performance in the next context. They can be self-critical and bring a keen sensitivity to criticism. They also have the ability to thrive and develop from feedback, implicit or explicit, in their communicative encounters. Consider how OI (in #3) reflects on the difference of the /i/ sound in her com-munity and the host community and collaboratively develops an insight with her

husband. Others too displayed a capacity for reflection and metalinguistic awareness, though they didn't have formal training in linguistics.

Such practice-based and adaptive learning can produce astounding results.
Consider the richness of repertoires in the case of PZ whom we met above. He is
able to learn from diverse venues, using his adaptive skills:

> 17. PZ (Zimbabwe, male, Priest in Leeds): I can speak six different lan-
> guages, four of which I learnt outside the school, two are self taught from
> my days of living at the farm where my father worked and I was playing
> with the farmer's children. That is how I came to speak Afrikaans and then
> when I worked in Bulawayo, I learnt Ndebele. I spent some time in Que-
> bec, Canada and there I learnt French. Sotho and Tswana, I learnt them in
> South Africa when I was ministering there. These languages were learnt a
> long time ago before I even knew that I would one day be called to minister
> in England. Learning all these different languages has been important not
> only for my job in this country but in all the countries that I have been to.
> I am able to talk to people who speak different languages. (#29)

It is also interesting that he is able to draw from repertoires he developed many
years back for work in his current migrant context. Such proficiency is quite
common in many of the other participants interviewed.

Finally, skilled migrants bring the learning strategy of scaffolding to develop
their performative competence. They use scaffolds of many kinds to develop their
proficiency, including using their knowledge of one language to develop proficiency in another, and using various caregivers and agents to help them in learning.
Some obtain self-help materials such as dictionaries and computers. Such strategies help them develop their performative competence further. Consider how TT
explained how he and his spouse use each other's experiences outside the home
to scaffold their further learning of English:

> 18. TT (Tanzania, male, teacher in Bristol): There will be tensions as Eng-
> lish is my fourth language. This means I wouldn't know some words, some
> pronunciation and my accent is not like native speakers. I know this and
> I am learning everyday from my wife, students and colleagues. How do
> you handle/overcome these differences? I socialise with native speakers of
> English and at home I communicate in English with my wife and family.
> While learning Creole, my wife's native language, and she learns Kiswahili
> my native language. And we also read widely.

Note that TT accepts his limitations and shows openness to learning from
interactions with diverse interlocutors ("I know this and I am learning everyday from my wife, students and colleagues.") It appears that there is a lot of
practice and reflection going on at home at the end of the day when husband

and wife scaffold each other's learning from socialization with native English speakers. TT's statements also show that, despite their agentive dispositions and strategies, multilinguals display a realistic acknowledgement of power and the status of native speaker norms. Note, also, that it is not only English that they are learning; the couple is simultaneously learning each other's African languages through each other's help. TT also suggests that reading helps him scaffold the learning from his conversational interactions with native English speakers.

Conclusion

My argument in this chapter is that multilinguals bring a special kind of competence—one that I label performative competence—to negotiate the diverse, unpredictable, and changing language norms in the contact zone. What helps them to enact and enhance this performative competence is their cooperative disposition that they have developed through their socialization in their multilingual home communities. I give flesh to these two constructs through the narratives and opinions of skilled African migrants. We have to study more diverse participants and contexts to develop this orientation further. However, a reading of scholarship from other multilingual communities in South Asia (Khubchandani, 1997), South America (de Souza, 2002), and Africa (Makoni, 2002) suggests that such dispositions are shared by multilinguals from diverse class, ethnic, and educational backgrounds in these regions. Though the educated and professional background of my informants might make us feel that they can afford to be more agentive, we must note that such dispositions are displayed to varying degrees by multilinguals from different walks of life in the extant literature.

Meanwhile, there are important pedagogical implications deriving from this research and the orientation proposed in this chapter. We have to consider what pedagogies can open up the classroom as a space for social negotiations, ecological affordances, and practice-based learning (cf. García & Flores, this volume; Leung, this volume). Rather than asking what we can offer "deficient" multilingual students, we have to ask how we can let students bring into the classroom the dispositions and competencies they have already developed richly outside the classroom. This involves turning the classroom into a site for translingual socialization. Teacher have to permit, as much as they can, the conditions, resources, and affordances students find outside the classroom for the development of their performative competence. In this enterprise, teachers should be prepared to learn from their students.

However, arguing that their cooperative disposition provides the aptitude for performative competence doesn't mean that there is no room for improvement and further development among multilingual students. Multilinguals can develop their proficiency through favorable pedagogical strategies and resources.

In fact, if multilinguals are always open to learning, "lifelong and lifewide" (Duff, 2008, p. 257), they would have the disposition to treat classroom relations and activities also for their development. The fact that we see effective socialization into performative competence in everyday situations in social contexts doesn't mean that the classroom cannot help in developing critical awareness and reflective practice (cf. Blackledge et al., this volume; Li Wei, this volume). Teachers can welcome and encourage the cooperative disposition of multilingual students and provide a space to further develop the performative competence they bring with them.

Notes

1. This is a multisited qualitative study, funded by the Worldwide Universities Network, led by Penn State University. I thank the following co-PIs for their help in collecting data: Adrian Bailey, Leeds University, UK; Frances Giampapa, Bristol University, UK; Margaret Hawkins, University of Wisconsin, USA; Ellen Hurst, University of Cape Town, South Africa; Ahmar Mahboob, University of Sydney, Australia; Paul Roberts, York University, UK; and Sandra Silberstein, University of Washington, USA.
2. "I" refers to interviewers.
3. My informants sometimes refer to their local varieties in pejorative terms, such as "broken English," as here. We have to acknowledge that language ideologies are powerful and that the participants have thus often already bought into the labels used by dominant communities. Despite their agentive practices then, they still display influences from dominant communities. Perhaps they are also acknowledging the reality of language hierarchies through such labels. I am certainly not claiming that my informants display total liberation from limiting language ideologies!

References

Atkinson, D. (Ed.). (2011a). *Alternative approaches to second language acquisition*. Abingdon, UK: Routledge.

Atkinson, D. (2011b). A sociocognitive approach to second language acquisition: How mind, body, and world work together in learning additional languages. In D. Atkinson (Ed.), *Alternative approaches to second language acquisition* (pp. 143–166). Abingdon, UK: Routledge.

Atkinson, D., Churchill, E., Nishino, T., & Okada, H. (2007). Alignment and interaction in a sociocognitive approach in second language acquisition. *The Modern Language Journal, 91*, 169–188.

Blommaert, J. (2010). *The sociolinguistics of globalization*. Cambridge, UK: Cambridge University Press.

Bourdieu, P. (1977). *Outline of a theory of practice*. Cambridge, UK: Cambridge University Press.

Braunmüller, K. (2006, September). *On the relevance of receptive multilingualism in a globalised world: Theory, history and evidence from today's Scandinavia*. Paper presented at the First Conference on Language Contact in Times of Globalization, University of Groningen, Netherlands.

Byram, M. (2008). *From intercultural education to education for intercultural citizenship*. Clevedon, UK: Multilingual Matters.

Canagarajah, A. S. (1999). Interrogating the native speaker fallacy: Non-linguistic roots, non-pedagogical results. In G. Braine (Ed.), *Non-native educators in ELT* (pp. 77–92). Mahwah, NJ: Erlbaum.

Canagarajah, A. S. (2007). Lingua franca English, multilingual communities, and language acquisition. *The Modern Language Journal, 91*(5), 921–937.

Canagarajah, A. S. (2011). Codemeshing in academic writing: Identifying teachable strategies of translanguaging. *The Modern Language Journal, 95*(3), 401–417.

Canale, M., & Swain, M. (1980). Theoretical bases of communicative approaches to second language teaching and testing. *Applied Linguistics, 1*(1), 1–47.

Cook, V. (1999). Going beyond the native speaker in language teaching. *TESOL Quarterly, 33*(2), 185–209.

de Souza, L. M. (2002). A case among cases, a world among worlds: The ecology of writing among the Kashinawa in Brazil. *Journal of Language, Identity, and Education, 1*(4), 261–278.

Duff, P. A. (2008). Language socialization, higher education, and work. In P. Duff & N. Hornberger (Eds.), *Language socialization: Encyclopedia of language and education* (pp. 257–270). Boston, MA: Springer.

Duff, P. A., & Talmy, S. (2011). Language socialization approaches to second language acquisition: Social, cultural, and linguistic development in additional languages. In D. Atkinson (Ed.), *Alternative approaches to second language acquisition* (pp. 94–116). Abingdon, UK: Routledge.

Firth, A. (1996). The discursive accomplishment of normality. On "lingua franca" English and conversation analysis. *Journal of Pragmatics, 26*, 237–259.

Franceschini, R. (2011). Multilingualism and multicompetence: A conceptual view. *The Modern Language Journal, 95*(3), 344–355.

García, O. (2009). *Bilingual education in the 21st century: A global perspective.* Oxford, UK: Wiley-Blackwell.

Goffman, E. (1981). *Forms of talk.* Oxford, UK: Blackwell.

House, J. (2003). English as a lingua franca: A threat to multilingualism? *Journal of Sociolinguistics, 7*(4), 556–578.

Hymes, D. (1974). *Foundations in sociolinguistics: An ethnographic approach.* Philadelphia, PA: University of Pennsylvania Press.

Jørgensen, J. N. (2008). Poly-lingual languaging around and among children and adolescents. *International Journal of Multilingualism, 5*(3), 161–176.

Kachru, B. (1986). *The alchemy of English: The spread, functions and models of non-native Englishes.* Oxford: Pergamon.

Kaur, J. (2009). *English as a lingua franca: Co-constructing understanding.* Berlin, Germany: Verlag.

Khubchandani, L. M. (1997). *Revisualizing boundaries: A plurilingual ethos.* New Delhi, India: Sage.

Kuznetsov, Y. (2006). *Diaspora networks and the international migration of skills.* Washington, DC: World Bank.

Lantolf, J. (2011). The sociocultural approach to second language acquisition: Sociocultural theory, second language acquisition, and artificial L2 development. In D. Atkinson (Ed.), *Alternative approaches to second language acquisition* (pp. 24–47). Abingdon, UK: Routledge.

Larsen-Freeman, D. (2011). A complexity theory approach to second language development/ acquisition. In D. Atkinson (Ed.), *Alternative approaches to second language acquisition* (pp. 48–72). Abingdon, UK: Routledge.

Makoni, S. (2002). From misinvention to disinvention: An approach to multilingualism. In G. Smitherman, A. Spear, & A. Ball (Eds.), *Black linguistics: Language, society and politics in Africa and the Americas* (pp.132–153). London, UK: Routledge.

Mercer, C., Page, B., & Evans, M. (2008). *Development and the African diaspora*. London, UK: Zed Books.

Pennycook, A. (2010). *Language as a local practice*. London, UK: Routledge.

Pitzl, M-L. (2010). *English as a lingua franca in international business*. Saarbrucken, Germany: Verlag.

Posner, R. (1991). Der ployglotte dialog [The polyglot dialog]. *Der Sprachreport, 3,* 6–10.

Pratt, M. L. (1987). Linguistic utopias. In N. Fabb, D. Attridge, A. Durant, & C. MacCabe (Eds.), *The linguistics of writing: Arguments between language and literature* (pp. 48–66). Manchester, UK: Manchester UP.

Pratt, M. L. (1991). Arts of the contact zone. *Profession, 91,* 33–40.

Seidlhofer, B. (2004). Research perspectives on teaching English as a lingua franca. *Annual Review of Applied Linguistics, 24,* 209–239.

Singh, R. (Ed.). (1998). *The native speaker: Multilingual perspectives*. New Delhi, India: Sage.

Tomasello, M. (2008). *Origins of human communication*. Boston, MA: MIT Press.

5

IDENTITY, LITERACY, AND THE MULTILINGUAL CLASSROOM

Bonny Norton

Interest in identity, literacy, and multilingualism represents a shift in the field of language education from a focus on psycholinguistic models of language learning to include greater interest in the sociological and anthropological dimensions of language learning.[1] Those of us interested in identity and language teaching are concerned not only about linguistic input and output in second language acquisition (SLA), but also in the relationship between the language learner and the larger social world.[2] To address our interests, we have examined the diverse social, historical, and cultural contexts in which language learning and literacy development take place and how learners negotiate and sometimes resist the diverse positions those contexts offer them. In order to better understand these contexts, we are also interested in the extent to which relations of power within classrooms and communities promote or constrain the conditions under which language learners speak, listen, read, or write. We take the position that, when learners speak or remain silent, when they write, read, or resist, we need to understand the extent to which the learner is valued in a particular classroom, institution, or community. We ask, for example, whether a learner's gender, race, class, ethnicity, or sexual orientation may position learners in ways that silence and exclude. At the same time, however, we seek to understand the diverse ways in which learners may challenge both subtle and overt forms of discrimination and what implications this has for language teaching. We take the position, therefore, that language is more than a system of signs; it is social practice in which experiences are organized and identities negotiated.

Parallel to changes in conceptions of language are changes in prevailing conceptions of literacy in the field of education.[3] As Luke (1997) notes, while earlier psychological perspectives conceived of literacy as the acquisition of particular behaviors, cognitive strategies, and linguistic-processing skills, more recent insights from ethnography, cultural studies, and feminist theory have led to increasing recognition that literacy is not only a skill to be learned but a practice that is socially constructed and locally negotiated. In this view, literacy is best understood in the context of larger institutional practices, whether in the home, the school, the community, or the larger society. These institutional practices, in turn, could be understood with reference to what is called the "literacy ecology" of communities, in which there is frequently inequitable access to social, economic, and political power (Barton, 2007; Hornberger, 2003; Martin-Jones & Jones, 2000). The complex ways in which families, schools, and communities interact and differ in their literacy practices provide significant insights into the ways in which people learn, teach, negotiate, and access literacy both inside and outside school settings.

These parallel trajectories in the fields of language and literacy education, respectively, have much in common and have had a great impact on my own research on identity, literacy, and the multilingual classroom in the international community. In this chapter, I will present four multilingual contexts in which I have sought to explore the subtle connections between literacy, identity, and language teaching. These collaborative research projects reflect a trajectory of research over the last two decades, beginning with research in South Africa in the early 1990s, followed by research in Canada and Pakistan, and concluding with my ongoing research in Uganda. In South Africa, we studied resistant readings of texts used for assessment purposes (Norton Peirce & Stein, 1995); in Canada, we examined the appeal of *Archie* comics for young people (Moffatt & Norton, 2005, 2008; Norton, 2003; Norton & Vanderheyden, 2004); in Pakistan, we investigated perceptions of literacy amongst middle-school students in Karachi (Norton & Kamal, 2003); and in Uganda, we continue to investigate a wide range of language and literacy practices in different regions of the country.[4] In this chapter, I will present some of the key findings from each of these four global research sites, focusing on the relationship between literacy, identity, and language teaching in these multilingual contexts. The research is informed by, and continues to inform, my theoretical interest in investment and imagined identities, as discussed next.

Investment and Imagined Identities

The theoretical assumptions associated with research on identity, literacy, and multilingualism suggest that language learning is not a gradual individual process of internalizing a neutral set of rules, structures, and vocabulary of a standard language. Rather, such theoretical principles suggest that language learners need to struggle for ownership of meaning making, they need to learn to command the attention of their listeners, and they need to negotiate language as a system and as a social practice. In this regard, my work on the constructs of *investment* and *imagined communities and imagined identities* seeks to contribute to these debates.

Investment

In ongoing research (see Norton, 2000, 2012; Norton & Toohey, 2011; Norton Peirce, 1995), I have sought to integrate poststructuralist conceptions of identity and human agency by developing a construct I have called *investment*. Departing from current conceptions of "motivation" in the field of language learning, the concept of investment signals the socially and historically constructed relationship of learners to the target language and their sometimes ambivalent desire to speak, read, or write it. Investment is best understood with reference to the economic metaphors that Pierre Bourdieu uses in his work, in particular the notion of "cultural capital" (Bourdieu, 1977, 1991). The term cultural capital is used to reference the knowledge, credentials, and modes of thought that characterize different classes, which have differential exchange value in different social fields (May, 2011).

In my work, I have argued that if learners "invest" in language and literacy, they do so with the understanding that they will attain a wider range of symbolic and material resources, which will, in turn, increase the value of their cultural capital and social power. By symbolic resources, I refer to such resources as language, education, and friendship, while material resources refer to such resources as capital goods, real estate, and money. As the value of their cultural capital increases, so learners' sense of themselves, their identities, are reassessed. Hence there is an integral relationship between investment and identity.

Unlike more traditional notions of motivation, which often conceive of the language learner as having a unitary, fixed, and ahistorical "personality," the construct of investment conceives of the language learner as having a complex identity, changing across time and space, and reproduced in social interaction. Further, while scholars such as Dörnyei and Ushioda (2009) have sought to accommodate theories of the self in new constructs of motivation, it remains a psychological construct with a quantitative orientation, while investment must be seen within a sociological qualitative framework, seeking to understand the relationship between a learner's desire to learn a language, their changing identity, and relations of power in human interaction.

The construct of investment provides for a different set of questions associated with a learner's commitment to learning the target language. In addition to asking, for example, "To what extent is the learner motivated to learn this language?" the teacher or researcher asks, "What is the learner's investment in the language practices of this classroom or community?" Despite being highly motivated, a learner could be excluded from the language practices of a classroom and, in time, positioned as a "poor" or unmotivated language learner. Alternatively, the language practices of the classroom may not be consistent with the learner's expectations of good language teaching, and the language learner may not be invested in the language practices promoted by the teacher. The notion of investment has been taken up by other scholars in the field and is proving productive for understanding the complex conditions under which language and literacy learning take place,[5] including a special issue on investment that appeared in the *Journal of Asian Pacific Communication* (Arkoudis & Davison, 2008). Cummins has argued that the construct of investment has emerged as a "significant explanatory construct" (Cummins, 2006, p. 59) in the second language learning literature.

Imagined Communities and Imagined Identities

In daily life, people interact with members of many communities, including the neighborhood, the workplace, the school, and the religious institution. As Wenger (1998) suggests, however, people are also affiliated with communities of the imagination. Benedict Anderson (1991), who originally coined the term "imagined communities," observed that nations are imagined communities, because members of a given nation will never know most of their fellow-members but still remain connected to them through the power of the imagination. Thus, in imagining ourselves allied with others across time and space, we can still feel a sense of community with people we have not yet met and with whom we may never have a direct relationship.

In 2001, I applied the term imagined community to language learning and teaching theory (Norton, 2001) and was particularly interested in the relationship between imagined communities, imagined identities, and classroom resistance. This relationship can be illustrated with reference to data I obtained from a Polish student, Katarina, who was an adult immigrant language learner in Canada. Katarina withdrew from her English-language course after four months in response to her teacher's evaluative comment that Katarina's English was not "good enough" to take a computer course. What might be perceived as a particularly strong reaction to her teacher's comment is best understood with reference to Katarina's history, investments, and imagined identities.

In her native country, Katarina had been a teacher for 17 years and was a highly respected professional. In Canada, she eagerly sought recognition from people who were fellow professionals, and she wished to have a career in which she could meet like-minded people. As she said, "I choose computer course, not because I have to speak, but because I have to think." Katarina's imagined community was thus a community of professionals (cf. Canagarajah, this volume) and was as much a reconstruction of her professional past in Poland as it was an imaginative construction of her future in Canada. Katarina's language teacher was a member of this imagined community, a community in which Katarina believed she had already achieved a respected status. When Katarina felt that her teacher failed to acknowledge her professional identity, positioning her as an immigrant, she was greatly distressed. When, indeed, the teacher appeared to discourage Katarina from taking a computer course that would give her greater access to her imagined identity, Katarina refused to continue participating in the language class. I concluded that Katarina's act of resistance helped her to preserve the integrity of her imagined community and imagined identity.

These concepts have been further developed in diverse collaborative publications (cf. Early & Norton, 2012; Kanno & Norton, 2003; Norton & Early, 2011; Norton & Gao, 2008; Norton & Williams, 2012; Pavlenko & Norton, 2007) and have proven productive for other scholars in a variety of research sites.[6] There is a focus on the future when learners imagine who they might be, and who their communities might be, when they become multiliterate or multilingual. However, these imagined communities may well have a reality as strong as those in which learners have current daily engagement and might have a significant impact on their investment in language and literacy learning. My research suggests that a teacher's lack of awareness of learners' imagined communities and imagined identities could compromise a learner's investment in the language practices of the classroom.

Research Across Time and Space

In my research projects in different regions of the world, I have sought to develop and enrich the constructs of identity, investment, and imagined communities in the field of language learning and teaching. Of central interest in my research is to enhance opportunities for English language learning without compromising investments in multilingualism and multilingual literacy. At the same time, I seek to better understand learner investments in both the English language and multilingualism and the relationship between learner investment and learner identity. My hope is that an enhanced understanding of this relationship will, in turn, support and enrich multilingual pedagogical practices. I turn now to research studies on literacy, identity, and multilingualism in South Africa, Canada, Pakistan, and Uganda.

Resistant Readings in South Africa

Struggles over conceptions of literacy across multilingual contexts, and the effects of power on the construction of meaning, are the subject of my early collaborative research in South Africa, a country which was just beginning to emerge from its apartheid past. One particular research project, conducted with Pippa Stein in the early 1990s (Norton Peirce & Stein, 1995), focused on the pretesting of a reading text that was being considered for inclusion in a pre-admissions English-language test to the University of the Witwatersrand (Wits) in Johannesburg, where English is the medium of instruction. The passage in question, drawn from a local newspaper, described police action against a group of monkeys that had eaten fruit from the trees in a white suburban neighborhood of Durban. The piloting of the text, which we called the *Monkeys Passage*, was undertaken with a group of Black students, all English language learners, in an inner-city Johannesburg school. We found that the students had very different interpretations of the text when the conditions under which they read it changed. Under test conditions, the students read the passage as a simple story about monkeys stealing fruit, but in the communal discussion following the test, the students read the text as symbolic of apartheid injustice. One of the central questions we sought to address was why the meaning of the passage shifted so radically from one social occasion to the next.

The answer to this question, we argued, was a function of the changing identities of the students, with respect to the particular "genre" in which the meaning of the text was negotiated. Drawing on Kress (1989, 1993), we made the case that a genre is not the more conventional notion of oral or written "text type" as, for example, a sonnet, term paper, interview, or prayer. Rather, with reference to Kress, we made the case that a genre is constituted within and by a particular social occasion that has a conventionalized structure and that functions within the context of larger institutional and social processes. In this formulation, the social occasions that constitute a genre may be formulaic and ritualized, such as a wedding or committee meeting, or less ritualized, such as a casual conversation. The important point is that the conventionalized forms of these occasions and the organization, purpose, and intention of participants within the occasion give rise to the meanings associated with the specific genre. Furthermore, as Kress has demonstrated, the increasing difference in power relations between participants in an interaction has a particular effect on the social meaning of the texts within a particular genre. In essence, in genres where there is great power difference between the participants, the mechanism of interaction, the conventionalized form of the genre, is most prominent, while the substance of the interaction, the content, is less prominent.

During the test event, when Stein was administering the test, the students were powerless test takers; during the communal discussion, however, the students were informed and powerful community members. After the scripts had been duly collected and handed in, the power relations between Stein and the students altered dramatically. Stein sat informally on a desk, inviting comment and criticism. She was no longer the test maker and the students test takers; she was no longer the expert and they the novices. In this context, it was Stein who was the novice and the students the experts. Further, students were no longer isolated and silent: They interacted with one another animatedly; they debated, argued, and laughed together. They had the time to reflect and critique. On this more egalitarian social occasion, the substance of the interaction (the content of the text) became more prominent than the mechanism of the interaction (the testing rituals), and there was no longer a single legitimate reading of the text. Students could draw on their background knowledge and experience to analyze the social meaning of the text, and there was now a place for multiple readings.

Our central finding was that the meaning of a reading passage can shift in the context of different social occasions, shifting identities, and changing relations of power. The research supports the view that literacy cannot be understood apart from relationships between people, in a given time and place, with differential access to resources. During the second social occasion, the value ascribed to the Monkeys Passage was complex and contested. For some students—most students—the Monkeys Passage was positioned as a text reflecting race and class interests at the expense of less powerful interests. "It's about black people, who are the monkeys 'on the rampage' in white people's homes"; "It's about who owns the land"; "It's about violence in our society," said these students. For others, the text remained a simple story about monkeys. The implications for the assessment of language learners are profound (cf. Leung, this volume).

Archie *Comics and the "Literate Underlife" of Multilingual Students in Canada*

Archie comics, which address the lives of a group of adolescents in the United States, are popular in Canada, and indeed, many parts of the world, and are widely read by preadolescent children of diverse language backgrounds, 60% of whom are girls. In embarking on this research (Moffatt & Norton, 2005, 2008; Norton, 2003; Norton & Vanderheyden, 2004), our aim was not to promote or denounce *Archie* comics but to better understand the ubiquitous *Archie* reader and to determine if insights from *Archie* readers might have significance for language and literacy education. The research was conducted in a Vancouver, Canada, elementary school from 1998–1999 and involved 55 elementary students, aged 10 to 12, 25 of whom were language learners of English, the medium of instruction.

In our research we found that *Archie* comic readers were subject to an interesting set of power relationships in their home and school contexts. Students noted that their parents and teachers were frequently dismissive of their love of comic books, describing them as "garbage" and "a waste of time." *Archie* readers had incorporated such views in their own understandings of literacy, drawing a distinction between what they called "real reading" and "fun reading." "Real reading," in their view, was reading what the teacher prescribed; it was "educational"; it was "challenging," but it was seldom "fun." The reading of *Archie* comics was "fun" because readers could construct meaning, make hypotheses, and predict future developments without trying to second guess the teacher. The findings suggest that the inequitable relationships of power between teachers and parents, on the one hand, and children, on the other, may limit a young reader's engagement with text, sometimes rendering it a meaningless ritual.

A second important finding from the research was that the reading, lending, and borrowing of comics provided a common set of interests and activities that constituted what Finders (1997, p. 25) would describe as the "literate underlife" of preadolescent children. Of particular significance is that the rituals associated with comic books helped strengthen relationships between children of diverse linguistic backgrounds, enhancing their language and literacy development. As Dyson (1996, p. 492) notes, "Curricula must also be undergirded by a belief that meaning is found, not in artifacts themselves, but in the social events through which these artifacts are produced and used." Consider the following conversation between

Karen, the interviewer, and Parry, an 11-year-old bilingual speaker of Korean and English:

Karen: Now when you trade, are you trading with other Korean kids or are you trading with Canadian kids? Or, who are you trading with?
Parry: Both.
Karen: So some of your Korean friends read Archie also? Now when you trade with your Korean friends, do you speak in Korean with them about Archie, or is it in English?
Parry. English. Well sometimes Korean.

Toohey (1998, 2000) has demonstrated that rituals of lending and borrowing among schoolchildren are intricate practices that engage the identities of students in complex ways. In her study of a multilingual elementary school classroom in Canada, Toohey found that children would engage in borrowing and lending rituals in order to enter into social interaction with other students, which would in turn build relationships and peer networks. Our study confirmed this finding, and we found that borrowing and lending took place both within and outside the classroom. Of particular significance was the fact that these rituals, as 12-year-old Dylan noted, had the effect of bringing children of different linguistic backgrounds together, "Cause it would give them something to realize that these kids like some things that they like, that they are kids who like things that other kids like, which is a way of bringing them together."

Two related observations from the research are relevant to an exploration of the relationship between identity and literacy in language teaching. First, the *Archie* study suggests that the pleasure children derive from popular culture, in general, and *Archie* comics, in particular, is associated with a sense of ownership over meaning making. It is this sense of ownership that gives children the confidence to engage with popular culture both energetically and critically. For the *Archie* comic readers in our study, their goal in debating the merits of characters, events, and stories was not to anticipate other interpretations and critiques but to draw on their own knowledge and experience to reflect, engage, and defend. Second, although the study provides much evidence to suggest that the *Archie* reading community was vibrant and social, and strengthened relationships between children of diverse linguistic backgrounds, the children's investments in *Archie* comics received little recognition or validation from teachers or parents. The study suggests that literacy educators need to better understand rather than dismiss those practices that students find engaging and meaningful, whether in or outside classrooms.

Literacy and Imagined Identities in Pakistan Youth

In our 2001–2002 research study (Norton & Kamal, 2003), students in Karachi, Pakistan, took part in a global social action project called the Youth Millennium

Project, in which 80 middle-school students, calling themselves "The Reformers," collected stationery, books, and supplies for a local orphanage serving Afghan refugee children. Part of the project was also to teach the Afghan children "some simple English phrases." We were intrigued by the students' interest in literacy and their promotion of the English language. We were also curious about the vision of the future held by these students at a time of great social and political instability. We collected data on these issues through questionnaires, interviews, observations, and email exchanges. The following findings inform our understanding of the relationship between identity, literacy, and multilingualism in the Pakistani context.

First, we were interested to find that the students' conceptions of literacy were consistent with many current theories of literacy in the scholarly literature. The students held the view that literacy is not only about reading and writing but also about education more broadly. "Literacy plays a vital role in the progress of a country," said Saman, while Nida noted passionately "without education our beloved country Pakistan cannot develop." Other students, however, extended this view to include the notion that a literate person has greater ability to reason than one who is illiterate. Shahida, for example, noted that a literate person "can make better decisions" than an illiterate person, while Kamran said that, "if we are not literate we cannot do any work with thinking." These same students noted, in addition, that material resources are needed to promote both literacy and development. They pointed out, for example, that what they called the Afghan "childlabors" in their community could not access literacy classes because they were supporting their destitute families. The students were well aware of the resources of wealthier countries, with Ahmed noting somewhat optimistically "we know that in developed countries everyone is educated and goes to school; that is why they are rich and have no problems." For students in Pakistan, literacy must be understood with reference to social, economic, and political power.

Like their notions of literacy, the students' responses to the importance of English were complex and best understood in the context of Pakistan's ambivalent status in the international community. In seeking to teach the Afghan children "some simple English phrases," students were invested in the belief that English is an international language and the language of science, technology, and the media. As Shahida said, "The English language is an international language spoken all over the world and it is the language of science. Therefore to promote their education and awareness with modern technologies, it is important to teach them English."

Students noted that English serves as a common language not only across nations, but also within nations, and expressed the hope that knowledge of English would redress imbalances between developed and developing nations. With only a few exceptions, the students demonstrated little ambivalence towards the English language and perceived it as an important tool for social, economic, and political advancement, both within Pakistan, as well as the international community. When students were pressed to consider whether the spread of English had any negative consequences, only two students noted that a country's native languages could be compromised, and only one noted that the spread of English would be accompanied by the spread of Western culture, what he called "a bad sign." Students expressed the hope that a future Pakistan would be one in which all inhabitants were literate, knowledgeable about English, and technologically advanced. They desired a peaceful society, true to the principles of Islam and respected in the international community.

Multilingual learners in Pakistan were thus invested in literacy and the English language because they wanted to appropriate identities as "educated" people living in a "developed" country, with access to both symbolic and material resources. However, it was of concern to us that students might in fact overestimate the benefits that can accrue from the development of literacy and the spread of English (see May, 2008; Pennycook, 1998). Ahmed's assessment, for example, that people who are educated "are rich and have no problems" might lead to a crisis of expectations. Of even greater concern was the way in which pedagogical and social practices may be serving, perhaps inadvertently, to reinforce the view held by the students that people who are literate are more rational and intellectually able than those who are not literate. If students in Pakistan, and perhaps in other parts of the world, equate literacy with rationality and intellectual ability, while at the same time embracing English as *the* international language of science, media, and technology, this may perpetuate the view that those who are literate in English are more rational and intellectually able than those who are not literate in English. How to address this concern remains a central challenge for educators, policy makers, and researchers.

Digital Literacy and Multilingual Students in Uganda

In a number of our ongoing language and literacy projects in Uganda, which began in 2003, we have found that multilingual students of varying ages are highly invested in the development of digital literacy (Kendrick, Jones, Mutonyi, & Norton, 2006; Norton, Jones, & Ahimbisibwe, 2011; Norton & Williams, 2012). In one project, undertaken in southwestern Uganda in 2004–2005, we worked with 19 secondary-school girls in Senior 3 (ages 16 to 19) to explore the use of digital photography as a multimodal pedagogy (Kendrick et al., 2006; cf. Block, this volume). The dominant languages in this region of the country are Luganda, Lunyankole, and Lukiiga, although English is the medium of instruction in secondary schools. The purpose of our research activity was to provide the girls with a visual artistic way in which to explore and view specific aspects of their lives through the lens of the camera; to improve English language and literacy development by using photography as an entry point for discussion, reading, writing, and critique; and to become familiar with technology they had not used before. Through journal writing and conversations, the girls discussed what they learned through their participation in the photography project, such as the way in which their experience with the camera made them feel more confident about learning about other types of technology. Of particular note, however, was that almost all of the girls also mentioned their improvement in their English-language competence. When asked directly how (if at all) they believed that this project facilitated learning English, the girls mentioned reading comprehension (as a result of studying the manuals); writing (writing about their pictures and in their research journals); and listening and speaking (from group discussions, meetings, and presentations). In a conversation with Shelley Jones, a member of our research team, one of the girls (Rose) expressed the following point in relation to learning English (Kendrick et al., 2006, p. 110):

Shelley: How is learning English through doing a project like this different from learning English in the classroom?
Rose: In class teachers write on the blackboard and we just listen.
Shelley: In the . . . project how do you use English?
Rose: Communication.
Shelley: Do you learn more by studying English or by communicating in English?
Rose: Communicating.
Shelley: Why?
Rose: Because when you communicate, you think your own English.

In a follow-up study conducted in 2006 with 12 of these young women (Norton et al., 2011), we investigated whether a digital literacy course would help the young women gain access to information about HIV/AIDS through global health websites, available in English, Uganda's official language. In particular, we investigated the learners' investments in the language practices of the digital literacy course and the relationship between learner investments in digital literacy and learner identities. Our findings suggest that the learners' investments in the digital literacy course derived not only from the significance of HIV/AIDS to their lives but from the opportunity to appropriate a range of imagined identities that offered enhanced possibilities for the future. One participant called Tracy, for example, specified her interest in becoming part of a global academic community, as she desired "to talk with people from different countries like to acquire some information from outside universities," while Jenenie expressed an interest in expanding her knowledge and worldview by becoming "mentally modernized." Particularly profound was the comment by Henrietta that, in becoming digitally literate, they had "joined the group of knowledgeable people around the world."

The young women's investments in the language practices of the digital literacy course derived, in part, from the opportunity they had to access the English language in multiple new ways. For example, in response to the question, "How do you think you could benefit from learning to use the computer?" Henrietta noted that she would "understand more about English language," commenting further that, "I got communication. I have learnt the English language because the English in internet has been very create and it has arranged properly."

Discussion

In these four research sites, spanning three continents and two decades, we found that the multilingual students in our studies had complex investments in their respective literacy practices, particularly with regard to literacy in English. These investments were associated with a range of identities, including those of the imagination. In South Africa, as students' identities shifted on the two social occasions during the pretesting of the Monkeys Passage, the learners' investments in the text were renegotiated. During the test event, the first social occasion, students' investment in the text was associated with academic access and future possibility, leading to acts of compliance as "test takers." During the second social occasion, in which many students became "resistant readers," students' investment in the text was structured by a history of racism and discrimination in South African society, in which black students were relatively powerless subjects.

In the *Archie* comic study in Canada, students of diverse language backgrounds were invested in these popular cultural texts because they had a sense of ownership over meaning making and were able to enter social relationships and form peer networks, some across linguistic divides. With respect to reader identities, students were in a position of relative power as they read their *Archie* comics and could engage actively in the construction of meaning. In teacher-controlled texts, in contrast, the readers were in a position of relative powerlessness and sought primarily to second-guess the teacher's reading of the text. With reference to Kress's (1989) notion of genre, our research suggests that student investment in the text, and the identity "reader," is strengthened when students engage with the substance of the text rather than its conventionalized form. Further, our research suggests that the literate underlife of the classroom helped to build relationships across linguistic divides, creating vibrant multilingual peer networks. Such communities fell beneath the radar of parents and teachers, who, inadvertently perhaps, sought to discourage students' investments in comic book culture, losing promising opportunities for creative pedagogical practices.

Insights from multilingual Pakistani students are best understood in the context of their complex identities and investments in a time of social and political instability, both nationally and internationally. The research suggests that the struggle for literacy, access to English, and technological progress are interdependent and reflect the desire of students in a postcolonial world to engage with the international community from a position of strength rather than weakness. For these students, English and vernacular languages could coexist in mutually productive ways, and the appropriation of English did not necessarily compromise identities structured on the grounds of linguistic or religious affiliation. At the same time, however, the implicit conflation of literacy in English with rationality and intellectual ability was a cause of much concern and requires greater attention from educators, policy makers, and researchers.

In Uganda, the young multilingual women in two of our studies were invested in digital literacy because of the opportunity it gave them to explore a range of new identities, both in their everyday lives and in their desired futures. Digital photography, for example, enabled them to reflect on the conditions that constrained the range of identities available to them and those that provided enhanced possibility. The digital literacy course provided the opportunity for them to enter into wider global networks and to become, as Henrietta put it, "mentally modernized." The role of the English language was seen to be significant in the process of becoming digitally literate. What they sought, however, was innovation in the teaching of English; they expressed their reluctance to "just listen" in teacher-fronted classrooms. Much as the readers of *Archie* comics in Canada claimed ownership of meaning making in their engagement with popular culture, so the young women in Uganda sought to "think their own English" in their classrooms and communities (cf. Leung, this volume).

The Multilingual Turn in Language Education

The trajectory of research discussed in this chapter raises three central concerns that have particular relevance to the multilingual turn in language education. First, consistent with the research of language and literacy scholars interested in globalization (cf. Blommaert, 2010; Canagarajah, 1999; Luke, 2004; Pennycook, 2010; Ramanathan, 2005; Street, 2001), we learned from many of the students in our studies that if we wish to understand the meaning of literacy in the lives of multilingual learners, we cannot ignore the imperatives of the material world and the ways in which resources are distributed—not only nationally but internationally. Canagarajah (1999) makes a compelling case that, in developing countries in which there is a daily struggle for food, clothing, shelter, and safety, researchers cannot indulge in theoretical debates and abstract policies but need to address the material realities of the communities in which we conduct research. Luke (2004), similarly, argues that, while we as educators might debate the meaning of critical literacy, we may not do justice to the physical and material challenges of students in diverse communities throughout the globe. The multilingual students in South Africa, Canada, Pakistan, and Uganda were well aware of the relationship between literacy in English, the distribution of resources, and human possibility. For these students, and many other students in poorly resourced regions of the world, a community that is both literate and competent in English is also a community that has social, economic, and political power.

Second, this trajectory of research has led us to rethink the relationship between literacy and identity in the multilingual classroom. The written word, while still important, is only one of the many semiotic modes that multilingual students encounter in the different domains of their lives. From popular culture, drama, and oral storytelling to television, the Internet, and digital worlds, young people in different parts of the world are engaging in diverse and innovative ways with multiple "texts." The challenge for literacy educators is to reconceptualize classrooms as semiotic spaces in which learners have the opportunity to construct meaning with a wide variety of multimodal texts, including digital, visual, written, and spoken texts. Scaffolding such a curriculum are critical pedagogical theories in which learners are given opportunities to claim ownership of the meaning making process (cf. Norton & Toohey, 2004).

Third, it was more than two decades ago (Norton Peirce, 1989) that I confronted the question of how notions of communicative competence are framed within the field of English-language teaching (see also Leung, 2005, this volume; Kramsch & Whiteside, 2008; Wallace, 2003). I argued that a concern for the "rules of use" in the teaching of English internationally is an inadequate pedagogical goal if teachers are concerned about the relationship between language, identity, and human possibility. The research I have conducted across time and space suggests that these concerns remain current in the field of English-language teaching and that the debate has now been extended to include the impact of global technologies on language teaching (Block & Cameron, 2002; Lam, 2000; Rassool, 1999; Snyder & Prinsloo, 2007; Warschauer, 2003). Rassool (1999, p. 238), for example, argues that communicative competence within a technological global world refers to the interactive process in which meanings are produced dynamically between information technology and lived experience. The extent to which we are informed will, in turn, affect the extent to which we respond to and act upon our understanding. In this regard, she argues, the very principles of democracy are at stake.

Conclusion

In this chapter, I have drawn on my research with multilingual learners in South Africa, Canada, Pakistan, and Uganda to make the case that literacy practices in the multilingual classroom are not only about reading and writing but about relationships between text and reader, student and teacher, classroom and community, in local, regional, and transnational sites. As such, when students invest in a set of literacy practices, they also invest in a range of possible and imagined identities. As language educators, we need to take seriously the findings that suggest that if learners have a sense of ownership over meaning making, they can engage actively in a wide range of literacy practices; however, if there is little ownership over meaning making, learning becomes meaningless and ritualized. Further, the studies suggest that meaning making is facilitated when learners are in a position of relative power within a given literacy event and when learners' social, cultural, and linguistic identities are validated. As language educators, the research challenges us to consider what pedagogical practices will help students develop the capacity for imagining an enhanced range of identities for the future. What changes in language–teacher identity will be necessary for pedagogical practices to be more innovative and productive? As we gain greater appreciation for the relationship between literacy, identity, and multilingualism, such questions will become increasingly intriguing and important.

Notes

This chapter is based on a plenary address given at the IATEFL (International Association of Teachers of English as a Foreign Language) conference in Cardiff, United Kingdom, in April 2009 (see Norton, 2010).

1. See Block (2003); Firth and Wagner (1997); Y. H. Gao (2007); Morgan (2007); Norton and Toohey (2011); Ricento (2005); Swain and Deters (2007); Zuengler and Miller (2006).
2. See monographs by Block (2007); Clarke (2008); Goldstein (2003); Heller (2007); Kanno (2008); May (2008); Miller (2003); Nelson (2009); Norton (2000); Potowski (2007); Rampton (2006); Stein (2008); Toohey (2000).
3. Albright and Luke (2008); Anderson, Kendrick, Rogers, and Smythe (2005); Auerbach (1989); Barton (2007); Blommaert (2008); Comber and Simpson (2001); Cope and Kalantzis (2000); Gee (2007); Gutierrez and Rogoff (2003); Heath (1983); Hornberger (2003); Hull and Schultz (2001); Janks (2010); Kendrick (2003); Kress (2003); Martin-Jones and Jones (2000); New London Group (1996); Prinsloo and Baynham (2008); Ramanathan (2002); Street and Hornberger (2008).
4. Early and Norton (2012); Kendrick, Jones, Mutonyi, and Norton (2006); Mutonyi and Norton (2007); Norton and Early (2011); Norton, Jones, and Ahimbisibwe (2011); Norton and Williams (2012); Tembe and Norton (2008).
5. See, for example, Anya (2011); Bearse and de Jong (2008); Chang (2011); Cornwell (2005); Cummins (2006); De Costa (2010); Haneda (2005); Kim (2008); McKay and Wong (1996); Pittaway (2004); Potowski (2007); Ross (2011); Shin (2009); Skilton-Sylvester (2002); Tomita (2011).
6. See, for example, Carroll, Motha, and Price (2008); Chang (2011); Cortez (2008); Dagenais (2003); F. Gao (2012); Gordon (2004); Murphey, Jin, and Li-Chin (2005); Pavlenko (2003); Silberstein (2003); Song (2010); Torres-Olave (2006); Villarreal Ballesteros (2010); Xu (2012).

References

Albright, J., & Luke, A. (2008). *Pierre Bourdieu and literacy education*. Mahwah, NJ: Lawrence Erlbaum.

Anderson, B. (1991). *Imagined communities: Reflections on the origin and spread of nationalism* (Rev. ed.). New York, NY: Verso.

Anderson, J., Kendrick, M., Rogers, T., & Smythe, S. (Eds.). (2005). *Portraits of literacy across families, communities, and schools: Intersections and tensions*. Mahwah, NJ: Lawrence Erlbaum.

Anya, O. C. (2011). *Investments in communities of learners and speakers: How African American students of Portuguese negotiate ethno-racialized, gendered, and social-classed identities in second language learning* (Unpublished doctoral dissertation). University of California, Los Angeles, USA.

Arkoudis, S., & Davison, C. (Eds.). (2008). Chinese students: Perspectives on their social, cognitive, and linguistic investment in English medium interaction [Special issue]. *Journal of Asian Pacific Communication, 18*(1).

Auerbach, E. (1989). Toward a social-contextual approach to family literacy. *Harvard Educational Review, 59*, 165–181.

Barton, D. (2007). *Literacy: An introduction to the ecology of written language* (2nd ed.). Oxford, UK: Wiley-Blackwell.

Bearse, C., & de Jong, E. J. (2008). Cultural and linguistic investment: Adolescents in a secondary two-way immersion program. *Equity and Excellence in Education, 41*(3), 325–340.

Block, D. (2003). *The social turn in second language acquisition.* Washington, DC: Georgetown University Press.

Block, D. (2007). *Second language identities.* London, UK: Continuum.

Block, D., & Cameron, D. (Eds.). (2002). *Globalization and language teaching.* New York, NY: Routledge.

Blommaert, J. (2008). *Grassroots literacy: Writing, identity, and voice in Central Africa.* London, UK & New York, NY: Routledge.

Blommaert, J. (2010). *The sociolinguistics of globalization.* Cambridge, UK & New York, NY: Cambridge University Press.

Bourdieu, P. (1977). The economics of linguistic exchanges. *Social Science Information, 16*(6), 645–668.

Bourdieu, P. (1991). *Language and symbolic power* (G. Raymond & M. Adamson, Trans.). Cambridge, UK: Polity Press. (Reprinted from *Ce que parler veut dire.* Paris, France: Librairie Arthème Fayard, 1982)

Canagarajah, A. S. (1999). *Resisting linguistic imperialism in English teaching.* Oxford, UK: Oxford University Press.

Carroll, S., Motha, S., & Price, J. (2008). Accessing imagined communities and reinscribing regimes of truth. *Critical Inquiry in Language Studies, 5*(3), 165–191.

Chang, Y.-J. (2011). Picking one's battles: NNES doctoral students' imagined communities and selections of investment. *Journal of Language, Identity, and Education, 10*, 213–230.

Clarke, M. (2008). *Language teacher identities: Co-constructing discourse and community.* Clevedon, UK: Multilingual Matters.

Comber, B., & Simpson, A. (Eds.). (2001). *Negotiating critical literacies in classrooms.* Mahwah, NJ: Lawrence Erlbaum Associates.

Cornwell, S. (2005). *Language investment, possible selves, and communities of practice: Inside a Japanese junior college temple* (Unpublished doctoral dissertation). Temple University, Japan.

Cortez, N. A. (2008). *Am I in the book? Imagined communities and language ideologies of English in a global EFL textbook* (Unpublished doctoral dissertation). University of Arizona, USA.

Cope, B., & Kalantzis, M. (Eds.). (2000). *Multiliteracies: Literacy learning and the design of social futures.* New York, NY: Routledge.

Cummins, J. (2006). Identity texts: The imaginative construction of self through multiliteracies pedagogy. In O. García, T. Skutnabb-Kangas, & M. Torres-Guzman. (Eds.), *Imagining multilingual schools: Language in education and glocalization* (pp. 51–68). Clevedon, UK: Multilingual Matters.

Dagenais, D. (2003). Accessing imagined communities through multilingualism and immersion education. *Language, Identity and Education, 2*(4), 269–283.

De Costa, P. I. (2010). Language ideologies and standard English language policy in Singapore: Responses of a "designer immigrant" student. *Language Policy, 9*(3), 217–239.

Dörnyei, Z., & Ushioda, E. (Eds.). (2009). *Motivation, language identity and the L2 self.* Bristol, UK: Multilingual Matters.

Dyson, A. H. (1996). Cultural constellations and childhood identities: On Greek gods, cartoon heroes, and the social lives of schoolchildren. *Harvard Educational Review, 66*(3), 471–496.

Early, M., & Norton, B. (2012). Language learner stories and imagined identities. *Narrative Inquiry, 22*(1), 194–201.

Finders, M. (1997). *Just girls: Hidden literacies and life in junior high.* New York, NY: Teachers College Press.

Firth, A., & Wagner, J. (1997). On discourse, communication, and (some) fundamental concepts in SLA Research. *The Modern Language Journal, 81,* 286–300.

Gao, F. (2012) Imagined community, identity, and Chinese language teaching in Hong Kong. *Journal of Asian Pacific Communication, 22*(1), 140–154.

Gao, Y. H. (2007). Legitimacy of foreign language learning and identity research: Structuralist and constructivist perspectives. *Intercultural Communication Studies, 16*(1), 100–112.

Gee, J. P. (2007) *Social linguistics and literacies: Ideology in discourses* (3rd ed.). Abingdon, UK: Routledge.

Goldstein, T. (2003). *Teaching and learning in a multilingual school: Choices, risks, and dilemmas.* Mahwah, NJ: Lawrence Erlbaum Associates.

Gordon, D. (2004). "I'm tired. You clean and cook." Shifting gender identities and second language socialization. *TESOL Quarterly, 38*(3), 437–457.

Gutierrez, K., & Rogoff, B. (2003). Cultural ways of learning: Individual traits or repertoires of practice. *Educational Researcher, 32*(5), 19–25.

Heath, S. B. (1983). *Ways with words: Language, life, and work in communities and classrooms.* Cambridge, UK: Cambridge University Press.

Haneda, M. (2005). Investing in foreign-language writing: A study of two multicultural learners. *Journal of Language, Identity, and Education, 4*(4), 269–290.

Heller, M. (2007). *Linguistic minorities and modernity: A sociolinguistic ethnography* (2nd ed.). London, UK: Continuum.

Hornberger, N. (Ed.). (2003). *Continua of biliteracy.* Clevedon, UK: Multilingual Matters.

Hull, G., & Schultz, K. (2001). Literacy and learning out of school: A review of theory and research. *Review of Educational Research, 71*(4), 575–611.

Janks, H. (2010). *Literacy and power.* New York, NY: Routledge.

Kanno, Y. (2008). *Language and education in Japan: Unequal access to bilingualism.* Basingstoke, UK: Palgrave Macmillan.

Kanno, Y., & Norton, B. (Eds.). (2003). Imagined communities and educational possibilities [Special issue]. *Journal of Language, Identity, and Education, 2*(4), 241–249.

Kendrick, M. E. (2003). *Play, literacy, and culture: Converging worlds.* Bern, Switzerland: Peter Lang Publishing.

Kendrick, M., Jones, S., Mutonyi, H., & Norton, B. (2006). Multimodality and English education in Ugandan schools. *English Studies in Africa, 49*(1), 95–114.

Kim, J. (2008) *Negotiating multiple investments in languages and identities: The language socialization of Generation 1.5 Korean Canadian university students* (Unpublished doctoral dissertation). University of British Columbia, Canada.

Kramsch, C., & Whiteside, A. (2008). Language ecology in multilingual settings: Towards a theory of symbolic competence. *Applied Linguistics, 29*(4), 645–671.

Kress, G. (1989). *Linguistic processes in sociocultural practice.* Oxford, UK: Oxford University Press.

Kress, G. (1993). Genre as social process. In B. Cope & M. Kalantzis (Eds.), *The powers of literacy: A genre approach to teaching writing* (pp. 22–37). London, UK: Falmer Press.

Kress, G. (2003). *Literacy in the new media age.* London, UK & New York, NY: Routledge.

Lam, W. S. E. (2000). L2 literacy and the design of the self: A case study of a teenager writing on the internet. *TESOL Quarterly, 34*(3), 457–482.

Leung, C. (2005). Convivial communication: recontextualizing communicative competence. *International Journal of Applied Linguistics, 15*(2), 119–144.

Luke, A. (1997). Critical approaches to literacy. In V. Edwards & D. Corson (Eds.), *Encyclopedia of language and education, Vol. 2: Literacy* (pp. 143–152). Dordrecht, The Netherlands: Kluwer Academic Publishers.

Luke, A. (2004). Two takes on the critical. In B. Norton & K. Toohey (Eds.), *Critical pedagogies and language learning* (pp. 21–29). New York, NY: Cambridge University Press.

Martin-Jones, M., & Jones, K. (2000). *Multilingual literacies.* Philadelphia, USA & Amsterdam, The Netherlands: John Benjamins.

Martin-Jones, M., & Jones, K. (Eds.). (2000). *Multilingual literacies: Reading and writing different worlds.* Amsterdam, The Netherlands: John Benjamins Publishing.

May, S. (2008). *Language and minority rights.* London, UK & New York, NY: Routledge.

May, S. (2011). The disciplinary constraints of SLA and TESOL: Additive bilingualism and second language acquisition, teaching and learning. *Linguistics and Education, 22*(3), 233–247.

McKay, S., & Wong, S. C. (1996). Multiple discourses, multiple identities: Investment and agency in second language learning among Chinese adolescent immigrant students. *Harvard Educational Review, 66*(3), 577–608.

Miller, J. (2003). *Audible difference: ESL and social identity in schools.* Clevedon, UK: Multilingual Matters.

Moffatt, L., & Norton, B. (2005). Popular culture and the reading teacher: A case for feminist pedagogy. *Critical Inquiry in Language Studies, 2*(1), 1–12.

Moffatt, L., & Norton, B. (2008). Reading gender relations and sexuality: Preteens speak out. *Canadian Journal of Education, 31*(1), 102–123.

Morgan, B. (2007). Poststructuralism and applied linguistics: Complementary approaches to identity and culture in ELT. In J. Cummins & C. Davison (Eds.), *International handbook of English language teaching* (pp. 1033–1052). New York, NY: Springer.

Murphey, T., Jin, C., & Li-Chin, C. (2005) Learners' constructions of identities and imagined communities. In P. Benson & D. Nunan (Eds.), *Learners' stories and diversity in language learning* (pp. 83–100). Cambridge, UK: Cambridge University

Mutonyi, H., & Norton, B. (2007). ICT on the margins: Lessons for Ugandan education. *Language and Education, 21*(3), 264–270.

Nelson, C. (2009). *Sexual identities in English language education: Classroom conversations.* New York, NY: Routledge.

New London Group. (1996). A pedagogy of multiliteracies: Designing social futures. *Harvard Educational Review, 66*, 60–92.

Norton, B. (2000). *Identity and language learning: Gender, ethnicity and educational change.* Harlow, UK: Longman/Pearson.

Norton, B. (2001). Non-participation, imagined communities, and the language classroom. In M. Breen (Ed.), *Learner contributions to language learning: New directions in research* (pp. 159–171). London, UK: Pearson Education Limited.

Norton, B. (2003). The motivating power of comic books: Insights from Archie comic readers. *The Reading Teacher, 57*(2), 140–147.

Norton, B. (2010). Identity, literacy, and English language teaching. In B. Beaven (Ed.). *IATEFL 2009 Cardiff Conference Selections.* Canterbury, UK: IATEFL.

Norton, B. (2012). Investment. In P. Robinson (Ed.), *Routledge encyclopedia of second language acquisition* (pp. 343–344). New York, NY: Routledge.

Norton, B., & Early, M. (2011). Researcher identity, narrative inquiry, and language teaching research. *TESOL Quarterly, 45*(3), 415–439.

Norton, B., & Gao, Y. (2008). Identity, investment, and Chinese learners of English. *Journal of Asian Pacific Communication, 18*(1), 109–120.

Norton, B., Jones, S., & Ahimbisibwe, D. (2011). Learning about HIV/AIDS in Uganda: Digital resources and language learner identities. *Canadian Modern Language Review, 67*(4), 569–590.

Norton, B., & Kamal, F. (2003). The imagined communities of English language learners in a Pakistani school. *Journal of Language, Identity, and Education, 2*(4), 301–307.

Norton, B., & Toohey, K. (Eds.). (2004). *Critical pedagogies and language learning.* New York, NY: Cambridge University Press.

Norton, B., & Toohey, K. (2011). Identity, language learning, and social change. *Language Teaching, 44*(4), 412–446.

Norton, B., & Vanderheyden, K. (2004). Comic book culture and second language learners. In B. Norton & K. Toohey (Eds.), *Critical pedagogies and language learning* (pp. 201–221). New York, NY: Cambridge University Press.

Norton, B., & Williams, C. J. (2012). Digital identities, student investments, and eGranary as a placed resource. *Language and Education, 26*(4), 315–329.

Norton Peirce, B. (1989). Toward a pedagogy of possibility in the teaching of English internationally: People's English in South Africa. *TESOL Quarterly, 23*(3), 401–420.

Norton Peirce, B. (1995). Social identity, investment, and language learning. *TESOL Quarterly, 29*(1), 9–31.

Norton Peirce, B., & Stein, P. (1995). Why the "Monkeys Passage" bombed: Tests, genres, and teaching. *Harvard Educational Review, 65*(1), 50–65.

Pavlenko, A. (2003). "I never knew I was a bilingual": Reimagining teacher identities in TESOL. *Journal of Language, Identity, and Education, 2*(4), 251–268.

Pavlenko, A., & Norton, B. (2007). Imagined communities, identity, and English language teaching. In J. Cummins & C. Davison (Eds.), *International handbook of English language teaching* (pp. 669–680). New York, NY: Springer.

Pennycook, A. (1998). *English and the discourses of colonialism.* New York, NY: Routledge.

Pennycook, A. (2010). *Language as a local practice.* New York, NY: Routledge.

Pittaway, D. (2004). Investment and second language acquisition. *Critical Inquiry in Language Studies, 4*(1), 203–218.

Potowski, K. (2007). *Language and identity in a dual immersion school.* Clevedon, UK: Multilingual Matters.

Prinsloo, M., & Baynham, M. (Eds.). (2008). *Literacies, global and local.* Philadelphia, PA: John Benjamins.

Ramanathan, V. (2002). *The politics of TESOL education: Writing, knowledge, critical pedagogy.* New York, NY: Routledge Falmer.

Ramanathan, V. (2005). *The English-vernacular divide: Postcolonial language politics and practice.* Clevedon, UK: Multilingual Matters.

Rampton, B. (2006). *Language in late modernity: Interaction in an urban school.* Cambridge, UK: Cambridge University Press.

Rassool, N. (1999). *Literacy for sustainable development in the age of information.* Clevedon, UK: Multilingual Matters.

Ricento, T. (2005). Considerations of identity in L2 learning. In E. Hinkel (Ed.), *Handbook of research on second language teaching and learning* (pp. 895–911). Mahwah, NJ: Lawrence Erlbaum Associates.

Ross, B. M. (2011). *Language, identity, and investment in the English language of a group of Mexican women living in southwestern Pennsylvania* (Unpublished doctoral dissertation). Pennsylvania State University, USA.

Shin, J. (2009). *Critical ethnography of a multilingual and multicultural Korean language classroom: Discourses on identity, investment and Korean-ness* (Unpublished doctoral dissertation). University of Toronto, Canada.

Silberstein, S. (2003). Imagined communities and national fantasies in the O.J. Simpson case. *Journal of Language, Identity, and Education, 2*(4), 319–330.

Skilton-Sylvester, E. (2002). Should I stay or should I go? Investigating Cambodian women's participation and investment in adult ESL programs. *Adult Education Quarterly, 53*(1), 9–26.

Snyder, I., & Prinsloo, M. (Eds.). (2007). The digital literacy practices of young people in marginal contexts [Special issue]. *Language and Education: An International Journal, 21*(3), 171–179.

Song, H. (2010). *Imagined communities, language learning and identity in highly skilled transnational migrants: A case study of Korean migrants in Canada* (Unpublished master's thesis). University of Manitoba, Canada.

Stein, P. (2008). *Multimodal pedagogies in diverse classrooms: Representation, rights and resources.* London, UK & New York, NY: Routledge.

Street, B. (Ed.). (2001). *Literacy and development: Ethnographic perspectives.* New York, NY: Routledge.

Street, B., & Hornberger, N. (2008). *Encyclopedia of language and education,* (Vol. 2). Boston, MA: Springer.

Swain, M., & Deters, P. (2007). "New" mainstream SLA theory: Expanded and enriched. *The Modern Language Journal, 91*, 820–836.

Tembe, J., & Norton, B. (2008). Promoting local languages in Ugandan primary schools: The community as stakeholder. *Canadian Modern Language Review, 65*(1), 33–60.

Tomita, Y. (2011). *The role of form-focused instruction: Learner investment in L2 communication* (Unpublished doctoral dissertation). University of Toronto, Canada.

Toohey, K. (1998). "Breaking them up; taking them away": Constructing ESL students in Grade 1. *TESOL Quarterly, 32*, 61–84.

Toohey, K. (2000). *Learning English at school: Identity, social relations and classroom practice.* Clevedon, UK: Multilingual Matters.

Torres-Olave, B. M. (2006). *"If I didn't have professional dreams maybe I wouldn't think of leaving"* (Unpublished master's thesis). University of British Columbia, Canada.

Villarreal Ballesteros, A. C. (2010). *Professional identity formation and development of imagined communities in an English language major in Mexico* (Unpublished doctoral dissertation). University of Arizona, USA.

Wallace, C. (2003). *Critical reading in language education.* Basingstoke, UK: Palgrave Macmillan.

Warschauer, M. (2003). *Technology and social inclusion: Rethinking the digital divide.* Boston, MA: MIT Press.

Wenger, E. (1998). *Communities of practice: Learning, meaning, and identity.* New York, NY: Cambridge University Press.

Xu, H. (2012). Imagined community falling apart: a case study on the transformation of professional identities of novice ESOL teachers in China. *TESOL Quarterly, 46*(3), 568–578.

Zuengler, J., & Miller, E. (2006). Cognitive and sociocultural perspectives: Two parallel SLA worlds? *TESOL Quarterly, 40*(1), 35–58.

6

COMMUNICATION AND PARTICIPATORY INVOLVEMENT IN LINGUISTICALLY DIVERSE CLASSROOMS

Constant Leung

The main purpose of this chapter is to present a reflexive examination of the notion of communication in English Language Teaching (ELT). The widespread demand for English as an additional or complementary language in different world locations has spawned a thriving English Language Teaching profession, sustained an internationalized academic community, and created a textbook market for transnational publishing houses. Promoting learners' capacity to communicate meaning through language with others is routinely presented as a key pedagogic goal. In particular, the concept of communicative competence, understood here as the capacity to communicate with others through language effectively, has informed a good deal of the curriculum, pedagogic, and assessment developments in ELT in the past 40 years (cf. Canagarajah, this volume; Li Wei, this volume). Historically, the advent of the concept of communicative competence in language teaching in the 1970s was widely seen as a moment when the traditional grammar-focused approaches gave way to a more socially and culturally sensitive approach to language modeling, curriculum design, and classroom pedagogy. This sociocultural turn was promoted energetically by leading theorists, researchers, and senior professionals in ELT, and it has since been consolidated into a teaching approach known as communicative language teaching (CLT) (for further discussion see Howatt & Widdowson, 2004, Chapter 20; Leung, 2010). It would be no exaggeration to say that communicative competence has come to be seen as a professional "kite mark" signaling intellectual respectability and desirable qualities in real-life curriculum applications. For instance, the Common European Framework of Reference for Languages (CEFR, Council of Europe, 2001, Chapter 2), a high-status transnational curriculum framework for language education and simultaneously an assessment framework for language proficiency, claims to be conceptually grounded in communicative competence.

However, continuing ambiguities in the relationship between certified communicative competence (e.g., proficiency test scores) and observed capacity to communicate in context (Ingram & Bayliss, 2007; Kerstjens & Nery, 2000; Lee & Greene, 2007; Paul, 2007) suggest, inter alia, that professionally critical self-questioning is necessary (cf. May, this volume). The widespread use of English as a complementary language and/or lingua franca in different world locations, and the increasing use of English as an additional language (EAL) in contemporary ethnolinguistically diverse English-speaking countries for important social and educational functions have signaled other emergent complexities. All of this points to the need to take stock.

In this discussion the first question to be addressed is: How is the concept of communication, particularly expressed as communicative competence, being understood and operationalized in ELT some 40 years after its initial development? ELT is a broadly configured field; teaching programs are located in a variety of educational contexts (e.g., universities and schools in public and private sectors), and for different purposes (e.g., English for specific purposes for professionals and English-language classes for refugees and asylum seekers). For reasons of scope and space, I will first explore this question by looking at the CEFR and a selection of internationally marketed textbooks as telling examples. Then I will turn my attention to English (as a subject) in the National Curriculum in England; although it is conceptualized primarily as a mainstream school subject with a first-language orientation, it also serves as a curriculum and assessment framework for EAL, and both communication and competence are writ large in the content descriptions. At this point, I will be suggesting that *language forms* and *norms of use* are the central concerns in many of the influential curriculum and pedagogic materials; communication, or more precisely *communicative capacity* (what it takes to achieve communication), is assumed to follow from knowing vocabulary and grammar and some norm-based conventions of use. After that, I will argue that a "follow-the-rules" view of communicative competence can only provide partial purchase on what it takes to achieve communication. In this part of the discussion, spoken interaction data from linguistically diverse classrooms will be used to highlight the need to take account of the importance of social participation (Auerbach, 1992). The data are drawn from a corpus of audio–video recordings of noncontrived classroom activities collected in a two-year study of the language and literacy practices in ethnolinguistically diverse schools and universities in London[1] (see Leung & Street, 2012, for further details). Overall then, I will be arguing for, paradoxically given its conceptual provenance, a more situation-oriented and participatory view of communication and communicative competence that would help clarify curriculum and pedagogic goals.

This discussion does not claim to provide an exhaustive survey of curriculum and pedagogic enactments of the idea of communication, nor does it offer a retrospective evaluation of the concept of communicative competence in relation to ELT. It is understood that the concept of communicative competence emerged from an intensive period of intellectual discussion involving many scholars. The term *communicative competence* is used to signal a set of related ideas. Likewise, CLT draws on a range of ideas and principles associated with this move away from grammar-focused pedagogy (see Savignon, 2005; Spada, 2007). It is not the purpose of this discussion to endorse any particular representation of CLT found in different textbooks and teacher-training materials. Instead, the aim is to portray the ways in which the ideas associated with communicative competence are being incorporated into ELT. Put more precisely, the aim is to capture a sense of how communicative competence is understood and embedded in curriculum frameworks, teaching materials, and pedagogic activities.

The methodological approach adopted here is that of analytic induction—an effort to "show how general principles deriving from some theoretical orientation manifest themselves in some given set of particular circumstances" (Mitchell, 1984, p. 239). In other words, this is an attempt to provide a telling case for further discussion. In passing, one should perhaps mention that the notion of competence is itself a much debated subject (see Winch, 2011). For the purpose of this discussion, it would be sufficient to adopt a broad definition that "[c]ompetences are the sum of knowledge, skills and characteristics that allow a person to perform actions" (Council of Europe, 2001, p. 9). The notion of communication is now generally recognized to be multimodal (Jewitt, 2008; Kress, 2000; cf. Block, this volume). My comments in this discussion are, however, restricted to the English-language dimension of communication because of the specific reference to ELT, which has been largely monolingual in orientation (May, 2011). Readers will find references to multilingual communication and translanguaging in other chapters (see Canagarajah, this volume; García & Flores, this volume; Li Wei, this volume).

Communicative Competence at Large

Academic and professional affiliations to the concept of communicative competence are far too numerous to cite here. It is, however, possible to see the systemic penetration of this concept in two established educational-cum-professional locales: the Common European Framework of Reference for Languages (CEFR; Council of Europe, 2001) and internationally marketed English-language textbooks.

CEFR: Learning, Teaching, Assessment

The CEFR is an important reference point because the curriculum and assessment framework it presents is explicitly linked to the concept of communicative competence (Council of Europe, 2001, Chapter 2). It is officially described as

> a comprehensive descriptive scheme offering a tool for reflecting on what is involved not only in language use, but also in language learning and

teaching. The Framework provides a common basis and a common language for the elaboration of syllabuses, curriculum guidelines, textbooks, teacher training programmes, and for relating language examinations to one another. (Martyniuk, 2005, p. 11)

In the relatively short time since its publication it has been adopted by policy makers, curriculum planners, and examination authorities in many different countries. Although it was initially designed for use within Europe for modern-languages education, it has now been incorporated into many educational systems and assessment schemes in other parts of the world. For instance, student performance in modern languages in New Zealand schools is assessed against the CEFR proficiency levels (Scarino, 2005), as is the Test of Chinese as a Foreign Language produced in Taiwan (Lan, 2007). The globalized ELT enterprise has also embraced it as a key reference point. For instance, the International English Language Testing System (IELTS) and Test of English as a Foreign Language (TOEFL), two of the world's largest English-language tests (in terms of the number of test takers), are aligned to CEFR proficiency levels. Their alignment with the concept of communicative competence is significant in this discussion because these tests are regularly used as part of the student selection apparatus for English-speaking universities.

An analysis of the CEFR descriptors from an epistemological perspective would help us to see the conceptual orientation of this framework. Communicative competence is seen as comprising three components: linguistic, sociolinguistic, and pragmatic. The following glosses are provided:

> *Linguistic competences* include lexical, phonological, syntactic knowledge and skills . . . independently of the sociolinguistic value of its variations and the pragmatic functions of its realizations . . .
>
> *Sociolinguistic competences* refer to the sociocultural conditions of language use [which include] rules of politeness, norms governing relations between generations, sexes, classes and social groups . . .
>
> *Pragmatic competences* are concerned with the functional use of linguistic resources (production of language functions, speech acts), drawing on scenarios or scripts of interactional exchanges. (Council of Europe, 2001, p. 13)

These three components are embedded in six proficiency levels (A1, A2, B1, B2, C1, C2), each comprising a set of competence descriptors covering spoken and written language use in a range of contexts, for example, interviews (Council of Europe, 2001, p. 82) and service encounters (p. 80). For illustrative purposes we will take the lowest level (A1) and the highest level (C2) of the Global Scale descriptors as examples (Council of Europe, 2001, p. 24). For ease of identification, the descriptors are presented as separate points and are assigned a lower-case letter:

A1

(a) "Can understand and use familiar everyday expressions and very basic phrases aimed at the satisfaction of needs of a concrete type."

(b) "Can introduce him/herself and others and can ask and answer questions about personal details such as where he/she lives, people he/she knows and things he/she has."

(c) "Can interact in a simple way provided the other person talks slowly and clearly and is prepared to help."

C2

(a) "Can understand with ease virtually everything heard or read."

(b) "Can summarize information from different spoken and written sources, reconstructing arguments and accounts in a coherent presentation."

(c) "Can express him/herself spontaneously, very fluently and precisely, differentiating finer shades of meaning even in more complex situations." (Council of Europe, 2001, p. 24)

At A1 level, descriptor (a) is concerned with the speaker learner's capacity to use language knowledge for routine everyday communication. Descriptor (b) appears to be an extension of (a) in that it specifies the range of communicative functions the learner can perform. Descriptor (c) states the limited capacity for language communication of A1-level speaker learners. Taken as a whole, the A1 descriptors are mainly focused on everyday communication at a low level of grammatical competence. Sociolinguistic and pragmatic competences are not explicitly mentioned; in all likelihood they have been subsumed as part of routine everyday expressions.

At C2 level, descriptor (a) is concerned with the speaker learners' capacity to use language knowledge for understanding contingent spoken and written communication. Descriptor (b) indicates the range of the speaker learner's capacity to comprehend and produce spoken and written language that is discoursally coherent. Descriptor (c) draws attention to the speaker learner's capacity to use language to produce meaning in socially sensitive ways. Unlike the descriptors in A1 level, all three competences—linguistic, sociolinguistic, and pragmatic—are covered.

Looking across the different purpose- and context-specific scales within the CEFR, it would seem that the lower level proficiency descriptors are more focused on use of grammatical knowledge at the vocabulary and sentence levels than sociolinguistic and pragmatic competences. For instance, at A1 level of the Transactions To Obtain Goods And Services scale (Council of Europe, 2001, p. 80) the descriptors are: "Can ask people for things and give people things" and "Can handle numbers, quantities, cost and time," whereas at the highest level, the descriptors cover use of sociopragmatic knowledge explicitly—for example, "Can outline a case for compensation, using persuasive language to demand satisfaction and state clearly the limits to any concession he/she is prepared to make." Perhaps it is not surprising to find that the descriptors at lower levels are more concerned with grammatical competence, since low-proficiency speaker learners are normally expected only to be able to understand and communicate meaning in a basic way. In this sense, the CEFR appears to conform to the widely accepted view that, at high-proficiency levels, the speaker learner is expected to show a capacity to use language effectively, in line with recognized sociocultural expectations in context.

Epistemologically, the formulation of the CEFR descriptors suggests that communicative competence is conceived as language knowledge residing in the individual and, at advanced levels of proficiency, a capacity to use this knowledge in socioculturally conventionalized ways. Phrases in the A1 and C2 Global Scale descriptors such as "can understand . . . and "[c]an summarize information from different spoken and written sources" reflect this "capacity in the individual" perspective (Council of Europe, 2001, p. 24). It is, however, not suggested here that the CEFR does not take the social dimension of communication into account. Indeed, the use of language and literacy socially in context is very much part of the basic assumptions built into the framework. This aspect of the framework is clearly shown in the invocation of sociolinguistic competence in the Sociolinguistic Appropriateness Scale (Council of Europe, 2001, p. 122) that, inter alia, contains the following descriptors:

> A1 "Can establish basic social contact by using the simplest everyday forms of: greetings and farewells; introductions."
> B2 "Can sustain relationships with native speakers without unintentionally amusing or irritating them or requiring them to behave other than they would with a native speaker."
> C2 "Appreciates fully the sociolinguistic and sociocultural implications of language used by native speakers and can react accordingly." (Council of Europe, 2001, p. 122)

In the above descriptors, and many others, the social dimension is clearly visible. But the social is understood as an established convention that exists independently of the individual speaker learner and regardless of the social dynamics of any situated social interaction. On this view, speaker learners are meant to enact the language repertoire they have acquired in a preordained social world where sociocultural and pragmatic conventions provide powerful scripts from which speakers do not (or at least should not) depart. The range of context/purpose-specific scales (e.g., "Obtaining goods and services" scale) indicate that, on the whole, the CEFR is mainly concerned with transactional efficacy. The CEFR descriptors are mainly framed as "can do" statements. The question here is: Do these can-do descriptors adequately cover the range of meaning making topoi (themes, motifs) in which teachers and students interact with one another in curriculum and other school activities?

Textbooks

Given the significant pedagogic role textbooks play in ELT pedagogy, particularly in parts of the world where the demand for English language is strong (e.g., the Pacific Rim region), they are a good place to see pedagogic and curriculum principles at work. Many of the current textbooks explicitly affiliate themselves to communicative competence, or at least to a notion of "communicative English" (e.g., Saslow & Ascher, 2006). The influence of this affiliation can be seen in terms of language and carrier content, learning activities, and/or approaches to modeling language use, a snapshot of which is offered here. No claim is made here as to representativeness of commercially produced textbooks in the market; nor is this discussion intended as an evaluation of the pedagogic efficacies of the textbooks being mentioned (for a detailed discussion on the analysis of ELT textbooks see Gray, 2010a, 2010b). The three examples included in this discussion have been chosen largely because they are currently available, are produced in the United States and the United Kingdom (both major publishing centers of ELT materials), can be seen as part of the mainstream offerings within the ELT market, and, most importantly, they claim to be communicative in orientation. As a general observation, the contents of these textbooks largely consist of, unsurprisingly, vocabulary- and grammar-focused teaching materials for spoken and written language. The point of interest for this discussion is how far the various language-focused content materials have been designed to contribute to the development of a communication capacity (i.e., not just learning knowledge of English vocabulary and grammar for its own sake) that echoes the tenets of communicative competence as discussed above.

The first example comes from one of the *Top Notch* series written by Saslow and Ascher (2006). This is an American-produced series offering a six-level communicative English course to adults and young adults that "prepares students to interact successfully with both native and non-native speakers of English" and helps students to achieve a "Top Notch communicative competence" (Saslow & Ascher, 2006, p. ix). The content of the learning units is divided into separate sections on vocabulary, social language, grammar, speaking activities, pronunciation, listening, reading, and writing.

In the preamble to teachers it is stated that the series treats:

> English as an international language, rather than the language of a particular country or region. In addition, *Top Notch* helps students develop a cultural fluency by creating an awareness of the varied rules across cultures for: politeness, greetings and introductions, appropriateness of dress in different settings, conversation do's and taboos, table manners, and other similar issues. (Saslow & Ascher, 2006, p. ix)

This cross-cultural sensitivity is reflected in different parts of the content material. For instance, the sample dialogues for listening and practicing intonation in

Unit 1 (Saslow & Ascher, 2006, p. 4) reflect an awareness of cultural sensitivity at an interpersonal level—as part of this practice exercise, students are provided models of asking permission to address a new acquaintance by their first name such as, "Do you mind if I call you Kazuko?" In this activity, as in many others, students are asked to work with one another to apply the language knowledge they are learning actively in conversation and/or shared reading and writing tasks. The idea seems to be that students should be encouraged to be culturally sensitive and should assume that ways of addressing other people vary in different places. In a unit named "Cultural Literacy," there is a section entitled "Be culturally literate." It provides a list of vocabulary for listening and practice. The words include:

> *etiquette* the "rules" of polite behaviour
>> When travelling, it's important to be aware of the etiquette of the culture you will be visiting.
> *cultural literacy* knowing about and respecting the culture of others and following their rules of etiquette when interacting with them
>> In today's world, cultural literacy is essential to success and good relations with others (Saslow & Archer, 2006, p. 8).

The second example is drawn from the series *English: No Problems* (Quinones & Korol, 2004). This series is oriented to adult education in the United States, with particular reference to adult migrant English language learners. On the back cover of the *Student Books* (of all proficiency levels), it is claimed that the series has been designed in such a way that students can easily connect with communication activities. The concept of "Equipped for Future" (EFF) is used to underpin the design of the book. The preamble in the *Student Book* states:

> Each unit in the student books includes a two-page unit opener followed by three lessons . . . A cumulative unit project concludes each unit. Every unit addresses all four language skills—listening, speaking, reading, and writing. Each lesson focuses on characters operating in one of the three EFF-defined adult roles—parent/family member at home, worker at school, or citizen/community member in the larger community. (Quinones & Korol, 2004, p. vi)

There is a section in each of the units entitled: "In the US." In the unit "Selling," we find this advice under "In the US," that asks students to take account of institutional or domain-specific norms:

> In general people in the US act quite formal in a business situation. However, some businesses are more informal. For that reason, it's often difficult to know exactly how to act in business situations. Here are some things you can do.
>   If you are going to have an interview with a company, get all the information you can about that company from books, web sites, and people. Network with friends, classmates, and acquaintances, especially US-born people.

Don't forget the library. Ask the librarian to help you find a book on business customs. In any business situation, watch what other people are doing. They can be models for the way you act. (Quinones & Korol, 2004, p. 30)

This advice is followed by an exercise on "Compare Cultures." Students are informed that in the United States providing resumes and attending interviews is part of the job application process. Students are asked to talk to their peers and classmates and compare what getting a job means in different countries.

The third example comes from the *Intermediate Student's Book* (4th edition) of the "New Headway" series written by Soars and Soars (2009). This British-produced series is explicitly aligned to the CEFR language proficiency levels, and the intermediate level is meant to be straddled between Levels B1 and B2 of the CEFR. Unit 1 of this student book is on the theme of "A World of Difference," which has a strapline showing the teaching content: "Tenses • Auxiliary verbs • What's in a word? Everyday situations" directly underneath the unit heading. This grammar and real-life language motif is repeated for all the units in the book. The actual teaching content and learning activities are focused on grammar, vocabulary, everyday English usages (associated with different themes such as "our changing world"), reading, listening, speaking, and writing.

Many of the exercises are interactive and communicative in the sense that they require students to work together. For example, the "One World Quiz" exercise that opens the "A World of Difference" unit requires students to discuss their individual answers together:

In which country **do** men and women **live** the longest?
a Japan   b Germany   c The USA

(Soars & Soars, 2009, p. 7)

In the "Reading and Speaking" section (Soars & Soars, 2009, pp. 10–11), the two reading texts are about two families, one in Kenya and one in China. As a warm-up activity students are asked to discuss questions about their own family, for example, "Who is in your immediate family?" Students are then divided into two groups. Each group is asked to read the text on one of the two families, then to do some comprehension questions with members of their reading group. After that, the two reading groups come together and compare the information they have read, for example, "What similarities and differences can you find?" This is then followed by an activity on vocabulary learning in which students' attention is directed to a set of highlighted words in the reading texts and to do a word-meaning/definition matching exercise.

In the "Spoken English" section with a subtitle: "Sounding polite," the student is advised that:

1   In English conversation it can sound impolite to reply with just *yes* or *no*. We use short answers with auxiliaries.
     "Did you have a good day?" "Yes, I did/No, I didn't."

2   It also helps if you add some more information.
    "Do you have much homework?" "Yes, I do. Loads. I've got Geography, French, and Maths." (Soars & Soars, 2009, p. 8)

Together, these samples of textbook content suggest that three senses of communication are at work. First, where the language-focused exercises are designed to encourage students to work with one another, it can be argued that the learning activities themselves are designed to generate opportunities for classroom interaction and active language use, albeit in textbook- and/or teacher-directed ways; task completion requires sharing of ideas and opinions through the use of spoken and written language. In a limited sense this can be seen as a kind of authentic communication (and therefore rehearsal for future communication). Second, the carrier content (the written, audio, and graphic texts on which language learning exercises are built, for example, the text for a reading comprehension exercise) tends to contain awareness-raising and/or socioculturally sensitizing information. For instance, the reading passage on family life in Kenya and China can be seen as an attempt to foreground a multicultural orientation. Insofar as comparative cultural awareness is held to be good for effective communication with people from different backgrounds, this can be seen as part of the pedagogic effort to build up students' communication capacity. Third, pragmatically informed advice is built into some of the grammar exercises. The advice on the undesirable social meaning of short answers using just "yes" or "no" is an example of this; the student is expected to learn conventionally established sociocultural meanings and norms of a target language community as knowledge.

English in the Mainstream

In many educational jurisdictions, linguistic-minority students are being expected to participate in curriculum activities in their additional/second language. For instance, in England all linguistic-minority students, irrespective of their English-language proficiency, are expected to participate in age-appropriate curriculum activities through the medium of English. The age-related subject content specifications in the statutory National Curriculum in England are meant to be applicable to all students, irrespective of language backgrounds. It is also a statutory requirement that their English-language proficiency is assessed on the mainstream English curriculum (and associated attainment scales) that has competence as a key concept (Qualifications and Curriculum Authority, 2007). As a subject in the National Curriculum, English has a language dimension and a literature dimension. For the present purpose, I will focus on the language dimension only. So how is language conceptualized in this English curriculum? To illustrate this, I will refer to the Key Stage 4 (senior secondary, aged 14–16) part of the curriculum (Qualifications and Curriculum Authority, 2007). There are four key concepts underpinning the English curriculum: competence, creativity, cultural understanding, and critical understanding. Of these four concepts, competence relates to the language dimension most closely:

Competence

> Competence in reading, writing and speaking and listening enables students to be successful and engage with the world beyond the classroom. They are able to communicate effectively and function in a wide range of situations and contexts. Competence includes being able to speak or write correctly, read or listen reliably and accurately. (Qualifications and Curriculum Authority, 2007, p. 84)

This gloss on competence is further elaborated by a number of characterizations, for instance:

a   Expressing complex ideas and information clearly, precisely and accurately in spoken and written communication.
b   Reading, understanding the detail and gaining an overview of texts from a wide range of sources.
c   Demonstrating a secure understanding of the conventions of written language, including grammar, spelling and punctuation. (Qualifications and Curriculum Authority, 2007, p. 84)

It can be argued that competence, as understood in this curriculum, plays an enabling role for the other key concepts. For instance, the following elements of the other key concepts all presuppose competence: "[m]aking fresh connections between ideas, experiences, texts and words" (Qualifications and Curriculum Authority, 2007, p. 84), "[u]nderstand that texts from English literary heritage have been influential and significant over time and exploring their meaning today" (Qualifications and Curriculum Authority, 2007, p. 84), and "[e]ngaging with the details of ideas and texts" (Qualifications and Curriculum Authority, 2007, p. 84).

In terms of conceptualizing language, there is an uncanny resemblance between the National Curriculum subject English and the CEFR in that both seem to be predicated on the idea that language competence is made up of language knowledge that resides in the individual student, and students are expected to progressively use this knowledge in socioculturally conventionalized ways over time. The expected progression, from Level 1 (lowest) to Level 8 (highest), in the attainment-level descriptions bears this out. For instance, if we look at "Speaking and Listening" for secondary-aged students:

Level 4 (expected to have been achieved by most junior secondary students)

> Pupils talk and listen with confidence in an increasing range of contexts. Their talk is adapted to the purpose: developing ideas thoughtfully,

describing events and conveying their opinions clearly. They listen carefully in discussions, making contributions and asking questions that are responsive to others' ideas and views. They adapt their spoken language appropriately and use some of the features of standard English vocabulary and grammar. (Department for Education, 2011, p. 19)

Level 7 (expected to be achieved by some senior secondary students)

Pupils are confident in matching their talk to the demands of different contexts, including those that are unfamiliar. They use vocabulary in precise and creative ways and organize their talk to communicate clearly. They make significant contributions to discussions, evaluating others' ideas and varying how and when they participate. They use standard English confidently in situations that require it. (Department for Education, 2011, p. 19)

Communication and Communicative Capacity: Theory and Application

The curriculum frameworks and the textbook samples discussed above, taken as a whole, signal strongly that the concept of communication has been understood primarily as a body of linguistic knowledge whose use is informed by the sociocultural and pragmatic conventions and norms associated with the typified scenarios in a putative target-language community. Communicative capacity, seen in this light, is concerned with having linguistic knowledge and knowing how to use it in socially and culturally sanctioned ways to make meaning. Competence is defined essentially by grammatical and sociocultural norms of use. A fundamental assumption here is that key aspects of communicative competence can be specified in advance; in that sense, communicative competence is understood as an inert and stable phenomenon. A conceptually interesting question here is: How far is this understanding of communication and communicative competence consistent with the theoretical underpinnings at the onset of communicative language teaching (CLT)?

The paper on communicative competence by Canale and Swain (1980), generally regarded as a seminal publication that represented the summation of the then accelerating move towards the social turn in language teaching (see also Canagarajah, this volume), provides some key framing statements. Two points from this paper bear on the present discussion. The first is that, ontologically, it is stated that "[i]t seems entirely reasonable to assume . . . that there are rule-governed, universal, and creative aspects of sociolinguistic competence just as there are of grammatical competence" (Canale & Swain, 1980, p. 6). The idea that competence, be it linguistic or sociolinguistic, is rule-governed and universal (taken to mean that a particular set of norms of grammar and use can be attached to a particular communicative act, irrespective of time, place, and participants) seems to support the knowledge-driven approach underpinning the CEFR and the curriculum and pedagogic materials discussed earlier. Perhaps one should note that, in passing, the creative aspects of sociolinguistic competence are likened to the rule-governed creativity in grammar; that is, creativity in terms of a set of permitted rules, not creativity in terms of innovative interpretation or generating practices that depart from the existing conventions. The second point is that this knowledge-driven approach is supported by Canale and Swain's epistemological view that "communicative competence will be viewed as a sub-component of a more general language competence, and communicative performance viewed as one form of more general language performance" (Canale & Swain, 1980, p. 7). So, within this purview, language, and therefore language knowledge, lies at the heart of competence, not communication or communicative capacity.

Bachman (1990) proposes a more detailed breakdown of communicative competence for language assessment. The Bachman model, as this influential multi-component multilevel reconfiguration has come to be known, conceptualizes competence in hierarchical terms. The overall competence (top level) consists of two subcomponents: organizational competence and pragmatic competence. Organizational competence, at the next level below, comprises grammatical competence (vocabulary and syntax) and textual competence (e.g., cohesion and rhetorical organization), and pragmatic competence is made up of illocutionary competence (e.g., ideational and manipulative functions) and sociolinguistic competence (e.g., sensitivity to variety and register and cultural practices). This more detailed spelling out of the (sub)components of communicative competence has been acknowledged as being very useful for designing language tests for specific situations and purposes (e.g., a language test for university applicants). On the assumption that the language use associated with, say, nursing can be observed and modeled, the more detailed elaboration enables test developers to pin down what should be included in the test content (for further discussion, see Leung, 2010).

In the round then, both the theoretical foundations and the present-day curriculum and pedagogic manifestations of the concept of communicative competence have tended to work with an inert and decomposed knowledge view, and this view continues to enjoy widespread circulation, despite a body of work that has pointed to the need to take a dynamic view of the social dimension (e.g., Brown, 2003; Chalhoub-Deville, 1997; Leung, 2005; McNamara, 1997; McNamara & Roever, 2006). Perhaps an inert and enumerative view is inherently friendly to language education because it lends itself to a describable and teachable knowledge base and because the possession of knowledge needed for communication is highly suggestive of communicative capacity. However, as Widdowson (2001) observes, enumerating the component parts of communicative competence provides only a partial account. In actual communication language users have to enact their knowledge of the component parts and exploit the relationships between them. So to get to grips with communicative competence it is necessary to look at "the whole as a function and not as a sum of its parts" (Widdowson, 2001, p. 13).

Participatory Engagement in Communication

While an inert view of communication and communicative competence may be expedient for purposes of curriculum specification and material development, it runs headlong into difficulties when confronted with some of the complex and contingent ways in which English (and other languages) is being used, particularly in social interactions involving participants from diverse ethno-lingua-cultural backgrounds (see Scollon & Scollon, 1995 for a discussion). Two contemporary communication settings are relevant to this discussion: the use of English by speakers from diverse language backgrounds in English-speaking environments, for example, schools and colleges in London, and the use of English as a lingua franca by speakers from diverse language backgrounds in primarily non-English speaking environments. For reasons of focus and scope, my discussion here is focused on the former (cf. Canagarajah, this volume).

Ethnolinguistic diversity is now a norm in many areas of the world. Over 50% of the student population of London's secondary schools, for instance, is reported to be from ethnic minority backgrounds (Hamnet, 2011), and over 35% of these students are speakers from diverse (non-English) language backgrounds (von Ahn, Lupton, Greenwood, & Wiggins, 2010). In this section, I will draw on some of the data from a recent empirical study carried out in London schools and universities where both the students and the teaching staff were from diverse language and cultural backgrounds. In this ethnographically oriented study, a key source of data comprised audio–video recordings of noncontrived classroom teaching–learning activities collected in three subject areas: biology, business studies, and English. The classroom interaction data were analyzed, inter alia, in terms of participant discourse roles and commitments (Scollon, 1996). The analysis suggests that some aspects of language expression and interpersonal pragmatics are not easily recognized by conventional conceptualizations of communicative competence. The following data extracts illustrate the case in point.

Extract 1 below is drawn from the data collected in a first-year BA class in sociolinguistics. The university is located in London. There were 20 students in this class, a majority of whom were from an ethnic minority and/or EAL background; the teacher was a first-language English speaker. At the onset of Extract 1, the teacher had spent 30 minutes (approximately) on sociolinguistic concepts such as standard language and dialect. The teacher-fronted talk was interspersed with short question-and-answer interludes. At this moment of the discussion, the teacher (T) had just given an account of the distinction between *overt* and *covert* prestige conferred on different varieties of language in a given society. The teacher made the point that some people might value a particular variety of language that did not have high prestige in the public domain generally. Such support for a supposedly non-prestigious variety of language could be seen as an instance of covert prestige. The focal student (S), from an ethnolinguistic minority background, interjected at this point.

Extract 1[2]

01	S:	you know the covert prestige thing(.)it's kind of contradictory to what
02		it really means(.)difficult to know what it means(.)because the overt
03		one is privileged open language(.)but aah people in you know in high
04		places you know such as musicians(.)obviously in high places(.)you
05		know(.)are using this other type of language which is in a way privilege
06		because they can use it(.)and like a majority of people are using
07		the same language(.)so it kind of contradicts the meaning of the covert
08		prestige in a way
09	T:	yeah I mean these are(.)these are just terms that(.)what happens uh
10		someone in the field let's say sociolinguistics will use uh will
11		coin the usage of a term to order to help them understand you know a
12		certain context or a certain aspect of language use(.)and that will gain
13		currency
14	S:	so does it take uh(.)or (confuse) to you where the language is coming
15		from(.)like for example(.)it's coming from music here which is
16		easily(.)you know(.)so it won't really be taken into consideration(.)
17		where you know everyone in society will use it it's not coming from(.)
18		an institution such as education
19	T:	well I think there's(2)what's considered(.)acceptable or standard uh(.)
20		again there're forces working outwards and inwards(.)and also from the
21		top down(.)and from the bottom up . . .

Lines 01–03 suggest that the student had understood the teacher's account of the conceptual distinction between overt and covert prestige. However, she wanted to point out that public opinion or support is a slippery notion—what constitutes public support depends on whose opinion we count. Her statements from Lines 03–08 and from 14–18 are attempts to express and prosecute this complex reasoning. This student was clearly engaged in an academic discussion with her teacher. She was under no pressure or obligation to speak; she wanted to respond. Furthermore, she authored the content and presented it on her own authority (see Scollon, 1996, for an analytic framework of discourse roles). All of this strongly suggests that the student was very keen to participate in the class proceedings.

From the point of view of language articulation though, the student did not prosecute her case clearly. The main contention is stated in Lines 01 and 02, but after that there is no direct engagement with the argument. In Lines 03–08, "musicians' language" is used to exemplify the fact that the language variety used by a particular group of people might also be adopted by wider society. This is clearly an interesting counterargument to that provided by the teacher. But the point is presented as a description of an observed case without any rhetorical framing or linkage to the concept under discussion. The language expressions have not been formulated cogently, for example, the deictic meanings of "it," "musician," and "the majority of people" are unclear. The style is very relaxed and informal (e.g., "You know the covert prestige thing"); the argument is implicit (e.g., "musicians . . . are using this other type of language which is in a way privilege because they can use it"). This kind of vague language requires a good deal of interpretive work by interlocutors.

If we are looking to map this instance of spoken language use on a communicative competence-oriented curriculum and assessment framework such as the CEFR, the descriptor that most closely corresponds to the quality of the utterance is:

B1 Formal discussion and meetings:

> "Can put over a point of view clearly, but has difficulty engaging in debate." (Council of Europe, 2001, p. 78)

Clearly this instance of language use does not quite fit the threshold level for university entrance (usually benchmarked between B2 and C1 levels), for instance:

B2 Formal discussion and meetings:

> "Can express his/her ideas and opinions with precision, present and respond to complex lines of argument convincingly." (Council of Europe, 2001, p. 78)

Nevertheless, judging from the teacher's fairly lengthy effort to respond, one would say that the student succeeded in communicating a complex argument and in the process engaged the teacher and others in a discussion. Participatory engagement on the part of the participants in this interaction seems to be an important issue. I will return to this point in a moment.

The second data extract was drawn from the start of an Advanced Subsidiary level (17-year-olds) biology lesson in a London school. The students had just come into the room, sat down and started to copy the information about the lesson on the whiteboard in their notebooks (this seemed to be a routine activity). The exchange below between the focal student, an English–Somali bilingual, and the teacher, a first-language English speaker, took place just after the teacher started to introduce the lesson topic.

Extract 2:

01	T:	so we are going to look at seeds today and compare how seeds are used
02		It's in your text book if you want to have a look but it is too
03		confusing for some people so maybe you want to leave it [T moving
04		around in the midst of the students near the front of the classroom,
05		slightly leaning towards the students in front of her]

06	S:	that's well horrible(.)are you calling me dumb now [S sitting near T]
07	T:	if I was I would tell you to your face but I am not [T walking past S]
08	S:	but you are implying it aren't you
09	T:	no not at all(.)so first question for you . . . [T resumes content-
10		focussed talk]

The atmosphere in this lesson was generally convivial. The students and the teacher seemed to have developed a shared understanding of the classroom routines, and there was an air of informality in the social chat between the students and the teacher. In Lines 02 and 03, the teacher seemed to be teasing the students by suggesting that they might not be capable of handling the information in the textbook. The focal student entered into the banter by feigning indignation and accused the teacher of personal insult (Line 06). The teacher responded to the student's mock indignation by offering an apparently straight answer (Line 07). In Line 08 the student persisted with her effort to engage the teacher. At this point, the teacher moved to close this particular exchange (Line 09) and returned to biology content matters. The exchange passed without further comment in the rest of the lesson. The classroom atmosphere remained friendly and relaxed throughout the lesson. In this interaction, the participants were engaged in a delicate exchange posed between ludic insult and business-like classroom talk (see also Blackledge, Creese, & Takhi, this volume). Both the teacher and the focal student had to negotiate how far to go with the ludic moment and to maintain the participatory footing associated with "doing a lesson." Insofar as the lesson proceeded more or less happily after this exchange, there is a good case to suggest that the participants had to sensitively gauge their linguistic and pragmatic moves and had managed to achieve a kind of "let-it-pass" closure. Again, it is very difficult to map this exchange on to the CEFR scales. The closest descriptor is:

C2 Overall spoken interaction:

"Has a good command of idiomatic expressions and colloquialisms with awareness of connotative levels of meaning. Can convey finer shades of meaning precisely by using, with reasonable accuracy, a wide range of modification devices. Can backtrack and restructure around a difficulty so smoothly the interlocutor is hardly aware of it." (Council of Europe, 2001, p. 74)

The mention of idiomatic expressions and colloquialisms provides some analytic traction on the lexical level, but the descriptor as a whole does not even begin to address the subtle local interpersonal management work that was key to the "successful" settlement. In that sense, Extract 2 can be seen as outside the conceptual frame of the CEFR. To be sure, these (and many other) instances of "outside-the-frame" participant language use are very much part of the mix that also comprises more conventionally predictable language use, such as teacher–student dialogue following a broad and familiar exchange sequence of: teacher asking a question—student giving an answer—teacher evaluating the student's answer (generally known as Initiation-Response-Evaluation ,IRE, or Initiation-Response-Feedback, IRF, pattern, see Mehan [1979], also Blackledge et al., this volume). However, these outside-the-frame instances are highly suggestive of the fact that having language knowledge (vocabulary, grammar, and established social conventions of use) is just one aspect of the capacity to communicate. Actual communication, particularly in terms of the ways in which language is used to bring it about, is altogether more contingent and fluid. Much would depend on how the participants see the context, their purpose(s), and the institutional and/or situated social constraints bearing on them. And in multiethnic and multilingual situations, where participants do not necessarily share a common language and cultural background, their interaction is likely to throw up more contingency, as conventionalized social meanings and language use can be given different interpretations or even bypassed. In this regard, some of the work in the English as a lingua franca (ELF) field offers relevant insights (see also Canagarajah, this volume). As Seidlhofer (2009) observes, when speakers of diverse language and cultural backgrounds interact with one another through ELF, the interaction process itself can heighten variability in terms of functions and forms; in her terms, "ELF is . . . best understood as a dynamic, locally realized enactment of a global resource" (Seidlhofer, 2009, p. 62)[3] While the context of use of English in a London classroom is not the same as that of ELF, ethnolinguistic diversity among the participants has intensified the dynamic and locally enacted aspect of meaning making and language use.

In a discussion on competence for intercultural communication, Kramsch (2010; see also Kramsch & Whiteside, 2008) suggests that such competence should transcend tolerance towards or empathy with others or understanding others in their own cultural context. Developing this idea further, Kramsch argues for a notion of symbolic competence that "goes further than . . . interpret[ing] events according to truths conventionally agreed upon. Symbolic competence is also engaged in the symbolic power game of challenging established meanings and redefining the real" (Kramsch, 2010, p. 6).[4] This competence is proactive in that it does not confine itself to reproducing what has been learned, it also seeks to define and shape new and different uses (see Warriner, 2010, for a further discussion; see also Li Wei, this volume). At a higher level of conceptualization, this view is related to a Hymesian precept: that it is important to recognize difference between language as system (e.g., grammar) and speech as instances of meaning making. Blommaert (2009) elaborates on speech thus:

> Speech is language-in-society, i.e. an *active* notion and one that deeply situates language in a web of relations of power, a dynamics of availability and accessibility, a situatedness of single acts vis-á-vis larger social and historical patterns such as genres and traditions. Speech is language in which people have made investments—social, cultural, political, individual-emotional ones. (Blommaert, 2009, p. 264)

Language communication thus involves both language as system and language as speech. Speech implies participatory involvement on the part of the speaker in social interaction. This view destabilizes a fundamental tenet of the conventional view of communicative competence. While it is possible to enumerate lexical, grammatical, and sociolinguistic knowledge (however defined) and to calibrate them at various competence levels, speech cannot be prescribed and calibrated in the same way. To communicate with others, speakers in any given situation have to, minimally: (a) decide to participate in social interaction and (b) make use of available linguistic and sociolinguistic resources to make meaning and to respond to others' meaning(s) in context contingently. Communicative competence, as it has been conceptualized hitherto in ELT, has tended to be highly explicit in terms of language knowledge and social conventions of use. The actual participation in communication with others is, however, taken for granted. Furthermore, it is presupposed that having a prespecified level of knowledge of language and social conventions of use is a prerequisite for communication in any given situation (e.g., to communicate at university one has to have B2 level knowledge as a minimum). The classroom data extracts shown earlier suggest that the importance of "knowledge" has to be understood alongside the importance of participatory involvement on the part of all the interlocutors. Auerbach (1992), in a discussion on a participatory approach to curriculum development, observes that

> a curriculum that aims to be centered on issues of importance to participants must be tailored to each group of students. It can't be developed before the educator ever comes into contact with the class, but rather has to be built on the particular conditions, concerns, and contributions of specific groups of participants at a particular point in time. (Auerbach, 1992, p. 13)

If ELT claims to be interested in communicative uses of English (and not just use of English as a display of speaker language knowledge), then there is a need to give greater prominence to the idea of participatory involvement as a key but not prescribed aspect of communication. Quite clearly, the normatively set level and/or kind of knowledge in terms of language and conventions of use can be used to facilitate communication, but communication can take place even when a speaker does not show the requisite level of normative knowledge. Participatory involvement is, however, a critical component for communication to occur at all. This line of argument can be abstracted as follows:

The conventional view of communicative competence comprises:

Language knowledge (L) + Knowledge of conventions of use (KCU) (Assuming a capacity to combine L and KCU in use).

For communication to occur certain prespecified knowledge is required (hence the concept of competence is normative and can be graded):

$$Normative\ L\ (Ln) + Normative\ KCU\ (KCUn).$$

By extension, unsuccessful communication would likely happen if a speaker has:

$$No\text{-}normative\ L\ (Lnn)\ and/or\ Nonnormative\ KCU\ (KCUnn).$$

However, from the earlier discussion, communication comprises:

$$L + KCU\ (+ Capacity\ to\ combine\ L\ and\ KCU\ in\ use) +$$
$$Participatory\ involvement\ in\ event/task\text{-}related\ interaction\ (PI).$$

Communication can occur when:

$$Normative\ L\ (Ln) + Normative\ KCU\ (KCUn) + PI$$
$$Nonnormative\ L\ (Lnn) + Nonnormative\ KCU\ (KCUnn) + PI.$$

But communication cannot be said to have taken place when there is no participatory involvement:

$$Normative\ L\ (Ln) + Normative\ KCU\ (KCUn) + PI\varnothing$$
$$Nonnormative\ L\ (Lnn) + Nonnormative\ KCU\ (KCUnn) + PI\varnothing.$$

Conclusion

Seen in this way, there is a very good reason to suggest that the conventional formulations of communication that emphasize the language and language use related knowledge component are in need of conceptual extension. Language knowledge (broadly defined) is clearly important for communication, but without speakers' participatory involvement, no amount of knowledge of language and social conventions of use can bring about communication, let alone achieve competence. So the concept of communicative competence should be seen as comprising both language knowledge (as discussed here) and participatory involvement. The weighting of each of the two components would need to be understood in relation to the purpose at hand in any given situation. For instance, the focal student in data Extract 1 would be regarded as communicatively competent if the focus is on engaging in a conversation in which other participants show involvement and share some content knowledge of the issue(s) under discussion; on the other hand, she might need to upgrade the language expression side of her communication if she were to present her ideas in a discussion where the other participants were not familiar with her ideas. In both scenarios though, participatory involvement makes the act of communication possible.

Extending this observation to language assessment, the analysis of classroom interaction reported above would suggest that any attempt at evaluating situated communicative competence should be separated from assessment of decontextualized display of normative language knowledge and associated conventions and rules of use. More specifically, the assessment of spoken communicative competence would need to dispense with any preconceived notion of "expected" or "appropriate" spoken language use in ethnolinguistically diverse settings, particularly with regard to classroom-based formative assessment. Summative assessment, particularly in the form of large-scale standardized tests, would need to reconsider the use of "standardized" interaction templates that prescribe test-takers' and examiners' contributions in prespecified ways. In principle, successful communicative outcomes will need to take account of the participatory involvement of all interlocutors.

From a research point of view, this reconfiguring of communication and communicative competence, however, creates new conceptual challenges. For example, if communicative competence, particularly the participatory involvement component, can only be understood and evaluated in context, what constitutive weighting should one be giving to factors such as participant role, content knowledge, gender, and power that can impact on the way in which participants engage with one another? To begin to answer this question in respect of any given context, situated empirical accounts of language communication would have to be developed in order to see how communication is actually being done and how participants act and react to one another in the accomplishment of meaning making. As Hymes (1991) observes "competence is what actual persons can actually achieve, variable, vulnerable, a function of social circumstance" (Hymes, 1991, p. 50).

From a curriculum design point of view, a question arising out of this discussion is: Should we treat the knowledge component and the participation component as two separate elements in language education? If this split were to be adopted by curriculum designers, language teachers and test developers would have to accept that in addition to teaching "language," they would have to find ways to encourage students to develop dispositions that would enable them to participate in language communication using both preformulated repertoires and contingent means of engagement. Furthermore, in ELT teaching materials and curriculum specifications, there is a strong tendency to focus on normatively established English-language repertoires exclusively. While this may be understandable in terms of conventionalized subject focus and even commercial imperatives (e.g., textbook marketing), professional experience tells us that students from diverse backgrounds can call upon their additional multilingual and multicultural resources to achieve communication and to further their learning (see also Canagarajah, this volume; García & Flores, this volume). All of this suggests a need to embrace a much wider notion of language and communication. This recasting of a long-established mindset would involve language educators in exploring issues of social and cultural values, language attitudes, and ideologies among themselves and with their students. In the longer run, language educators may need to challenge some of the prevailing public and professional opinions and values that assume that, for additional language speakers from diverse language backgrounds, normative language knowledge and observance of conventionalized ways of use alone would facilitate communication.

Notes

1. Economic Social Research Council (United Kingdom) funded research project RES-062-23-1666 Modelling for Diversity: Academic Language and Literacies in School and University (2009/2011); the researchers were Constant Leung and Brian Street.
2. Transcription key:

   S—student
   T—teacher/tutor
   (.) pause of up to 1 second
   (number) pause longer than 1 second
   (word) unclear words
   [ ] noises and comments related to the utterance

3. For a further discussion on ELF, see Jenkins, Cogo, and Dewey (2011).
4. It should be noted that the CEFR regards communicative competence as a specific aspect of general competences that consists of knowledge (gained from experience and/or formal learning), skills and know how (use of knowledge and other abilities to carry out tasks such as driving or speaking a language), and existential competence, "the sum of the individual characteristics, personality traits and attributes which concern, for example, self-image and one's view of others and willingness to engage with other people in social interaction" (Council of Europe, 2001, pp. 11–12). This personality-based competence is conceptualised quite differently from Kramsch's (2010) symbolic competence.

References

Auerbach, E. R. (1992). *Making meaning, making change: Participatory curriculum development for adult ESL literacy.* McHenry, IL: Center for Applied Linguistics and Delta Systems.

Bachman, L. (1990). *Fundamental considerations in language testing.* Oxford, UK: Oxford University Press.

Blommaert, J. (2009). Ethnography and democracy: Hymes's political theory of language. *Text & Talk, 29*(3), 257–276.

Brown, A. (2003). Interviewer variation and the co-construction of speaking proficiency. *Language Testing, 20*(1), 1–25.

Canale, M., & Swain, M. (1980). Theoretical bases of communicative approaches to second language teaching and testing. *Applied Linguistics, 1*(1), 1–47.

Chalhoub-Deville, M. (1997). Theoretical models, assessment frameworks and test construction. *Language Testing, 14*(1), 3–22.

Council of Europe. (2001). *Common European Framework of Reference for languages: Learning, teaching, assessment.* Cambridge, UK: Cambridge University Press.

Department for Education. (2011). *English: Speaking and listening (National Curriculum, England).* Retrieved from http://www.education.gov.uk/schools/teachingandlearning/curriculum/secondary/b00199101/english/ks4/attainment/speaking

Gray, J. (2010a). The branding of English and the culture of the new capitalism: Representations of the world of work in English language textbooks. *Applied Linguistics, 31*(5), 714–733.

Gray, J. (2010b). *The construction of English—Culture, consumerism and promotion in the global ELT coursebook.* Basingstoke, Hampshire, UK: Palgrave McMillan.

Hamnet, C. (2011). Concentration or diffusion? The changing geography of ethnic minority pupils in English secondary schools, 1999–2009. *Urban Studies* (online version). doi: DOI: 10.1177/0042098011422573

Howatt, A. P. R., & Widdowson, H. G. (2004). *A history of English language teaching* (2nd ed.). Oxford, UK: Oxford University Press.

Hymes, D. (1991). Is poetics original and functional? *Language and Communication, 11*(1/2), 49–51.

Ingram, D., & Bayliss, A. (2007). IELTS as a predictor of academic language performance: Part 1 (IELTS Research Report No. 7). London, UK: British Council.

Jenkins, J., Cogo, A., & Dewey, M. (2011). Review of developments in research into English as a lingua franca. *Language Teaching, 44*(3), 281–315.

Jewitt, C. (2008). Multimodality and literacy in school classrooms. *Review of Research in Education, 32*, 241–267.

Kerstjens, M., & Nery, C. (2000). Predictive validity in the IELTS Test: A study of the relationship between IELTS scores and students' subsequent academic performance (IELTS Research Report No. 3). London: British Council.

Kramsch, C. (2010). *The symbolic dimensions of the intercultural.* [Plenary speech]. Retrieved from http://journals.cambridge.org/action/displayFulltext?type=1&pdftype=1&fid=7931790&jid=LTA&volumeId=-1&issueId=&aid=7931788, Cambridge University Press, Cambridge, UK.

Kramsch, C., & Whiteside, A. (2008). Language ecology in multilingual settings: Towards a theory of symbolic competence. *Applied Linguistics, 29*(4), 645–671.

Kress, G. (2000). Multimodality. In B. Cope & M. Kalantzis (Eds.), *Multiliteracies: Literacy learning and the design of social futures* (pp. 182–202). London, UK: Routledge.

Lan, P. J. (2007). 基礎華語文能力測驗與歐洲共同架構的對應關係 [The relationship between Chinese Language proficiency and CEFR]. *台灣華文教學學會會刊 [Journal of Teaching Chinese as a Second Language], 3*(2), 39–47.

Lee, Y.-J., & Greene, J. (2007). The predictive validity of an ESL placement test: A mixed methods approach. *Journal of Mixed Research Methods, 1*(4), 366–389.

Leung, C. (2005). Convivial communication: Recontextualizing communicative competence. *International Journal of Applied Linguistics, 15*(2), 119–144.

Leung, C. (2010). Language teaching and language assessment. In R. Wodak, B. Johnstone, & P. Kerswill (Eds.), *The Sage handbook of sociolinguistics* (pp. 545–564). London, UK: Sage.

Leung, C., & Street, B. (2012). English in the curriculum—Norms and practices. In C. Leung & B. Street (Eds.), *English—A changing medium for education* (pp. 1–21). Bristol, UK: Multilingual Matters.

Martyniuk, W. (2005, May). *Relating language examinations to the Council of Europe's Common European Framework of Reference for Languages (CEFR).* Paper presented at the Multilingualism and Assessment: Achieving Transparency, Assuring Quality, Sustaining Diversity—Proceedings of the ALTE Conference, Berlin, Germany.

May, S. (2011). The disciplinary constraints of SLA and TESOL: Additive bilingualism and second language acquisition, teaching and learning. *Linguistics and Education, 22*(3), 233–247.

McNamara, T. (1997). 'Interaction' in second language performance assessment: Whose performance? *Applied Linguistics, 18*(4), 446–466.

McNamara, T., & Roever, C. (2006). *Language testing: The social dimension.* Oxford, UK: Blackwell Publishing.

Mehan, H. (1979). *Learning lessons: Social organisation in the classroom.* Cambridge, MA: Harvard University Press.

Mitchell, J. (1984). Typicality and the case study. In R. F. Ellen (Ed.), *Ethnographic research: A guide to conduct* (pp. 238–241). New York, NY: Academic Press.

Paul, A. (2007). IELTS as a predictor of academic language performance, part 2. In P. McGovern & S. Walsh (Eds.), *IELTS research reports vol. 7.* Manchester, UK: British Council.

Qualifications and Curriculum Authority. (2007). *The National Curriculum.* London: QCA.

Quinones, K., & Korol, D. (2004). *English no problems—Language for home, school, work and community.* New York, NY: New Readers Press.

Saslow, J., & Ascher, A. (2006). *Top Notch 3.* White Plains, NY: Pearson Education.

Savignon, S. (2005). Communicative language teaching: Strategies and goals. In E. Hinkel (Ed.), *Handbook of research in second language teaching and learning* (pp. 635–651). Mahwah, N J: Lawrence Erlbaum Associates.

Scarino, A. (2005). *Learning languages in the New Zealand curriculum.* Wellington, New Zealand: Ministry of Education Retrieved from http://nzcurriculum.tki.org.nz/Curriculum-resources/NZC-resource-bank/Learning-languages/Supporting-materials#resource-1139

Scollon, R. (1996). Discourse identity, social identity, and confusion in intercultural communication. *Intercultural Communication Studies, 6*(1), 1–16.

Scollon, R., & Scollon, S. W. (1995). *Intercultural communication.* Oxford, UK: Blackwell.

Seidlhofer, B. (2009). Orientations in ELF research: Form and function. In A. Mauranen & E. Ranta (Eds.), *English as a lingua franca: Studies and findings* (pp. 37–59). Newcastle, UK: Cambridge Scholars Publishing.

Soars, J., & Soars, J. (2009). *New headway—Intermediate student's book* (4th ed.). Oxford, UK: Oxford University Press.

Spada, N. (2007). Communicative language teaching: Current status and future prospects. In J. Cummins & C. Davison (Eds.), *International handbook of English language teaching* (Vol. 1, pp. 271–288). New York, NY: Springer.

von Ahn, M., Lupton, R., Greenwood, C., & Wiggins, D. (2010*). Languages, ethnicity and education in London.* London, UK: Institute of Education.

Warriner, D. S. (2010). Communicative competence revisited: An ethnopoetic analysis of narrative performances of identity. In F. M. Hult (Ed.), *Directions and prospects for Educational Linguistics* (pp. 63–77). New York, NY: Springer.

Widdowson, H. G. (2001). Communicative language testing: The art of the possible. In C. Elder, N. Brown, E. Iwashita, E. Grove, K. Hill, T. K. Lumley, T. McNamara, & K. O'Laughlin (Eds.), *Experimenting with uncertainty: Essays in honour of Alan Davies* (pp. 12–21). Cambridge, UK: Cambridge University Press.

Winch, C. (2011). Skill—A concept manufactured in England? In M. Brockmann, L. Clarke, & C. Winch (Eds.), *Knowledge, skills and competence in the European labour market: What's in a vocational qualification?* (pp. 85–101). London, UK: Routledge.

7

MULTILINGUALISM AND COMMON CORE STATE STANDARDS IN THE UNITED STATES

Ofelia García and Nelson Flores

The United States has never had a national system of education. Instead, it is individual states that set educational standards and adopt ways to assess student success. But the demands of a new global economy are changing the ways in which the United States does educational business. Perhaps the clearest manifestation of this change has been the adoption of what are known as the Common Core State Standards in English Language Arts and Literacy in History/Social Studies, Science and Technical Subjects, and in Mathematics by 46 of the 51 U.S. states[1] by late 2012. These standards outline what U.S. students across different states are expected to know and do. Two global forces have come together to shape these changes in U.S. education in the 21st century. On the one hand, a global economy has forced increased competition for open markets throughout the world, making the United States conscious of the imperative of educating all its children in ways that would prepare them for college and careers. On the other, this same globalization has increased the diversity of the U.S. student body, with more immigrant students than ever coming from nation-states with collapsed educational systems, a result of the growing privatization of public services in a neoliberal economy. Thus, the United States is at a crossroad—on the one hand, it demands educational common standards; on the other, it faces the greatest student diversity of all time.

This chapter will attempt to describe the educational tension produced by these two contradictory forces—one of uniformity, the other of diversity—and the possibilities inherent in the tension specifically for bilingual students. We use the term *bilingual* students to encompass those who, in the European Union, are referred to as *plurilingual* and in the United States and other contexts as *multilingual*. There are two reasons why we prefer the term bilingual to plurilingual or multilingual for students. First of all, the term bilingual is linked to a history of the

U.S. civil rights struggle, as well as to recent campaigns to eradicate and silence it. Thus, naming bilingualism, instead of talking about dual languages or multilingualism is our own act of resistance in bringing back the sociopolitical meaning of what Crawford (2004) has called "the B word."

In addition, as with other contributors to this volume, we view language not as a system of discrete sets of skills but as a series of social practices and actions that are embedded in a web of social relations (Pennycook, 2010; Street, 1985). In supporting *languaging* as action and practice, rather than language as a system of structures, we understand the linguistic repertoire of bilinguals as a fluid network of signs and features that have been socially assigned to different languages. That is, a bilingual repertoire is one fluid network of signs that is societally constructed as two or more "languages." For the so-called bilingual or multilingual speaker, there is only one linguistic repertoire from which speakers select social features to match the construction of what is socially defined as two or more languages. Thus, to us, a bilingual repertoire already indicates plurality beyond a monolingual one—and it is this understanding of bilingualism that we attempt to use as a lens for rereading the Common Core State Standards (CCSS) in ways that affirm rather than erase the fluid language practices of bilingual populations.

We start by describing the language diversity of the U.S. student population, and the sociohistorical context for the development of the CCSS. We comment on the content of the CCSS and the advances in the theory of language that ground them. We then analyze how theories of bilingualism and of the complex language practices of bilinguals (which we also take to encompass multilinguals) have been ignored in the standards and how the multilingualism of the U.S. student body has been neglected, commenting on the possible consequences of this exclusion for bilingual students, especially those who are new to English, as well as for U.S. society. Finally, we propose some ways in which the common core of the CCSS can be supported through building on the dynamism of bilingual students' diverse language practices. Rather than negate language differences, a bilingual reading of the CCSS can ensure an equitable education for U.S. bilingual students.

U.S. Student Diversity, Bilingualism, and Education

Much has been said about the ethnolinguistic diversity of students in the United States. Perhaps more than any other developed country, the United States has had much experience educating immigrant students who are new to English. But the challenges of the 21st century are different from those of the past. In the early 20th century, only three quarters of U.S. children attended school, and it wasn't until 1918 that every U.S. state required students to complete elementary school (Graham, 1974). In 1940, only half of American young adults had a high-school diploma (Urban & Wagoner, 2000). Furthermore, especially in southern U.S. states, schools were segregated until 1954 when the U.S. Supreme Court unanimously declared in Brown vs. Board of Education that segregated education of Blacks and Whites was unequal and unconstitutional. This segregation included people of Asian and Hispanic descent. Although Mexicans were considered White under state segregation laws, they were segregated through local practice; in 1930, 85% of schools in California and 90% of schools in Texas segregated Mexican students (Donato, Menchaca, & Valencia, 1991). The many immigrants who came through Ellis Island—the gateway to the United States—at the turn of the 20th century also experienced educational segregation. Children who spoke different languages were assigned to special reception classes or what became known as "steamer classes" for children "off the boat" from Europe in which there was only intensive work in English (Thompson, 1920/1971). The academic expectations for those who were racially or linguistically different were few.

But the educational expectations for all students, including those who are developing English, have grown in the 21st century. In 2002, the U.S. Congress signed No Child Left Behind (NCLB) into law, supporting higher standards and tying federal school funding to assessments. On July 24, 2009, President Barack Obama and Secretary of Education Arne Duncan announced Race to the Top, a U.S. Department of Education contest among states for over $4 billion to spur innovation and reform. State applications for the funds were given points based on several criteria, among which was that states would adopt a set of nationwide common core standards that had been released a month before. These higher expectations for all students have meant that students who are developing English, as well as those with disabilities, have received increased attention, as educators and state education departments grapple with how best to enable them to meet these standards.

Little has been said about the relationship between U.S. students' growing bilingualism and meeting educational standards in English only. Yet, one of every five 5-17-year-olds in the United States is bilingual. In 2010, 21% of 5-17-year-olds in the United States, or 11.3 million youth, spoke languages other than English (U.S. Census Bureau, 2010). Of 5-17-year-olds who are bilingual, 25% of them are considered English language learners because they speak English less than very well (U.S. Census Bureau, 2010). The CCSS do not acknowledge bilingualism in any way, and they are not read through the lens of bilingualism, though they could be. That is, nothing is officially said about how U.S. students who perform well in English academically may also have at their disposal other language practices that would enable them to expand even further their literacy and content knowledge. The CCSS document does devote two-and-a-half pages to English-language learners and acknowledges that "these students may require additional time, appropriate instructional support, and aligned assessments as they acquire both English-language proficiency and content area knowledge" (Common Core State Standards Initiative, n.d.-a). Nevertheless, U.S. states are scrambling to develop pathways by which students who are new to English may meet standards.

Students who are developing English, referred to as *English language learners*, differ in language, national origin, age, socioeconomic status, and histories. As with all students, they also differ in capacities. Some are newcomers to the United States, immigrants who have arrived in the last three years. But among the new-comers there are those who come with strong academic preparation, whereas others come with very low academic abilities. Those arriving with low literacy and academic preparation are often designated as Students with Interrupted Formal Education (SIFE). In addition to new arrivals, many of those who are classified as English language learners were born in the United States or have been schooled in the United States for many years. When students have been schooled in the United States for longer than three years and still are unable to pass the English literacy tests that individual states require, they are often referred to as Long Term English Learners (LTELs). Some of these students may have disabilities having to do with poor language and literacy processing. Others may have been inappropri-ately schooled, having attended poor under-resourced schools with weak teachers and curricula (Menken & Kleyn, 2009; Olsen, 2010). Despite their designation as English learners, these students are users of English although they struggle with the English used for academic purposes (Olsen, 2010). Generally, then, the edu-cational authorities address the English-language learning needs of three different groups of students who speak languages other than English:

1. English language learners who are newcomers.
2. English language learners who are students with interrupted formal educa-tion (SIFE).
3. Long-term English learners (LTELs).

But many American students speak and use English very well and are also pro-ficient in home languages other than English. Sometimes these bilingual students are also biliterate as a result of bilingual schooling. The U.S. education system seldom acknowledges the bilingual capacities of these American students. In the past decade, bilingual education programs that develop students' home languages have been curtailed and even banned in California, Arizona, and Massachusetts (Crawford, 2004; García, 2009).

As we will see, the English-only orientation of the CCSS fails to build on the complex language practices of bilingual students. Instead, educators have been primarily concerned with how to ensure that English language learners meet the CCSS, while failing to understand that they are "emergent bilinguals" (García & Kleifgen, 2010) with all the linguistic, cognitive, and educational potential that bilingualism could bring. Throughout this chapter, we use the term *emergent bilin-gual students* to refer to those categorized as English language learners because we want to name the bilingual potential of these students to meet the CCSS. We will return to this reconceptualization of English language learners in the section on Bilingualism and Common Core State Standards below, but we first turn to the history and reality of the Common Core State Standards and to the theory of language that they espouse.

The Common Core State Standards and Language

The Common Core State Standards were not an initiative of the federal government, but of states, under the leadership of the National Governors Association, an organization of state governors, and the Council of Chief State School Officers, an organization of public officials who head departments of elementary and secondary education in these states. The CCSS were motivated by the poor performance of the United States in the Program for International Student Assessment (PISA), a worldwide survey conducted every three years by the Organization for Economic Cooperation and Development (OECD) to 15-year-olds in mathematics, science, and reading. In 2009, the United States ranked 14th in reading, 17th in science, and 25th in math among the 65 countries included. Dane Linn, Director of the Education Division for the National Governors Association Center for Best Practices, summarized the charge for the CCSS saying, "Governors recognize the irrefutable links between a quality education, a productive workforce, and a sound economy. Our competitiveness relies on an education system that can adequately prepare our youth for college and the workforce" (cited in National Governors Association, 2009).

The Common Core State Standards are internationally benchmarked college- and career-ready standards (National Governors Association for Best Practices and Council of Chief State School Officers, 2010). There are differences between the expectations for how students use language and literacy in the standards and those that U.S. states have utilized before. Students are expected to:

*   Gather, comprehend, evaluate, synthesize, and report on information and ideas, using text-based evidence. This includes conducting original research and analyzing and creating print and non-print texts in media forms, old and new.
*   Engage with complex texts, not just literary but also informational, with informational texts making up half of the texts in 4th grade, 55% in 8th grade, and 70% in 12th grade.
*   Write to persuade, explain, and convey real or imaginary experience, with writing to convey experience decreasing in importance and making up 35% in 4th grade, 30% in 8th grade, and 20% in the 12th grade, while writing to persuade and explain take on more importance.

Furthermore, rather than the English Language Arts teachers being responsible for English-language development, there is shared responsibility among teachers in all content areas. An integrated model of literacy is espoused, with reading, writing, speaking, and listening closely connected.

Another important difference in the CCSS from prior standards is the relationship of language and literacy to content. Whereas in the old paradigm there was only overlap between language and content instruction in terms of vocabulary and grammar, the CCSS present an integrated model of learning where language, literacy, and content overlap significantly. The Stanford group on Understanding Language (2012) describe the overlap between language and content in the CCSS as consisting of discourse, text (complex text), explanation, argumentation, purpose, structure of text, sentence structures, and vocabulary practice (Common Core for ELLs, 2012). It is important that all students get practice understanding complex informational and disciplinary texts and that they ground their reading, writing, and speaking in English on evidence from texts.

It is evident that the theory of language in these CCSS has shifted from one that supported the linear buildup of structures and vocabulary to one that may be better understood as language as a form of human action, embodied in the social world of human relationships. That is, the CCSS emphasize languaging as action and practice, rather than language as a system of structures. Language is not pregiven, able to be decomposed into fragments that human beings are able to then "have" (cf. Leung, this volume) but as human action that someone performs in particular in a specific place (Becker, 1995; Maturana & Varela, 1987). The emphasis now is on the development of comprehension and rhetorical effectiveness, as well as participation in activity that simultaneously leads to understanding and more complex language use. This action-based perspective of language is explained by Van Lier and Walqui (2012), speaking about emergent bilingual learners:

> Language is an inseparable part of all human action, intimately connected to all other forms of action, physical, social and symbolic. Language is thus an expression of agency, embodied and embedded in the environment. . . . In a classroom context, an action-based perspective means that ELs engage in meaningful activities (projects, presentations, investigations) that engage their interest and that encourage language growth through perception, interaction, planning, research, discussion, and co-construction of academic products of various kinds. During such action-based work, language development occurs when it is carefully scaffolded by the teacher, as well as by the students working together. (Van Lier & Walqui, 2012, n.p.)

The theory of language inherent in the Common Core State Standards is consonant with the ways in which language is used in the 21st century. Students are asked to use the greater variety of texts—oral, visual, quantitative, print, and non-print—that technology has enabled. The purposes for which language is used have also changed—from recreation or factual declaration giving way to analysis, interpretation, argument, and persuasion. Even language itself has gone from being acknowledged as simply grammar and vocabulary of printed texts to include its many levels of meaning, figurative language, word relations, genres, and media. Finally, students are now being asked to perform language socially through cooperative tasks. It is not enough to organize information on one's own and write as an individual; it is important to build upon others' ideas, whether those of peers, teachers, or authors of texts, to find evidence to articulate one's own ideas, adjusting the presentation according to the different purposes or audiences (see also, Blackledge, Creese, & Takhi, this volume; Leung, this volume; Li Wei, this volume). Language for academic purposes in the 21st century has leapt outside the rigidity of a single oral or written text and the individual engaged in the text. We have finally acknowledged the social function and the flexible semiotic nature of multiliteracies that the New London Group (1996) first espoused.

Scholars interested in the education of emergent bilingual students have begun to study how to utilize the opportunities of the CCSS to improve their education (Coleman & Goldenberg, 2012). In particular, the Stanford *Understanding Language* team, led by Kenji Hakuta and María Santos, is developing resources and principles to ensure that emergent bilinguals meet the standards (http://ell.stanford.edu). A number of white papers on their website offer some excellent recommendations.[2] In addition, on May 18, 2012, they released a draft of *Six Instructional Principles*, presented to the Council of the Great City Schools (Understanding Language, 2012). The first instructional principle calls for "leveraging the native language and culture" (http://ell.stanford.edu/policy-news/council-great-city-schools-presentation), indicating their awareness of bilingualism as a resource (see also May, 2011). New York State is also working on its own *Bilingual Common Core Initiative*.

It is interesting to note, however, that although the advances in a theory of language for academic purposes have been substantial in the CCSS, and there is increasing attention as to how emergent bilinguals can meet the standards, there has been a total neglect of theories of bilingualism and of the complex language practices of bilinguals. And although the CCSS have heeded some of the lessons of New Literacy Studies (Street, 1985), moving away from viewing literacy as an autonomous skill, the CCSS have ignored the ideological framework of New Literacy Studies—the fact that social, cultural, political, and economic factors influence literacy practices (cf. Norton, this volume). The next section explores the two gaps in the CCSS with regards to bi/multilingualism: (1) the failure to account for the complex dynamic language use of bilingual students; and (2) the disregard for the growing bi/multilingualism of a U.S. audience and the different cultural contexts and backgrounds that shape literacy practices.

Bilingualism and the Common Core Standards

The language use of bilinguals is more dynamic than that of monolinguals because the tasks that they must perform are more varied, responding to more complex social and cultural practices, as well as a more diverse audience. As we will see, it is not enough to "language," to "do" or "perform" language; bilinguals have to "translanguage," and, in so doing, respond to the different cultural contexts and social backgrounds that shape their language practices. But the CCSS are silent on the potential of dynamic bilingualism and translanguaging, as well as of the greater diversity of audiences, contexts, and structures that bilingual students face.

Dynamic Bilingualism, Translanguaging, and the CCSS

The Common Core State Standards expect bilingual students to demonstrate the exact language competence of monolingual English speakers and to use English according to monolingual norms. But this stance ignores bilinguals' different language competence, as well as their diverse language practices.

As many have said, bilingualism is not simply double monolingualism, with bilinguals expected to be and do with each of their languages the same thing as monolinguals (García, 2009; Grosjean, 1982; Heller, 1999). That is, bilingualism is not simply additive, as if L1 + L2 = L1 + L2, with a second language added whole to a monolingual's repertoire and kept separate from a first language. Instead, bilingualism has been shown to be dynamic (García, 2009), with language practices multiple, interdependent, "and ever adjusting to the multilingual multimodal terrain of the communicative act" (García, 2009, p. 53; see also May, this volume).

Some scholars have pointed to the different cognitive orientation to competence of bilinguals when compared to monolinguals. Bilinguals are said to have different lives and minds from those of monolinguals, valued for their multicompetence (Cook, 1992; see Block, this volume; Ortega, this volume). As Herdina and Jessner (2002) have pointed out, the interactions of bilinguals' interdependent language systems create new structures that are not found in monolingual systems. These theories were made possible by Jim Cummins' early work on the language interdependence of bilinguals and of their Common Underlying Proficiency (Cummins, 1981), and the understanding that the two languages of bilingual individuals are not stored separately in the brain but are interdependent and rely on a common foundation.

Recently, many critical scholars have pointed to the differences in language competence between bilinguals and monolinguals based not on cognitive differences but on the different practices and socialization of bilinguals (Block, this volume; Canagarajah, 2007, this volume). Critical sociolinguists have used different terms to refer to the diverse dynamic practices of bilinguals, shuttling between practices that are socially seen as one or another language or treating their entire repertoire as an integrated system. Jørgensen (2008) refers to the combination of features that are not discrete and complete languages in themselves as "polylingualism." Jacquemet (2005) speaks of "transidiomatic practices" to refer to the communicative practices of transnational groups that interact using different communicative codes simultaneously present in a range of local and distant communicative channels. Canagarajah (2011) uses "codemeshing" to refer to the realization of the ability to shuttle between language practices in written texts. Many more have used the term translanguaging to refer to the flexible use of linguistic resources by bilinguals in order to make sense of their complex worlds.[3]

The term translanguaging was first coined in Welsh (*trawysieithu*) by Cen Williams (1994) to refer to a pedagogical practice where students are asked to alternate languages for the purposes of reading and writing or for receptive or productive use; for example, students might be asked to read in English and write in Welsh and vice versa (Baker, 2012).

The enactment of translanguaging as the manifestation of dynamic bilingualism differs substantially from the realization of additive bilingualism. Translanguaging does not refer to the use of two separate languages or even the shift of one language or code to the other, since there isn't *a* language. Rather, translanguaging is rooted in the belief that bilinguals select language features and "soft assemble" their language practices in ways that fit their particular sociolinguistic situation (García, 2009, in press). Translanguaging is an approach to bilingualism that is centered not on languages, but on the observable communicative practices of bilinguals. Translanguaging is part of the metadiscursive regimes that bilingual students in the 21st century must perform in order to sustain their language practices in interaction with their plural social, economic, and political contexts (García, 2011a).

Until very recently, translanguaging was not seen as appropriate in classrooms or as a pedagogical resource (cf. Li Wei, this volume). But there is now emerging evidence that translanguaging builds deeper thinking, affirms multiple identities, engages bilingual students with more rigorous content, and at the same time develops language that is adequate for specific academic tasks. Translanguaging, if properly understood and suitably applied in schools, can in fact enhance cognitive, language, and literacy abilities.[4] Cummins (2007) has called for bilingual instructional strategies in the classroom as a way of promoting "identities of competence among language learners from socially marginalized groups, thereby enabling them to engage more confidently with literacy and other academic work . . ." (Cummins, 2007, p. 238). As Larsen-Freeman and Cameron (2008) have argued:

> Learning a language is not just the 'taking in' of standard linguistic forms by learners, but the constant adaptation of their linguistic resources in the service of meaning-making in response to the affordances that emerge in the communicative situation, which is, in turn, affected by learners' adaptability. (Larsen-Freeman & Cameron, 2008, p. 135)

As mentioned above, the CCSS have been silent on issues of bilingualism and have certainly not addressed the question of dynamic bilingualism and translanguaging. And yet, the potential of translanguaging for bilinguals as both bilingual discourse and pedagogy to develop more appreciation of text function, greater comprehension of complex texts, more intricate text structures, and greater familiarity with sentence structures and vocabulary has been well recognized (see above). Without the acknowledgement of the potential of translanguaging, the CCSS may further contribute to the stigmatization of the language practices of bilinguals and doom them to academic failure. It would then be important to resist ways in which the CCSS may be used to manipulate language in academic contexts so as to maintain the asymmetries of power between monolinguals and bilinguals that presently exist in the United States.

Diversity of Audiences, Contexts, and Backgrounds and the CCSS

Bilingual students have to adapt their language use and literacy practices to the broader and more diverse audiences, contexts, and structures in which they "language." Technology has expanded the range of audiences and contexts for the languaging of bilinguals (see also, Blackledge et al., this volume; Norton, this volume; Li Wei, this volume). Whereas in the past, bilingual students' audiences for language practices other than those of the classroom were reduced to those of the home, technology has expanded space and contexts, providing bilingual students with access to voices and languaging from contexts other than classrooms and homes, both in familiar and formal context. The audience today is not simply the school authorities, educators, and classmates, or the home adults or siblings and peers, but those in distant lands and in-between spaces. Whereas the range of audience choices for monolingual students is narrower, enabling them to more easily target a specific audience, bilingual students have different audiences to satisfy through their complex language performances.

Sometimes bilingual students are in an English-language school system performing for a test or giving a formal presentation in English (cf. Leung, this volume). This means that they're deactivating all features of their language repertoire except those that are socially acceptable in the English-language educational system. But other times, they have informal interactions with peers in classrooms, lunchrooms, hallways, often other bilinguals who share many of the features in their bilingual repertoire. At these times, often in the same space in which the test or the formal presentation occurs, bilingual students translanguage, activating different features for effect. Yet other times, these bilingual students are in a mosque or synagogue within their ethnic communities where they're expected to activate only certain features of their bilingual repertoire to read a sacred text while deactivating others. In their neighborhoods, bilinguals often perform linguistically still using other features, different ones in the park, where they play with children with very different linguistic profiles than in the home, where they speak to parents, siblings, listen to radio, watch television, do homework, read, and write, activating different language features even within the same language event. Despite the books and homework bilingual students bring home in English, they now have computers at home where they search the Internet using other practices and where they chat or Skype using yet others.

Language performances are also linked to cultural contexts and social structures, which are much more varied for bilingual than for monolingual students. For example, in the United States, essayist literacy in English is privileged over other forms of literacy (Scollon & Scollon, 1981). Heath (1983) has shown how middle-class English-speaking homes socialize their very young children in this essayist tradition even before they arrive in school. But different cultures structure their texts in diverse ways and value different textual features (Kaplan, 1966). Texts are differently shaped and interpreted in various languages and cultures (Clyne, 1987; Connor, 1996; Eggington, 1987; Hinds, 1983). What counts as literacy varies situationally and relationally (cf. Norton, this volume). The expressive tradition and expository writing that is so common in the United States is difficult in places "where the central focus is either the text or the teacher as the central authority and source of information" (Watkins-Goffman & Cummings, 1997, p. 345). For example, writing in Spanish is often less direct (or, some may say, more subtle) than the argumentation that predominates in U.S. classrooms (Watkins-Goffman & Cummings, 1997). And diverse cultures have different views of critical analysis, as well as of supporting evidence (Ramanathan & Kaplan, 1996; Scollon & Scollon, 1981). For example, it is difficult for bilingual students who are schooled in reading the sacred script of the *Qur'an* to question the text, to argue with positions, and to be critical. As Bertha Pérez states: "[Literacy] is a technology or tool that is culturally determined and used for specific purposes. Literacy practices are culture specific ways of knowing" (Pérez, 1998, p. 22). It is then important to note that bilingual students negotiate many different cultural spaces, and thus they become more aware of issues of language and language use. This more complex understanding of language is very much in line with the CCSS, and thus bilingualism should be exploited as a resource to meet the CCSS.

Finally, because of their greater engagement with cultural and linguistic flows, bilingual students' background knowledge may not match that of monolingual students. Often their background knowledge—of different ways of being and doing, of different scripts and ways of languaging, of different disciplines and content—have little to do with those exploited in U.S. schools. If the CCSS were read through the lens of bilingualism, they would seek to also build on these complex cultural and linguistic resources.

To meet standards, the CCSS expects that language be used to analyze and evaluate texts through cooperative tasks (see also Leung, this volume). But some bilingual students are from cultures in which building upon others' ideas is considered cheating and in which arguing with people and texts and being critical is seen as inappropriate, and in some cases, even a sacrilege. It would then be important to recognize the differences in audiences, contexts, and background knowledge that may make bilingual students' languaging experience different from that of monolingual students. An effort must then be made to acknowledge the different language and literacy practices that bilingual students bring and to build upon them in order to have bilingual students and their teachers move beyond essentialized notions of language and culture and adopt *third spaces*. In these third spaces, bilingual students can perform language in ways that transcend both their home and school cultural norms. Only by feeling confident in one's linguistic and cultural identities can bilingual students be expected to draw upon their backgrounds as resources to learn rigorous content material, meet language, literacy, and content standards, and feel empowered as U.S. bilinguals. But the CCSS remain silent on how to build on the language practices of U.S. bilinguals in order to provide them with an equitable and rigorous education.

The next section provides an example of how to read the CCSS through a bilingual lens, resulting in what we might call Bilingual Common Core State Standards (BCCSS). First, BCCSS would provide different progressions of what bilingual students are able to do using English, the language other than English, or translanguaging in order to meet standards. These progressions would be different for various student profiles, taking into account all language practices for academic purposes, rather than the use of English only, or of standard English, to meet the academic standard. Second, BCCSS would legitimate translanguaging pedagogical strategies, both to scaffold instruction in English, as well as to acknowledge translanguaging as an important bilingual discourse that has the potential to expand thinking and understanding, at the same time that it provides practice for bilingual sustainability. Third, BCCSS would have to be carefully aligned with assessment that separates language proficiency from content knowledge by adjusting the language load in a language according to bilingual capacities or that taps the bilingual abilities of students, their translanguaging, to perform their content knowledge. The last section of this paper thus addresses the potential of Bilingual Common Core State Standards for the equitable education of all U.S. students.[5]

Extending Commonalities to Support Equity for Bilingual U.S. Students

Although the commonalities of the CCSS remain, this section makes evident that effectively including U.S. bilingual children in the CCSS would require a bilingual reading that would open up three possibilities:

1. To meet common standards, *bilingual progressions* of what students must be able to do have to be developed, adapted to different bilingual student profiles.
2. To meet common standards, *translanguaging pedagogical practices* of what teachers of bilingual students must be able to do have to be acknowledged.
3. To meet common standards, *dynamic bilingual assessments* of how bilingual students must be able to demonstrate their knowledge have to be developed.

We expand on each of these below.

Bilingual Progressions

As we mentioned above, not all bilingual students are the same. Emergent bilingual students may be new to English. But the English-language progressions cannot be the same for all, since students arrive in the United States from different countries with diverse educational systems and opportunities. Further, emergent bilingual students differ with regards to their social and economic profiles, as well as the age at which they enter the U.S. school system. In short, while the CCSS are moving all students toward a common benchmark, there must be spaces built into the framework for differentiating what emergent bilinguals at different English proficiency levels are expected to achieve as they work toward mastery of the CCSS. These differentiated English-language progressions would ensure that students are working toward the CCSS while also providing realistic expectations for students with various language proficiencies in a new language. The English-language progressions would align English-language development with the CCSS and ensure that the work in English is progressing toward grade-level competency as per CCSS.

An exploration of some of the different subgroups of students learning English can help clarify this point. A student who is newly arrived and is completely new to English cannot possibly be expected to perform at the same level as somebody who has been in the United States for several years and tests at an advanced level on an English-language proficiency test. An English-language progression would articulate to teachers what beginner students are expected to do as they move toward English-language proficiency and mastery of the CCSS and how this differs for somebody who is at an advanced level. To complicate matters even more, the English-language progression of emergent bilingual students who have low home-language literacy (the so-called SIFE), would be different from that of emergent bilingual students who arrive in the United States knowing how to use their home language for academic purposes. For these highly literate students, transfer of these language and literacy practices to English-only linguistic performances will be faster, and they can be expected to meet standards at a more accelerated pace than SIFE students. Bilingual students who can already perform academic tasks in English should be expected to meet the same language/literacy progressions as monolingual students. But bilingual students who have been unable to perform academic tasks in English (although they speak English) after three years, should be expected to have different progressions whenever the CCSS demands reading or writing performances. In short, an English-language progression that takes a bilingual perspective must confront the reality of the dynamic bilingualism of bilingual students and create tools for teachers to accommodate students across the continuum of bilingualism as they move them toward mastery of the CCSS.

In addition to English-language progressions that take into account the dynamic bilingualism of the U.S. student population, taking a bilingual perspective of the CCSS also entails making home-language development central to the educational programming for bilingual students. All bilingual students should also be able to use their heritage/home-language practices to meet rigorous academic standards. Thus, heritage/home-language progressions would also need to be developed. These, however, are even more complex than those for English, since, besides emergent bilingual students who are new to English whose home-language development has been interrupted by failing school systems abroad, most bilingual students who have gone to school in the United States have had their home-language development interrupted by the U.S. school system's monolingual approach. Thus, the heritage/home-language progressions must show a greater range of variation than those for English. Far too many bilingual students have been inappropriately placed in traditional foreign-language classes where their bilingualism is ignored or in classes for native English speakers where they struggle to be able to use the home language for academic purposes. Home-language progression benchmarks that are differentiated so as to account for the dynamic bilingualism of U.S. bilingual students could offer teachers tools in differentiating instruction for bilingual students across the continuum of biliteracy.

In order to develop heritage/home-language literacy, there must also be Native Language Arts standards. The creation of Native Language Arts standards aligned with the CCSS would send a powerful message about the importance of home-language development for bilingual students. This would assert the importance of building academic literacy in the home language and would provide an academic context for its practice. The research is overwhelming on the transferability of abilities from home languages to English and vice versa. By aligning home-language instruction with the CCSS, these benchmarks will ensure that Native Language Arts classes are rigorous and are supporting students in reaching the CCSS.

Finally, it would be important for BCCSS to match English-language progressions with heritage/home-language progressions, insisting that translanguaging as discourse be used to meet rigorous content standards. An example might make this clearer. Standard 1 for Reading Literature and Reading Informational Text in the 6th grade reads "Cite textual evidence to support (analysis of) what the text says explicitly as well as inferences drawn from the text" (Common Core State Standards, n.d.-b, p. 36). The details cite grappling "with works of exceptional craft and thought whose range extends across genres, cultures, and centuries." Although it also mentions "seminal US documents, the classics of American literature, and the timeless dramas of Shakespeare," it is possible to read these in translation, gaining, as the standard continues: "a reservoir of literary and cultural knowledge, references, and images; the ability to evaluate intricate arguments; and the capacity to surmount the challenges posed by complex texts." It is not necessary to wait until the English language is developed in order to meet this standard. It is possible to use texts in the students' home languages and to accept students' developing English. What is important is to demonstrate the complex ways in which language is used to learn and make meaning to demonstrate the capacities of a literate and educated individual, which are, according to the CCSS, to:

- demonstrate independence as self-directed learner;
- build strong content knowledge;
- respond to the varying demands of audience, task, purpose, and discipline;
- comprehend as well as critique;
- value evidence;

- use technology and digital media strategically and capably; and
- understand other perspectives and cultures.[6]

    All of this can be achieved by emergent bilingual students only if translanguaging is used to its full potential as English develops. On the other hand, all bilingual students would gain much from using the potential of translanguaging to read texts beyond those crafted in English and within a U.S. cultural context: to engage in research using sources in languages other than English; to participate in discussions taking place in other languages; and to write narratives using dialogue in languages other than English and events situated in other cultural contexts. Translanguaging is not simply a discursive scaffold for emergent bilinguals that disappears as bilingualism develops. Translanguaging is the norm for bilingual communities and it has great potential for teaching and learning. But translanguaging needs to be practiced and developed by teachers who use it as a pedagogical strategy, as we describe in the next section.

Translanguaging Pedagogical Strategies

To equitably educate bilingual students, it would be important to not only allow translanguaging to naturally occur in classrooms, but to have students explicitly practice it as a rhetorical choice for learning and knowing (Canagarajah, 2011). This means that teachers must hold a language philosophy that encourages voice, regardless of language features. They must also provide translanguaging models for analysis and encourage students to use translanguaging in any language or literacy performance. Furthermore, teachers must position bilingual students as bilinguals, at times talking to other bilinguals, and enable them to use their linguistic and cultural backgrounds as a resource to learn. The goal, therefore, should not be for students to use English exclusively once they are deemed proficient but rather for students to be able to use their entire linguistic repertoire strategically and develop unique voices that express their U.S. bilingual identities. As Canagarajah (2011) states: "The confidence in one's identity and background and the ability to draw from them as resources for one's communication are certainly empowering strategies for multilingual students" (Canagarajah, 2011, p. 408; see also Canagarajah, this volume).

Assessments

Assessments play a most important role in education. Up to now, assessments have measured growth and ultimate attainment of discrete language skills in one or another language (see also Leung, this volume). But the CCSS require that students integrate reading, writing, speaking, and listening and that language be used in dialogic interactions. The CCSS present a new challenge for test developers as they learn to assess not specific language skills but languaging, and even translanguaging, in action.

For bilingual students it would be important to create language-proficiency assessments that assess their ability to perform academically in English, their heritage/home language, or a combination of both. In addition, it would be most important to develop valid and reliable assessments that separate language proficiency from content knowledge. Technology is assisting with the development of internet-based adaptive tests that can adapt the language load, as well as the language use, to the bilingual students' linguistic profile. Thus, the language of the test can be simplified, translated, or changed to adjust to the students' languaging to ensure the assessment of language and literacy use, rather than just discrete language skills, and the assessment of content proficiency and knowledge independent of language. Internet-based adaptive tests are capable of being flexible multilingual tests that adjust to students' dynamic language practices. These tests can also provide visuals and glossaries to contextualize language for bilingual students.

Bilingualism has been assessed in the past simply by giving an additional test in the other language. But bilingual students cannot be assessed equitably simply as monolinguals, either in English or in their other language(s). In a world that would view bilingualism as a resource, Bilingual Common Core Standards would require that students draw from all their language practices as they perform bilingually in different modes and modalities, able to move back and forth between standard academic practices and those of their homes and communities and able to render their understandings of language and content while drawing on their entire linguistic repertoire. Filters in the internet are able to create unique information for each of us as we click, providing us with different ideas and information and constructing who we are (Pariser, 2011). In the same way, internet-based adaptive language assessment should be able to accommodate our bilingual selves. The technology is here, what remains is for the testing industry to give up traditional views of language and conventional validity and reliability constructs, while accepting the challenge of today's dynamic bilingualism (see also Leung, this volume).

Conclusion

The Common Core State Standards are an excellent opportunity to provide U.S. students with a rigorous and challenging education that would enable them to reach their full potential as learners and scholars. But to do so, the United States would have to come to terms with its own multilingualism and with the complex languaging of its bilingual students. We have noted how the language practices of bilinguals, their translanguaging, provide students with opportunities to expand the uses, audiences, contexts, and texts from which meaning and knowledge can be extracted. The complex language practices of bilinguals open up multiple worlds to comprehend and critique and offer plural perspectives and multifaceted evidence that provide further opportunities for rigorous analysis. These complex language practices are very much in line with the language and literacy practices espoused by the CCSS. To ensure that all bilingual students meet the rigorous requirements of the CCSS, bilingual students must be supported in their reasoning, their construction of explanations and solutions, and their argumentation from evidence, even if the language used to do so does not match the conventions of standard English grammar and usage. Only by building on bilingual practices will emergent bilingual students eventually be able to master the English-language conventions and the rigorous education that the CCSS espouses. At the same time, only by building on the bilingual practices of these students will U.S. public schools develop spaces that embrace, rather than marginalize, the home-language practices of bilingual students and meet the challenge of creating common standards while affirming the diversity of its student population.

Notes

1. We are including within this number Washington, DC, which, along with the 50 U.S. states, also has responsibility for education within their district.
2. With regards to language, see especially, Bunch, Kibler, and Pimentel (2012); Quinn, Lee, and Valdés (2012); Van Lier and Walqui (2012).
3. See Blackledge and Creese (2010); Creese and Blackledge (2010); García (2009); Hornberger and Link (2012); Lewis, Jones, and Baker (2012a, 2012b); see also Blackledge et al., this volume.
4. See Fitts (2006); García (2009); García and Kleifgen (2010); García (2011b); Heller and Martin-Jones (2001); Hornberger and Link (2012); Lewis (2009); Li (2010); Sayer (2008).
5. We know only of New York state's efforts to build on emergent bilinguals' home languages to meet CCSS.
6. See http://www.corestandards.org/the-standards/.

References

Baker, C. (2012). *Foundations of bilingual education and bilingualism* (5th ed.). Bristol, UK: Multilingual Matters.

Becker, A. L. (1995). *Beyond translation: Essays toward a modern philosophy.* Ann Arbor, MI: University of Michigan Press.

Blackledge, A., & Creese, A. (2010). *Multilingualism.* London, UK: Continuum.

Bunch, G., Kibler, A., & Pimentel, S. (2012, January). *Realizing opportunities for English learners in the Common Core English Language Arts and Disciplinary Literacy Standards.* Paper presented at the Understanding Language Conference, Stanford University, Stanford, CA. Retrieved from http://ell.stanford.edu/publication/1-realizing-opportunities-ells-common-core-english-language-arts-and-disciplinary

Canagarajah, A. S. (2007). Lingua franca English, multilingual communities, and language acquisition. *The Modern Language Journal, 91*, 921–937.

Canagarajah, A. S. (2011). Codemeshing in academic writing: Identifying teachable strategies of translanguaging. *The Modern Language Journal, 95*(3), 401–417.

Clyne, M. (1987). Cultural differences in the organization of academic texts: English and German. *Journal of Pragmatics, 11*(2), 211–247.

Coleman, R., & Goldenberg, C. (2012). The Common Core challenge for English language learners. *Principal Leadership* (February), 46–51.

Common Core for ELLs. (2012, May). *Challenges and opportunities. Language, literacy and learning in the content areas*. Paper presented at the Conference of the Council of the Great City Schools, Seattle, WA. Retrieved from http://ell.stanford.edu

Common Core State Standards Initiative (n.d.-a). *Application of common core state standards for English language learners.* Retrieved from http://www.corestandards.org

Common Core State Standards Initiative (n.d.-b). *Common core state standards for English language arts and literacy in history/social studies, science, and technical subjects.* Retrieved from http://www.corestandards.org

Connor, U. (1996). *Contrastive rhetoric: Cross-cultural aspects of second language writing.* New York, NY: Cambridge University Press.

Cook, V. J. (1992). Evidence for multicompetence. *Language Learning, 42*(4), 557–591.

Crawford, J. (2004). *Educating English learners: Language diversity in the classroom* (5th ed.). Los Angeles, CA: Bilingual Educational Services.

Creese, A., & Blackledge, A. (2010). Translanguaging in the bilingual classroom: A pedagogy for learning and teaching? *The Modern Language Journal, 94*, 103–115.

Cummins, J. (1981). The role of primary language development in promoting educational success for language minority students. In California State Department of Education (Ed.), *Schooling and language minority students: A theoretical framework* (p. 350). Los Angeles, CA: Evaluation, Dissemination and Assessment Center.

Cummins, J. (2007). Rethinking monolingual instructional strategies in multilingual classrooms. *Canadian Journal of Applied Linguistics, 10*(2), 221–240.

Donato, R., Menchaca, M., & Valencia, R. R. (1991). Segregation, desegregation, and integration of Chicano students: Problems and prospects. In R. Valencia (Ed.), *Chicano school failure and success: Research and policy agendas for the 1990s* (pp. 27–63). London, UK: Falmer.

Eggington, W. (1987). Written academic discourse in Korean: Implications for effective communication. In U. Connor & R. B. Kaplan (Eds.), *Writing across languages: Analysis of L2 text* (pp. 153–168). Reading, MA: Addison-Wesley.

Fitts, S. (2006). Reconstructing the status quo: Linguistic interaction in a dual-language school. *Bilingual Research Journal, 29*(2), 337–365.

García, O. In press. Becoming bilingual: Sociolinguistic and sociopolitical considerations. In C.A. Stone, E.R. Silliman, B.J. Ehren, & G.P. Wallach (Eds.), *Handbook on language and literacy: Development and disorders.* New York: Guilford Press.

García, O. (2009). *Bilingual education in the 21st century: A global perspective.* Malden, MA: Blackwell/Wiley.

García, O. (2011a). From language garden to sustainable languaging: Bilingual education in a global world. *Perspective. A Publication of the National Association for Bilingual Education*, Sept./Oct. 2011, 5–10.

García, O. (with Makar, C., Starcevic, M., & Terry, A.). (2011b) Translanguaging of Latino kindergarteners. In K. Potowski and J. Rothman (Eds.), *Bilingual youth: Spanish in English speaking societies* (pp. 33–55). Amsterdam, The Netherlands: John Benjamins.

García, O., & Kleifgen, J. (2010). *Educating emergent bilinguals. Policies, programs and practices for English language learners.* New York, NY: Teachers College Press.

Graham, P. A. (1974). *Community and class in American education, 1865–1918.* New York, NY: Wiley.

Grosjean, F. (1982). *Life with two languages.* Cambridge, MA: Harvard University Press.

Heath, S. (1983). *Ways with words: Language, life and work in the communities and classrooms.* Cambridge, UK: Cambridge University Press.

Heller, M. (1999). *Linguistic minorities and modernity: A sociolinguistic ethnography.* London, UK: Longman.

Heller, M., & Martin-Jones, M. (Eds.). (2001). *Voices of authority: Education and linguistic difference.* Westport, CT: Ablex.

Herdina, P., & Jessner, U. (2002). *A dynamic model of multilingualism: Perspectives of change in psycholinguistics.* Clevedon, UK: Multilingual Matters.

Hinds, J. (1983). Contrastive rhetoric: Japanese and English. *Text, 3*(2), 183–195. Retrieved from http://www.nga.org/cms/home/news-room/news-releases/page_2010/col2-con tent/main-content-list/title_national-groups-co-host-briefing-on-2009-pisa-results-world-class-education-for-global-competitiveness.html

Hornberger, N., & Link, H. (2012). Translanguaging and transnational literacies in multilingual classrooms: A bilingual lens. *International Journal of Bilingual Education and Bilingualism, 15*(3), 261–278.

Jacquemet, M. (2005). Transidiomatic practices: Language and power in the age of globalization. *Language and Communication, 25,* 257–277.

Jørgensen, J. N. (2008). Polylingual languaging around and among children and adolescents. *International Journal of Multilingualism, 5*(3), 161–176.

Kaplan, R. B. (1966). Cultural thought patterns in intercultural education. *Language Learning, 16*(1), 1–20.

Larsen-Freeman, D., & Cameron, L. (2008). *Complex systems and applied linguistics.* Oxford, UK: Oxford University Press.

Lewis, W. G. (2009). Current challenges in bilingual education in Wales. *AILA Review, 21,* 69–86.

Lewis, G., Jones, B., & Baker, C. (2012a). Translanguaging: Developing its conceptualisation and contextualisation. *Educational Research and Evaluation: An International Journal on Theory and Practice, 18,* 655–670.

Lewis, G., Jones, B. & Baker, C. (2012b). Translanguaging: Origins and development from school to street and beyond. *Educational Research and Evaluation: An International Journal on Theory and Practice, 18,* 641–654.

Li, W. (2010). Moment analyses and translanguaging space: Discursive construction of identities by multilingual Chinese youth in Britain. *Journal of Pragmatics, 43*(5), 1222–1235.

Maturana, H., & Varela, F. (1987). *The tree of knowledge: The biological roots of human understanding* (Rev. ed., R. Paolucci, Trans). Boston, MA & London, UK: Shambhala.

May, S. (2011). The disciplinary constraints of SLA and TESOL: Additive bilingualism and second language acquisition, teaching and learning. *Linguistics and Education, 22*(3), 233–247.

Menken, K., & Kleyn, T. (2009). The difficult road for long-term English learners. *Educational Leadership, 66*(7). Retrieved from http://www.ascd.org/publications/educational_leader ship/apr09/vol66/num07/The_Difficult_Road_for_Long-Term_English_Learners.aspx

National Governors Association. (2009). *Accelerating the agenda: Actions to improve America's High Schools.* Retrieved from http://www.nga.org

National Governors Association Center for Best Practices and Council of Chief State School Officers. (2010). *Common core standards.* Washington DC: National Governors Association Center for Best Practices, Council of Chief State Officers. Retrieved from http://www.corestandards.org/the-standards

New London Group. (1996). A pedagogy of multiliteracies. Designing social futures. *Harvard Educational Review, 66*(1), 60–92.

Olsen, L. (2010). A closer look at long term English learners: A focus on new directions. *STARlight, 7.* Retrieved from http://en.elresearch.org/issues/7

Pariser, E. (2011). *The filter bubble: What the Internet is hiding from you.* New York, NY: Penguin Press.

Pennycook, A. (2010). *Language as local practice.* London, UK & New York, NY: Routledge.

Pérez, B. (Ed.). (1998). *Sociocultural contexts of language and literacy.* Mahwah, NJ: Lawrence Erlbaum.

Quinn, H., Lee, O., & Valdés, G. (2012, January). Language demands and opportunities in relation to next generation science standards for ELLs. Paper presented at the Understanding Language Conference, Stanford University, Stanford, CA. Retrieved from http://ell.stanford.edu/publication/3-language-demands-and-opportunities-relation-next-generation-science-standards-ells

Ramanathan, V., & Kaplan, R. B. (1996). Audience and voice in current L1 composition texts: Some implications for ESL student writers. *Journal of Second Language Writing, 5*, 21–34.

Sayer, P. (2008). Demystifying language mixing: Spanglish in school. *Journal of Latinos and Education, 7*(2), 94–112.

Scollon, R., & Scollon, S. B. K. (1981). *Narrative, literacy, and face in interethnic communication.* Norwood, NJ: Ablex.

Street, B. (1985). *Literacy in theory and practice.* Cambridge, UK: Cambridge University Press.

Thompson, F. V. (1971). *Schooling of the immigrant.* Montclair, NJ: Patterson Smith. (Reprinted from *Schooling of the immigrant* by F. V. Thompson, 1920, New York, NY: Harper & Brothers)

Understanding Language. (2012). *Six key principles for ELL instruction.* Retrieved from http://ell.stanford.edu

Urban, W. J., & Wagoner, J. L. (2000). *American education: A history* (2nd ed.). Boston, MA: McGraw-Hill.

US Census Bureau. (2010). *American Community Survey, 2006–2010. 5 year estimates.* Retrieved from http://factfinder2.census.gov/faces/tableservices/jsf/pages/productview.xhtml?pid = ACS_10_5YR_S1601&prodType = table

Van Lier, L., & Walqui, A. (2012, January). *Language and the Common Core Standards.* Paper presented at the Understanding Language Conference, Stanford University, Stanford, CA. Retrieved from http://ell.stanford.edu/publication/4-language-and-common-core-state-standards

Watkins-Goffman, L., & Cummings, V. (1997). Bridging the gap between native language and second language literacy instruction: A naturalistic study. *Bilingual Research Journal, 21*(4), 334–347.

Williams, C. (1994). Arfarniad o Ddulliau Dysgu ac Addysgu yng Nghyd-destun Addysg Uwchradd Ddwyieithog [An Evaluation of Teaching and Learning Methodologies in the Bilingual Secondary Education Context] (Unpublished doctoral dissertation). University of Wales, Bangor.

8

WHO'S TEACHING WHOM? CO-LEARNING IN MULTILINGUAL CLASSROOMS

Li Wei

Transnational migration on a global scale in the last two decades has raised a range of important issues for language education in different countries. Amongst them is the question of what to do with the languages in the pupils' linguistic repertoire that are not the school's language of instruction. Bilingual and multilingual education come in different shapes and forms. A "strong form" of bilingual education, described by Baker (2012), occurs where "language minority children use their native, ethnic, home or heritage language in the school as a medium of instruction with the goal of full bilingualism" (Baker, 2012, p. 232). Examples of such strong forms of bilingual and multilingual education may include the European schools that have been described by Housen (2002), among others, where linguistically and culturally diverse students are taught in nonlanguage subjects in multiple languages as well as learning additional languages. Multilingual proficiency and cultural pluralism are promoted through content learning and regular mixing of different language groups. It is fair to say that such schools are still in the minority and tend also towards the elite in the sense that they are not widely available to all pupils who are in need of bilingual and multilingual support. More common forms of bilingual education are often less structured, with less focus on balanced distribution of languages across the curriculum.

This chapter looks at a particular type of school for bilingual and multilingual children in Britain, especially for those of immigrant and/or minority ethnic backgrounds, which we call complementary schools. Whilst the complementary schools are not set up with an explicit goal of full bilingualism, nor do they actively encourage the use of the full linguistic repertoire of the pupils, in practice, both the teachers and the pupils use a wide range of linguistic resources and behave in a highly multilingual manner. Indeed, evidence shows that such schools are a *safe space* for the pupils to practice their multilingual identities and contest the monolingual and monocultural ideologies, which include the language-of-instruction policies of these schools (Blackledge & Creese, 2010a, 2010b; Martin, Bhatt, Bhojani, & Creese, 2006).

Systematic enquiries of complementary, heritage, or community language schools internationally have a relatively short history. There is a fast-expanding body of literature on the policies and practices of these schools in different national and linguistic contexts.[1] This chapter focuses on what is going on in the British complementary school classroom, with particular regard to teaching and learning practices through multiple languages. Whilst the findings of the research reported in this chapter have important implications for policies, my primary interest here is in the *co-learning* between teachers and pupils in terms of language and cultural knowledge and the effect of co-learning on identity development.

The chapter is structured as follows: I begin by discussing the notion of co-learning in the classroom that provides the theoretical foundation for the subsequent analysis. The connections between co-learning and other theoretical concepts in the study of language teaching are outlined. I then outline the complementary schools in the United Kingdom, which provide the context for the present study. The Chinese complementary schools and the research methods used for the present study are then described. The main body of the paper is devoted to an analysis of co-learning of language, co-learning of related cultural practices, and the co-construction of identity through co-learning, through a series of examples of classroom interaction between the teacher and the pupils. The chapter concludes with a summary of the findings and a discussion of their implications.

Co-learning in the Classroom

The classroom is an interesting site for the negotiation of power relations. Classroom-based learning typically involves the role set of teachers and learners. While cultural variations exist, the role of the teacher in the classroom context is traditionally seen as the source provider of information and the role of the learner as the recipient of that information. In the language classroom, the teacher provides models of language, either through their own speaking and writing or through samples of speech and writing by other, usually "native," language users, and the learner learns to use the target language according to the standard set by the teacher via such models.

Technological advancement and global migration have challenged the traditional configuration of the classroom role set and broken the boundary between formal classroom-based learning and learning in less formal contexts (cf. García & Flores, this volume; Norton, this volume). A massive amount of information is freely available on the internet at the press of a button. Learners no longer need to wait for their teachers to give them the information. They also find themselves sharing learning contexts with others from very diverse backgrounds, experiences, motivations, and needs. For the language teacher, they may be teaching a group of learners with highly mixed interests, abilities, learning histories, and exposures to the target language, while the language learner may be confronted with so many different models of the target language that notions of native, first, second, and foreign languages become blurred (see recent critical sociolinguistic work by Blommaert, 2010; Pennycook, 2010, for example).

This chapter deals with a specific language classroom context, where the traditional role set of the teacher and the learner, and the power relations implied in such a role set, is being challenged by sociocultural changes that are going on simultaneously in the community and society at large. I will evoke the notion of co-learning both as an analytic concept for the empirical data that I present and as a pedagogical practice that may benefit the co-participants in multilingual classrooms more generally.

The concept of co-learning has been used in a range of disciplines from artificial intelligence and computer simulation to global security systems and business information management. Interestingly, and somewhat paradoxically, co-learning as a concept is not talked about very much in educational research, where co-participation and co-construction of knowledge are more often discussed with a focus on equitable access to resources, equal contributions from individuals, and emergence of knowledge through the actual learning process. In essence, co-learning is a process in which several agents simultaneously try to adapt to one another's behavior so as to produce desirable global outcomes that would be shared by the contributing agents. Researchers of co-learning have been particularly interested in the emergence of conventions and the evolution of cooperation during its process (e.g., Macy & Skvoretz, 1998; Ossowski, 1999; Shoham & Tennenholtz, 1994, 1997). Brantmeier (n.d.) suggests that, in the classroom context, co-learning changes the role sets of teachers and learners from "dispensers and receptacles of knowledge" to "joint sojourners" on the quest for knowledge, understanding, and wisdom. The teacher would become a learning facilitator, a scaffolder, and a critical reflection enhancer, while the learner becomes an empowered explorer, a meaning maker, and a responsible knowledge constructor. As Brantmeier argues, "a facilitator doesn't get in the way of learning by imposing information. A facilitator guides the process of student learning" (Brantmeier, n.d., n.p.). A scaffolder "assesses the learner's knowledge and builds scaffolding to extend that knowledge to a broader and deeper understanding" (Brantmeier, n.d., n.p.). And a critical reflection enhancer asks the learner to "reflect on what is being learned and the process of learning (meta-reflection about process)" (Brantmeier, n.d., n.p.). In the meantime, an empowered explorer is "an independent or collective explorer of knowledge through disciplined means" (Brantmeier, n.d., n.p.). And a meaning maker and responsible knowledge constructor is "one who engages in meaningful knowledge construction that promotes relevancy to her/his own life" (Brantmeier, n.d., n.p.). Mutual adaptation of behavior is the key to co-learning. In order to achieve desirable learning outcomes, the teacher and the learner need to constantly monitor and adapt their actions and learn from each other.

Co-learning in the classroom does not simply involve the teacher in developing strategies to allow equitable participation for all in the classroom; co-learning requires much unlearning of cultural conditioning because, as Brantmeier (n.d.) points out, "it challenges the traditional authoritative, dominant and subordinate role sets in schooling environments and the unequal power relationships in wider spheres of our world" (Brantmeier, n.d., n.p.). It empowers the learner, and "builds a more genuine community of practice" (Brantmeier, n.d., n.p.). It moves the teacher and the learner towards a more "dynamic and participatory engagement" (Brantmeier, n.d., n.p.) in knowledge construction. According to Brantmeier, the characteristics of a co-learning relationship include:

- all knowledge is valued;
- reciprocal value of knowledge sharers;
- care for each other as people and co-learners;
- trust; and
- learning from one another.

And the characteristics of a co-learning classroom environment include:

- shared power among co-learners;
- social and individualized learning;
- collective and individual meaning making and identity exploration;
- community of practice with situated learning; and
- real-world engagement and action.

Research on co-learning in the classroom investigates how the coparticipants, teachers, and learners jointly build and manage their co-learning relationships, what they actually learn from each other, and what impact co-learning practices has on the co-participants' knowledge acquisition and identity development.

Co-learning and Language Teaching

Since the 1990s, there has been a transformation in language teaching, especially second- and foreign-language teaching, from an instructor-centered curriculum to what has been termed as the *learner-centered curriculum* (e.g., Nunan, 1988; see also Leung, this volume). The learner-centered curriculum is a negotiated process in which the curriculum is a collaboration between teachers and students. Whilst the focus is often on how the teacher plans, implements, and evaluates their language-teaching activities, emphasis is given to learner needs, learner motivation, and learner identity.

One of the consequences of the learner-centered curriculum is a realization of learner diversity. Due in part to ever-increasing international migration and intercultural encounters, it is now commonplace for language classes to have learners with very different linguistic, cultural, and educational backgrounds, some having very complex migration and language-learning experiences (cf. García & Flores, this volume). They bring with them "funds of knowledge"—"the historically accumulated and culturally developed bodies of knowledge and skills essential for households and individual functioning and well-being" (Moll, Amanti, Neff, & Gonzalez, 1992, p. 133, see also Moll & Gonzalez, 1994). Such funds of knowledge contain rich cultural and cognitive resources that can be used in the classroom in order to provide culturally responsive, meaningful, and effective teaching (cf. Norton, this volume). Teachers, as well as the learners, have much to gain from using these funds of knowledge in the classroom, not only to make the classrooms more inclusive but also to engage in real-world meaning making and identity exploration, which are crucial yet often neglected aspects of learning.

Multilingualism is now widely recognized to be a major source of funds of knowledge.[2] The ability to use home or community languages and to draw on funds of knowledge associated with worlds beyond the classroom and the school is part of what Kramsch and Whiteside (2008) call *symbolic competence*—"the ability not only to approximate or appropriate for oneself someone else's language, but to shape the very context in which the language is learned and used" (Kramsch & Whiteside, 2008, p. 664. See also Kramsch, 2006; Leung, this volume). As Kramsch and Whiteside point out,

> Social actors in multilingual settings seem to activate more than a communicative competence that would enable them to communicate accurately, effectively, and appropriately with one another. They seem to display a particularly acute ability to play with various linguistic codes and with the various spatial and temporal resonances of these codes. (Kramsch & Whiteside, 2008, p. 664)

Extending Bourdieu's notion of *sens pratique,* which is exercised by a habitus that structures the very field it is structured by in a quest for symbolic survival (Bourdieu, 2000, p. 150), Kramsch and Whiteside (2008) argue that a multilingual *sens pratique* multiplies the possibilities of meaning offered by the various codes in presence. As they suggest,

> In today's global and migratory world, distinction might not come so much from the ownership of one social or linguistic patrimony (e.g. Mexican or Chinese culture, English language) as much as it comes from the ability to play a game of distinction on the margins of established patrimonies. (Kramsch & Whiteside, 2008 p. 664)

It should be recognized that the language teacher community has also gone through enormous diversification. Native speaker teachers are no longer regarded as the standard bearer (e.g., Braine, 2010; Llurda, 2005). Multilingual and multicultural teachers bring their own funds of knowledge and have their own symbolic competence. The question that I am particularly interested in exploring is, then, what and how do the teachers and learners co-learn in the multilingual and multicultural classroom?

Complementary Schools in Britain

Complementary schools have been a major sociopolitical and educational movement in Britain since the 1950s. Initially they were formed by the Black community as a means of tackling racism towards, and underachievement amongst, Black children. In the 1960s and 1970s, British Muslim communities set up a number of faith schools, especially for girls. Some of these schools later received governmental recognition along with other faith schools. But the vast majority of complementary schools in today's Britain are cultural and language schools, usually run outside the hours of mainstream schools, that is, at weekends.[3] According to the national resource center ContinYou's register (http://www.continyou.org.uk/), there are currently over 2,000 such schools (see also Kempadoo & Abdelrazak, 1999). However, such figures are likely to be an underestimate, as these schools are voluntary organizations and many are very small and informal and thus may not wish to appear on official registers for a variety of reasons.

Complementary schools have attracted a certain amount of public debate in Britain vis-à-vis the definition of schooling, government's involvement in educational management, and alternative pedagogical practices (e.g., Chevannes & Reeves, 1987; Halstead, 1995; Hewer, 2001; McLaughlin, 1995). But on the whole there is a lack of awareness of complementary schools by both mainstream school teachers and the general public. Many mainstream teachers are not aware that a significant number of their pupils also attend complementary schools at the weekend, nor do they know what is being taught, or how, in these schools. For their part, complementary schools do not usually attempt to interact with other educational institutions (see Creese et al., 2008; Kenner, 2007). This includes complementary schools of other minority ethnic communities. So a teacher at a Turkish complementary school in the northeast of London may not have spoken to a Gujarati school or a Chinese school teacher in the same area. They tend to operate entirely within their own communities.

While the establishment of the complementary schools is sometimes seen as a challenge to the dominant ideology of monoculturalism in Britain, the ideology of the complementary schools themselves is rarely questioned. For instance, most complementary schools have an implicit policy of one language only (OLON), usually the minority ethnic language of course, or one language at a time (OLAT). It discourages the use of English and the mixing of languages and treats the pupils as if they were the same as those from their ancestral countries, be it China, Turkey, India, or some other, even though they are British by any definition. I have raised the question elsewhere (Li & Wu, 2008, 2009) about the implications of such policies.

To me, OLON and OLAT policies are another form of the monolingual ideology, particularly in light of the complexities of the multilingual repertoires of the pupils, the teachers, and the parents (cf. García & Flores, this volume). Although it is understandable that the complementary schools want to insist on using specific community languages in this particular domain, the long-term consequence of the compartmentalization of community languages and cultural affiliations is an issue of concern.[4]

The Present Study

The present study draws data from a number of complementary schools for ethnic Chinese children in the major British cities of London, Manchester, and Newcastle.[5] The current Chinese community is one of the largest immigrant communities in Britain, developed primarily from post-war migrants who began to arrive in the 1950s. The vast majority of the post-war Chinese immigrants were from Hong Kong. They were Cantonese and/or Hakka speakers. Many of them were peasants and laborers who left an urbanizing Hong Kong to seek a better living in Britain. They tend to be engaged in largely family-based catering businesses and other service industries. Over a quarter of the Chinese community in Britain now are British born.[6]

There were informal reports of "home schooling," that is, children being taught by their parents and others at home, amongst these Chinese migrant families in the 1950s and 1960s in cities such as London, Liverpool, and Manchester where there were significant numbers of Chinese residents (Benton & Gomez, 2007). The very first Chinese schools, complementary schools in effect, emerged on the basis of such collectives of families, providing private education to their children. The reasons for the emergence of such schools were complex. There is no doubt that racial discrimination played a role. But the fact that the vast majority of the Chinese were, and still are, engaged in service industries has led to scattered settlements right across Britain. It is often said that any town or village in Britain with around 2,000 residents will have at least one family-run Chinese takeaway. While this may be stereotypical, the implication is that the Chinese children of these families would have little or no contact with other Chinese children if there was no Chinese complementary school. The establishment of the Chinese schools must thus be seen as a major achievement of the community in their determination to support themselves. According to the UK Federation of Chinese Schools and the UK Association for the Promotion of Chinese Education, the two largest national-level organizations for Chinese complementary schools, there are over 200 Chinese complementary schools in the United Kingdom.[7] They are located in major urban centers. Many families have to travel for hours to send their children to the schools. They receive little support from the relevant local education authorities. They are almost entirely self-financed. Parents pay fees to send the children, and local Chinese businesses offer sponsorships and other support (e.g., paying for the hire of premises and facilities). Many of the schools use teaching materials provided free of charge by voluntary organizations and other agencies in mainland China, Hong Kong, and Taiwan. The teachers are mainly enthusiastic middle-class Chinese parents and university students.

In the last decade or so, a pattern has emerged. There are now four types of Chinese schools in Britain: (1) schools for Cantonese-speaking children from Hong Kong immigrant families; (2) schools for Cantonese-speaking children of Hong Kong immigrant families with particular religious affiliations, that is, run by the church; (3) schools for Mandarin-speaking children from mainland China; and (4) schools for Mandarin-speaking children of Buddhist families, mainly from Taiwan. Most of the schools run classes over the weekend for up to three hours. Parents play a crucial role in the schools—parents pay, parents govern, and parents teach. A typical Chinese complementary school in Britain looks like this: It rents its premises from a local school or education center. There is a temporary reception desk at the entrance for parents to speak to the teachers about any issues of interest. A shop is available for the children to buy snacks and drinks. Space is provided for the staff to have tea and coffee during break time and to have meetings. The children are grouped according to proficiency in Chinese. There are traditional Chinese dance, arts, and sports sessions before or after the language and literacy sessions. Many schools also provide English-language lessons for parents.

With regard to language, four issues are noteworthy: (i) There is a clear policy that only Chinese, whatever variety it may be, should be used by the teachers and pupils, even though in practice both teachers and pupils alternate between Chinese and English regularly (see further, Li & Wu, 2008). Li Wei (2011) discusses how switching by the children between Chinese and English, as well as between speech and writing, in the complementary-school classroom is used creatively not only in the process of learning but also as an act of identity and rebellion against the OLON or OLAT policies. (ii) Like most complementary schools in Britain, the Chinese schools have literacy teaching as their key objective, as there is a widespread perception amongst the parents that the British-born generations of minority ethnic children have lost the ability to read and write in their ethnic languages. (iii) There are significant differences between the teachers and the pupils' linguistic proficiency and preference. The teachers tend to be native speakers of Chinese, have had a substantial monolingual experience as Chinese speakers, and prefer to use Chinese most of, if not all, the time. In contrast, the pupils have had limited and context-specific input in Chinese, have high proficiency in English, and use English as the lingua franca with their peers, including other children of Chinese ethnic origin. The children's English-language proficiency, in most cases, is much more sophisticated than that of the teachers. Li and Wu (2009) examined examples of how children manipulate the discrepancies in the language proficiencies and preferences in Chinese and English between themselves and their teachers to their own advantage in the classroom, for example, through correcting the teachers' pronunciation of certain

English words and the use of idioms that are unknown to the teacher. (iv) All the Cantonese schools also teach Mandarin and the simplified characters that are associated with it. However, none of the Mandarin schools teaches Cantonese or the traditional complex characters. This may be seen as a sign of the changing hierarchies amongst varieties of the Chinese language as a result of the rising politico-economic power of mainland China. Mandarin, the variety that is most popularly used in mainland China, is fast gaining currency in the Chinese over-seas diasporas that are traditionally Cantonese or Hokkien speaking (see further Li & Zhu, 2010a, 2010b). It also raises issues of the complexities of different modalities in learning Chinese (see, e.g., Li, 2011).

The data for the present chapter come out of a series of research projects inves-tigating multilingual practices in complementary schools and families in London, Manchester, and Newcastle. In each of the cities, we chose one Cantonese school and one Mandarin school. And in all the schools, extensive ethnographic obser-vations were made. After initial meetings with the administrators in each school explaining the purpose of the research project, information sheets were distributed to teachers, parents, and pupils and permissions sought for further data collection. We were allowed access to observe classroom interaction and to collect data in a range of settings, including break time and formal school events such as prize-giving ceremonies. A selection of teachers, administrators, parents, and pupils were interviewed, and recordings, both audio and video, were made in the classroom as well as during break time. We chose to focus on the 10–12-year-old groups in all the schools we studied, although some of the classes also included children as young as eight, or as old as 14, years. All the examples discussed below are taken from the transcripts of audio-recorded interactions.[8]

Co-learning of Language

Example 1 is taken from a Mandarin class in the Cantonese school in London. The teacher has written the Chinese characters for a particular type of cookie, 曲奇, on the whiteboard because she thought it was an unfamiliar word for the pupils. As it happens, the word is a Cantonese transliteration of English and some of the pupils recognize the characters, as they have seen them in local shops. The Cantonese pronunciation of the characters is *kuk-kei*, as G2, one of the pupils, says in Example 1. But the teacher, not knowing Cantonese, pronounces the word in Mandarin, which sounds very different from the English source, *cookie*. The two pupils explain to the teacher that the Cantonese pronunciation of the characters is in fact very similar to the English word. What is particularly remarkable is that when the teacher seeks confirmation ("Is it?"), G2 replies in Cantonese, *haila*, meaning yes and reinforcing the fact that they are Cantonese speakers. So whilst the pupils are learning Mandarin, their knowledge of Cantonese helps with the proceeding of the class, while the teacher gains knowledge about the origin of the Chinese word by learning from the pupils.

Example 1. (T: a female teacher in her late twenties; G1 and G2 are two 11-year-old female pupils.)

T: 曲奇 (quqi). 一种饼干, 知道吗?
Quqi. A kind of cookie, you know?

G1: What?

T: 曲奇 (quqi).

G2: *kuk-kei. kuk-kei.*

T: Yes.

G1: So why did you say *qiu* . . . something *qiu* . . .

T: 曲奇 (quqi).

G2: No. *kuk-kei.*

G1: 广东话是 *kuk-kei?*
In Cantonese it is kuk-kei.

G2: It's Cantonese. *kuk-kei* is Cantonese.

T: 是吗?
Is it?

G2: 係啦!
Yes!

We have observed many comparable instances where the pupils' knowledge of Cantonese has proved to be particularly useful in the teaching and learning of specific words and phrases, many of which are transliterations of English. Examples include 沙律 (*salad*) in Cantonese *saaleot* and in Mandarin 色拉 *sela*; 芝士 (*cheese*), in Cantonese *zisi* and Mandarin *zhi-shi*. The Mandarin teachers, while assuming an influential status in the class and teaching what is assumed to be a high-status variety of Chinese, gain by learning from the pupils.

Example 2 is taken from a class of 8-year-olds in the Cantonese school in Newcastle. The teacher is going through a series of pictures of fruit and vegetables and asks the pupils to name them in Mandarin. When the teacher points to the picture of potatoes, B1 answers in English. The teacher asks for the Chinese name, and G1 answers in Cantonese. The teacher does not know the Cantonese word for potato. So she asks for clarification. B2 repeats what G1 said. The teacher realizes that they are speaking Cantonese. She seems to accept it with her "OK" and then asks for an alternative. B1 answers in English, again, but this time with a Cantonese utterance final particle. The teacher takes the opportunity to stress that this is a Chinese class and asks for the Chinese name. B1 attempts at a literal translation. *Tang* means sweet but it is a noun, as in confectionery, and *shu* means potato. *Tian* means sweet and it is an adjective. One can see that he is trying to work out what is the correct form of the word. G2 repeats B1's first attempt, *tang shu* (confectionery potato), in a mildly mocking way and some of the pupils in the class giggle. The teacher then offers the correct term, explaining that in some parts of China it is known as *hong shu* (literally: red + potato) and in some other places, *bai shu* (white potato). G2 understands it and says in English "red and white." The teacher then offers another term, *digua* (literally: earth melon), adding that this is how it is known in her hometown dialect. But she then says that *digua* is potato. G1 reckons that sweet potato would need to have an adjective before it. So she says *tian digua*. But in fact, *digua* means sweet potato and the teacher has made a slip in the previous turn. When she corrects G1, and herself, by saying *digua* is sweet potato, B2 repeats the Cantonese term that he and G1 offered in the first place, *faansyu*, as if in protest.

Example 2. (T: Female teacher in her early thirties. B1 and B2 are boys and G1 and G2 are girls. They are all about eight years old.)

T:　　好了。下一个,是什么?
　　　Good. Next, what is it?
B1:　Sweet potato.
T:　　中文是什么?
　　　What is it in Chinese?
G1:　蕃薯 (faan syu) ?
　　　Sweet potato.
T:　　什么?
　　　What?
B2:　蕃薯 (faan syu)?
　　　Sweet potato.
T:　　OK. 还可以叫什么?
　　　What can it also be called?
B1:　Sweet potato 啦。
　　　PA [particles]
T:　　中文!!
　　　Chinese.
B1:　糖薯 (tang shu), 甜薯 (tian shu)?
　　　candy potato, sweet potato
G2:　糖薯 (tang shu)!
　　　candy potato

(Giggles)

T:　　红薯 (hong shu), 也有的地方叫白薯 (bai shu)?
　　　some places call it bai shu
B2:　Red and white.
T:　　我们家那边叫地瓜 (digua).
　　　In my hometown we call it digua.
G2:　地瓜 (digua)?
T:　　地瓜 (digua) 就是 potato.
　　　Digua is potato.
G1:　So it's 甜地瓜(tian digua)?
　　　So it's sweet digua

T: No, 地瓜 (digua) 就是 sweet potato.
        No, digua is sweet potato.
B2:   蕃薯啦 (faan syu la)?

Example 3 was recorded in one of the Mandarin schools in London. The teacher is trying to explain the meaning of the phrase 摆乌龙 (*bai wulong*), or in traditional characters 擺烏龍, and in Cantonese, *baai wulung*. As in Examples 1 and 2, the phrase comes from a Cantonese transliteration of the English phrase *own goal*, and the verb *baai/bai* could mean *play*, *place*, or *display*. Nowadays, the phrase is widely used amongst speakers of different varieties of Chinese to mean "made a mess of things." Like the teacher in Example 1, the teacher in this example does not seem to know the origin of the phrase that he is teaching. He makes a connection between the word *wulong* (transliteration of *own goal*) with the name of a type of Chinese tea which has the same written characters. Unlike Example 1 though, the pupils in the present example do not seem to know the origin of the phrase either, as they are not Cantonese speakers so they have not challenged the teacher on the meaning of the phrase. What they do challenge is the mispronunciation of the English translation of the phrase that the teacher makes. He pronounces the word *mishap* as /mɪ ʃeɪp/. B1 is clearly puzzled. After the teacher explains it with other translations, but still including the mispronunciation in English, G1 realizes what is meant and offers the "correct" pronunciation. When the teacher shows his lack of knowledge of the correct pronunciation, the pupils start to teach him. And the teacher learns. The class then proceeds smoothly. One cannot help wondering though that, if there was a Cantonese speaker present bringing further funds of knowledge to the discussion, the teacher and the pupils would have learned much more beyond the correct pronunciation of an English word. Nevertheless, the teacher has gained some knowledge of English pronunciation.

Example 3. (T: Male Mandarin teacher in his late twenties. B1 and B2 boys about 13 years old; G1: a 12-year-old girl.)

T: (Speaking slowly as he writes on the whiteboard) 摆-乌-龙 (bai wulong).
        Mess up. 乌龙 (wulong), black dragon. 乌龙茶 知道吗?
        Wulong Tea, do you know?
        Black Dragon tea. 乌龙 (wulong)? means /mɪ ʃeɪp/.

(Silence)

T: 乌龙 (wulong) /mɪ ʃeɪp/. 摆乌龙 (bai wulong). Mess up.
B1:   What?
T: Made a mistake. Accident. /mɪ ʃeɪp/.
G1:   /mɪʃæp/, you mean?
B1:   Oh I see.

T: What?

B2:   /mɪshǽp/. It's /mɪshǽp/.

B1:   Not /mɪ ʃeɪp/.

T: /mɪshǽp/.

B1:   Yes.

Elsewhere, I have discussed other examples of the pupils teaching the teachers the standard ways of saying certain phrases or pronouncing certain words in English (e.g., Li & Wu, 2009). The teachers in the Chinese complementary schools generally readily accept that the pupils' English is much better than theirs and many actively seek to learn from the pupils, just as many Chinese parents routinely ask their British-born children for the "correct" way of saying things in English.

Example 4 comes from a Cantonese class in the Manchester Cantonese school that we studied. The teacher is trying to teach numerals in the traditional Chinese written characters rather than the Arabic numbers. The pupils, who are used to the latter, cannot see the point of learning the Chinese characters and contest the way they are being taught. One pupil, Y, explicitly says "But we don't use them now."

Example 4 (T: Female teacher in her forties. G, P, and Y are girls and H is a boy, all about 11 years old.)

T: 嗱, 改好正的那些拿出堂課簿, 抄黑板的字。

      Nah, those who finished the corrections, take out your exercise book and copy the characters on the blackboard.

G: (moaning) Oooh . . . What for?

T: 第一個是壹字, 第二個是貳字, 這些是中國的數字。

      The first character is word 'One,' the second is word 'Two.' These are Chinese number words.

P: (confirming understanding): 哦。

      Oh.

T: 壹是代表一, 貳是代表二, 叄是代表三, 肆是代表四。.

      'One' represents 'one', 'Two' represents 'two', 'Three' represents 'three', 'Four' represents 'four'.

H: 喺堂課簿。

      In the exercise book.

T: 是啦, 在堂課簿。

      Yes, in the exercise book.

G: (sigh) 唉。

      Ai.

T: 壹至拾。不是一至十次。壹是代表一的'一'字。是中國的文字。中國的數字一是這樣寫. . . .

      'One' to 'Ten,' not one to ten times. 'One' represents 'one.' These are Chinese characters. Chinese number words are written like these. . . .

T: 這些是以前中國用的壹字。
      This is the word 'One' which used to be used in China.
Y: 但我們現在不用。
      But we don't use them now.
T: 現在不用，但比你們認識一下，因爲有時會在報章上看到。所以給你們認識，這個是壹、貳、叁、肆、伍、陸、柒、玖、玖、拾。快點抄到堂課簿上。因爲在報紙上，有時你們會 見到這些字。
      Not being used now, but just to let you know these. Sometimes you'll see them in newspaper or magazine articles. So, (I'm) letting you know these. This is 'One,' 'Two,' 'Three,' 'Four,' 'Five,' 'Six,' 'Seven,' 'Eight,' 'Nine,' 'Ten.' Copy into your exercise book quickly. Because you'll sometimes see these words in newspapers.

Shortly after this exchange, the teacher asked the class what other systems of numerals they knew. Some said that they knew the Roman numerals. The teacher was very enthusiastic about learning them and asked two of the pupils to write them out on the blackboard. She actually remarked to the class, "Oh I learned a lot today." In fact, during our interviews with the teachers, many of them claim that learning from the pupils is one of the most enjoyable aspects of working in the complementary schools.

One further example I want to discuss in this section was recorded in the Mandarin school in London. In this example, the teacher is explaining the text 送爷爷回家 meaning *taking granddad home.* But her English translation "took grandfather to the home" does not only sound bookish, it is also pragmatically misleading. Chinese learners of English often have problems with the use of articles in English. The teacher evidently does not know the difference between *home,* which can be used as an adverb, and *the home.* This causes one of the pupils to remark on the Chinese tradition of looking after the elderly within their own families rather than sending them to care centers. What is interesting here is that, while B1 realizes that he misunderstood the teacher because of the way she phrased it, the teacher does not seem to realize that the word *home* can also refer to care centers for the elderly.

Example 5. (T: Female teacher in her mid-twenties. B: Boy of 12 years old.)

T: (Reading the textbook) 送爷爷回家, *took grandfather to the home.*
      send granddad home
B: Aren't the Chinese supposed to be nice to their grandparents?
T: Yes, of course.
B: Why is she sending him to a home then?
T: What?
B: You said she sent the granddad to a home.
T: 对, 家 home。回家 going home。

B: Not an old people's home then.

T: What?

B: Doesn't matter.

This example also illustrates the discrepancies in the cultural knowledge that exists between the teachers and the pupils. Many of the teachers have been in Britain for only a short period of time. The pupils, on the other hand, are mostly British born. They have relatively little in common in terms of their cultural background and life experience. This lack of commonality between the teachers and the pupils can potentially cause difficulties in the classroom and beyond, unless they engage in co-learning in an active and positive way.

Let us now turn to other examples that illustrate more specifically the issue of co-learning of culture rather than language.

Co-learning of Cultural Values and Practices

Example 6 is taken from a recording of an exchange between two boys and the teacher in the Mandarin complementary school in London. The teacher has mentioned the word 统一 (*unite*) several times. That has triggered the question from B1. B2 offers his explanation, which is correct, except that he talks about Taiwan and China as two separate countries. This is a highly contentious political issue and the mainland Chinese government and a significant number of the politicians in Taiwan use a discourse that treats Taiwan as an integral part of China, even though, as B2 points out, the mainland and Taiwan are often separately represented at international events. The teacher clearly follows the official line and states that the mainland and Taiwan are not two countries and that Taiwan is part of China. He explains B2's observation by referring to the UK situation and how the different nations in the United Kingdom[9] are represented in sports. He further rejects B1's assertion that Scotland is a different country and reinforces his position by stressing the word United in the United Kingdom.

Example 6. (T: Male teacher in his early thirties. B1 and B2 are boys about 13 years old.)

B1:   Are the Chinese still fighting?

T: No, why?

B1:   So why are you always talking about 统一?
       unite

B2:   It's about Taiwan and China. They are two countries, and they want to be united.

T: No. 不是两个国家。台湾是中国的一部分。
       Not two countries. Taiwan is part of China.

B2:   No, they are not.

T: They are.

B2:   They are not. In the Olympics, there were separate teams. I saw it.

T: It's like Scotland or Northern Ireland. 都是英国, 但是世界杯 football 还有rugby也 是分开的了。

All part of the UK. But for the World Cup football and rugby, they can be separately represented.

B1:   Scotland is a different country.

T: No it is not.

B2:   It is. XXX (a girl in the class) is from Scotland. She was born in . . . where were you born again?

B1:   Dundee.

T: 但它是统一的了。不是两个国家. The UNITED Kingdom 知不知道?!

But it is united. Not two separate countries. The United Kingdom, don't you understand?!

As has been discussed in Li and Wu (2010), the process of teaching and learning can be seen as a process of socialization through which certain values and ideologies, as well as facts and practices, are transmitted and exchanged amongst the coparticipants. Out of this process, new values, ideologies, knowledge, and identities may emerge. The mainland and Taiwan relationship issue is a politically sensitive one amongst the Chinese worldwide, but it is rarely directly discussed in everyday social interaction. It is interesting to observe such a direct engagement with the issue in a British complementary school classroom. The teacher is taking a very clear and strong stance in the present example. The pupils seem to have a somewhat different understanding of the situation. Whether or not the pupils' views would be changed by the teacher's stance is impossible to tell. But one thing is certain: By engaging in the discussion, both the teacher and the pupils have been made aware of the different positions on the issue.

Example 7 is an instance of the teacher moving from various Chinese folk festivals to the key phrase 盼望 (*panwang*), meaning *longing for*. But the examples she gives in collocation with it all concern certain sociocultural ideals, such as having a "united homeland" and "united family." In contrast, the pupils are all longing for the less serious things such as holidays, sporting events, and in an apparent act of rebellion, the end of the Chinese complementary school year.

Example 7 (T: Female teacher in her forties. Q and B are girls, and the others boys, all between 10 and 11 years old.)

T: 那是第五个词了。第四个词:盼望。盼望怎么说? 比如说, 我们都盼望什么? 盼望,expect, look forward to. Write down the explanation beside the words, in case you forget it later. 盼望, the 4th one, means look forward to. 比如说, 我们都盼望什么?

That's the fifth word. The fourth word? 'Panwang' (long for). How do you use 'Panwang'? For example, what do we long for? 'Panwang' expect, look forward to. Write down the explanation beside the words, in case you forget it later. 'Panwang', the fourth one, means look forward to. For example, what do we 'panwang'?

P1:   过节.
       Having festivals.

P2:   圣诞节。
       Christmas.

T: 世界杯?
       World cup?

P3:   No.

P4:   吃月饼。
       Eating mooncakes.

T: 我们都盼望吃月饼? Sounds a little strange.
       We all long for eating mooncakes?

B: Birthday! My birthday!

T: 我们都盼望着过圣诞节。B盼望着过生日。盼望 can be a little big for all these occasions. 比如说, 我们都盼望着祖国统一, 对吧? 我们都盼望着祖国 get reunited.
       We all long for Christmas. B longs for her birthday. 'Panwang' can be a little big for all these occasions. For example, we all long for our mother country to get reunited, right? We all long for our mother country to get reunited.

L: 盼望中文学校完了。
       Long for Chinese school to run out.

(All laugh.)

T: L, be serious, OK?

L: I am serious, I'm looking forward to it.

T: 比如说, 我们都盼望家人团聚。
       For example, we long for family reunion.

T: For example, if you are here in Manchester, your parents are back in China, and you have been separated for years, you are looking forward to the reunion of the family.

Very similarly, in Example 8, the teacher is making sentences with the phrase 期待 (qidai), also meaning *longing for,* in collocation with a "united motherland," family reunion, peace, and friendship, while the pupils are making fun of each other, as well as making light of the learning task. B deliberately transliterates his classmate's girlfriend's name, Jennifer, in a funny Chinese phrase literally meaning *real clay Buddha,* and the phrase *moon bathing* is clearly a parody of *sun bathing.*

Example 8. (From a Mandarin class of 13-year-olds in Newcastle. T: Female teacher in her forties. B, a boy.)

T: "期待" 可以说什么? 期待 祖国统一, 期待家人团聚, 期待和平友好。
    What can you say with qidai (longing for)? Longing for a united motherland; longing for family reunion; longing for peace and friendship.

B: xxx (name of another boy in the class) 期待真泥佛跟他晒月光。
    xxx is longing for Jennifer to moon bathing with him.
    (All laugh.)

Another example that shows the discrepancy between what the values that the teacher wants to pass onto the pupils and what the pupils are interested in is Example 9, where the teacher makes sentences with the verb 团结 *tuanjie* (unity/unite) by citing examples of propaganda slogans from mainland China, while the pupils use the word in association with football.

Example 9. (T: Female teacher in her early thirties. B1 and B2: 11-year-old boys.)

T: 团结(tuanjie)。团结就是力量, 团结起来争取更大胜利。团结(tuanjie), united.
    Unity/Unite. Unity is strength. Unite to strive for greater success.
B1: Manchester United.
B2: Yeah, United will win.

Co-construction of Identity

What impact does the kind of socializational teaching, as we see in the above examples, have on the development of the pupils' identity? As here, we have shown elsewhere that the pupils in the Chinese complementary schools often resist the teachers' socializational teaching by posing challenging questions and making fun of the classroom activities (e.g., Li & Wu, 2010; see also Blackledge et al., this volume). Many of them associate China with food, music, and everyday culture. While most of them are aware of certain aspects of Chinese history, some of the old folk tales, and archaeological artifacts, their primary interests in things Chinese are Chinese pop songs, comics and youth magazines, and various card and computer games. Yet, little of what the young British Chinese seem to be interested in is reflected in the teaching in the Chinese complementary schools. Their actual, complex, lived experiences as British Chinese youth are not at all reflected in the teaching and learning in this particular context. For the schools and the teachers, and many of the parents for that matter, on the other hand, the emphasis seems to be on a set of traditional values and practices, many of which are imagined rather than real (cf. Norton, this volume). They also tend to think of the children as primarily Chinese and they want them to be very much similar to those in China.

The children, on the other hand, think of themselves primarily as British youths of Chinese heritage. The issue of identity is sometimes discussed explicitly in the Chinese complementary school classrooms, as the final example illustrates.

Example 10. (From the Mandarin school in London. T: Female teacher in her early thirties. G1 and G2 are girls and B1 and B2 boys, all between 11 and 12 years old.)

T: 我们中国人。
      We are Chinese.

B1:   我们不是中国人。
      We are not Chinese.

T: 你不是中国人是什么人?
      You are not Chinese?

B2:   英国人。
      British.

G1:   英国华侨。
      British Chinese.

T: OK.

G2:   海外华人。
      Overseas Chinese.

G1:   是华人还是华侨。
      Should it be huaren *(ethnic Chinese) or* huaqiao? *(Chinese citizens residing outside China).*

T: 严格地说,应该是华人。
      Strictly speaking, it should be huaren *(ethnic Chinese).*

B1:   华人。
      Huaren *(ethnic Chinese).*

T: 对。你们是海外华人。
      Correct. You are overseas Chinese.

G1:   英国华人。
      British Chinese.

T: 也可以。
      Also correct.

B1:   那你呢?
      Then what are you?

T: 我? 我是中国人。
      Me? I am Chinese.

B1:   So you don't have a British passport.

T: No.

B2:   Isn't your husband British?

T: Yes, I have permanent residence.

B1:   So you are not British.

T: 我可以说是华侨。
      I can say that I am huaqiao (*Chinese citizen residing outside China*).
B2:   British Chinese.
T: No. I am a Chinese living in Britain. You are British Chinese.
B1:   Or Chinese British.
B2:   Like they call it Chinese American or American Chinese.
B1:   ABC (American-born Chinese).
T: You are BBC (British-born Chinese).

Here, the Chinese phrase 中国人 (*zhongguo ren*) is linguistically ambiguous as it can refer to the general ethnic category or Chinese citizens or nationals. What the pupils object to is being described as Chinese citizens or nationals. But the two terms often used to describe Chinese people living outside China are also confusing. 华人 (*huaren*) means persons of Chinese ethnic origin, and 华侨 (*huaqiao*) means Chinese citizens who are living outside China. However, when the English term Overseas Chinese is used, it often includes both groups of people. Many of the governmental and nongovernmental organizations for overseas Chinese affairs do not make a clear distinction between the two groups and they are both invited to events in the British Chinese embassy—for instance, Chinese National Day celebrations and Chinese New Year receptions. Remarkably, the pupils in the present example seem to be interested in the fine technical details and one of them asks the teacher directly what she is. The teacher first gives a clichéd reply that she is Chinese. After the pupils' challenges, however, she has to reflect on it and gives a more precise answer. The pupils also begin to reflect on who they are. What starts as a technical discussion of some terminological issues has thus led to a meaningful discussion and enhanced awareness of their identities.

Conclusion

I have tried in this chapter to use the concept of co-learning to investigate the teaching and learning that goes on in a specific kind of language classroom— British Chinese-language(s) complementary schools. Co-learning challenges the traditional sets in the classroom, especially the unequal power relationships between the teachers and the pupils. It takes the teacher and the learner to a more "dynamic and participatory engagement" in knowledge construction by empowering the learner and by building a more genuine community of practice. In such an environment, different kinds of knowledge are not only equally appreciated but also actively exchanged.

Complementary schools such as the ones we have examined in this chapter offer an interesting environment for co-learning. The funds of knowledge the teachers and pupils bring into the classroom include language, culture, and life experiences. What is particularly interesting, as the examples discussed in this chapter show, is the differences in the teachers and the pupils' linguistic proficiencies in Mandarin, Cantonese, and English, their attitudes and attachments to the different languages and language varieties, the cultural values that are inherent in the languages as well as those that they gain from their different life experiences, their migration histories and developmental trajectories, and their social positions in the community and the wider society. The vast majority of the teachers have a relatively short experience of living in Britain and many also have little contact with the Chinese communities apart from service encounters. Some of them are educational transients who are in Britain for their studies and who have every intention of returning to China in due course. They of course bring with them knowledge of contemporary China, which they do use in their teaching. But the vast majority of pupils in the Chinese complementary schools are British born and have no intimate knowledge of China. Very few of them have ever lived in China for any significant period of time. They are British youth of ethnic Chinese background. These differences may cause tensions and conflicts, as studies in Li and Martin's (2009) collection demonstrate. But they also provide exciting learning opportunities and resources. When the teachers and the pupils are engaged in co-learning, these resources are fully utilized and opportunities taken. Their knowledge therefore gets enriched. The conventional power relations between the teacher and the pupil are being challenged in the process of co-learning. A new set of relations is negotiated.

One particular aspect of the co-learning using different funds of knowledge, the above examples show, concerns the pupils' knowledge of Cantonese and the lack of it on behalf of many of the teachers, especially those in Mandarin classes. Although the social hierarchy between Mandarin and Cantonese is changing fast amongst the Chinese diasporas due to globalization and the increased politico-economic power of mainland China, Cantonese speakers bring with them specific cultural knowledge that is immediately relevant to the everyday life of the community in which these Chinese complementary schools are located. So, while at the global level Mandarin clearly has higher status, at the local level Cantonese plays a key role that brings with it specific power and influence. For instance, the provision of services such as restaurants, travel agencies, accountancies, and health clinics in the Chinese communities in Britain is still dominated by Cantonese. And there are many times more Cantonese schools than Mandarin ones. When the Cantonese pupils use their knowledge of the language skilfully in the classroom, they can obtain an especially powerful position, and when the non-Cantonese-speaking teachers are prepared to learn from the pupils, they gain knowledge, power, and respect.

Co-learning in the complementary school classroom also has significant effects on the identity development of both the teachers and the pupils. The reflexive process of co-learning provides an interesting opportunity for the co-participants to think further about who they are, what they know, and what they can learn from others. New identities and new ideas of identities emerge out of the co-learning process.

Notes

1. See Blackledge and Creese (2010a); Brinton, Kagan, and Bauckus (2007); Duff and Li (2009); He and Xiao (2008); Hornberger (2005); Li and Martin (2009); May and Aikman (2003); Nicholls (2005).
2. See Boyd, Brock, and Rozendal (2004); Gee (1996); Perry and Delpit (1998); Saxena and Martin-Jones (2003); Smitherman (2000).
3. See Li (2006) for a review of the historical developments of complementary schools in Britain; see also Blackledge, Creese, and Takhi, this volume.
4. See Blackledge and Creese (2010b); Blackledge et al., this volume; Creese et al. (2006); Martin, Creese, Bhatt, and Bhojani (2004).
5. These data were collected as part of an ESRC funded project *Investigating Multilingualism in Complementary Schools in Four Communities*. RES-000–23–1180 and AHRC project SGDMI/PID134128. The research team of the ESRC project consisted of A. Creese, T. Baraç, A. Bhatt, A. Blackledge, S. Hamid, Li Wei, V. Lytra, P. Martin, C.-j. Wu, and D. Yağcıoğlu-Ali. The AHRC project was led by Zhu Hua.
6. A more detailed account of the current sociolinguistic situation of the British Chinese community can be found in Li (2007).
7. See http://www.ukfcs.info/ and http://www.ukapce.org.uk/.
8. The examples are given in standard Chinese and English orthography. Mandarin is represented in simplified Chinese characters and Cantonese in traditional full characters. The pronunciation of the Chinese words is given only where it is relevant to the discussion, in Pinyin for Mandarin and in Jyutping for Cantonese, in brackets immediately after the Chinese characters. The English translation is given underneath the Chinese transcript in italics.
9. Britain comprises the three nations of England, Scotland, and Wales. The United Kingdom also includes the province of Northern Ireland.

References

Baker, C. (2012). *Foundations of bilingual education and bilingualism* (5th ed.). Bristol, UK: Multilingual Matters.

Benton, G. & Gomez, E.T. (2007) *The Chinese in Britain, 1800–present: Economy, transnationalism, and identity.* Basingstoke: Palgrave.

Blackledge, A., & Creese, A. (2010a). *Multilingualism: A critical perspective.* London, UK: Continuum.

Blackledge, A., & Creese, A. (2010b). Opening up flexible spaces: Ideology and practice in complementary schools. In V. Lytra and P. Martin (Eds.), *Sites of multilingualism: Complementary schools in Britain today* (pp. 3–17). Stoke on Trent, UK: Trentham Books.

Blommaert, J. (2010). *The sociolinguistics of globalization.* Cambridge, UK: CUP.

Boyd, F., Brock, C. H., & Rozendal, M. S. (Eds.). (2004). *Multicultural and multilingual literacy and language: Contexts and practices.* New York, NY: Guilford Press.

Bourdieu, P. (2000). *Pascalian meditations* (R. Nice, Trans.). Stanford, CA: Stanford University Press.

Braine, G. (2010). *Nonnative speaker English teachers: Research, pedagogy, and professional growth.* London, UK: Routledge.

Brantmeier, E. J. (n.d.). *Empowerment pedagogy: Co-learning and teaching.* Retrieved from http://www.indiana.edu/~leeehman/Brantmeier.pdf

Brinton, D. M., Kagan, O., & Bauckus, S. (Eds.) (2007). *Heritage language education: A new field emerging.* London, UK: Routledge.

Chevannes, F., & Reeves, M. (1987). The Black voluntary school movement. In B. Troyna (Ed.), *Racial inequality in education* (pp. 147–169). London, UK: Tavistock.

Creese, A., Barac, T., Bhatt, A., Blackledge, A., Hamid, S., Lytra, . . . Yagcioglu-Ali, D. (2008). *Multilingualism in complementary schools in four linguistic communities* (ESRC Report no: RES-000–23–1180). Birmingham, UK: University of Birmingham.

Creese, A., Bhatt, A., Bhojani, N., & Martin, P. (2006). Multicultural, heritage and learner identities in complementary schools. *Language and Education, 20*(1), 23–43.

Duff, P. A., & Li, D. (Eds.). (2009). Indigenous, minority, and heritage language education in Canada: Policies, contexts and issues. *The Canadian Modern Language Review/La Revue canadienne des langues vivantes, 66*, 1.

Gee, J. P. (1996). *Social linguistics and literacies: Ideology in discourses.* London, UK: Routledge-Falmer.

Halstead, M. (1995). Voluntary apartheid? Problems of schooling for religious and other minorities in democratic societies. *Journal of Philosophy of Education, 29*, 257–272.

He, A. W., & Xiao, Y. (Eds.). (2008). *Chinese as a heritage language: Fostering rooted world citizenry.* Mānoa, HI: National Foreign Language Resource Center, University of Hawai'i.

Hewer, C. (2001). Schools for Muslims. *Oxford Review of Education, 27*, 515–527.

Hornberger, N. H. (Ed.). (2005). Introduction: Heritage/community language education: US and Australian perspectives. *International Journal of Bilingual Education and Bilingualism, 8*(2&3), 101–108.

Housen, A. (2002). Processes and outcomes in the European Schools Model of multilingual education. *Bilingual Research Journal, 26*(1), 45–64.

Kempadoo, M., & Abdelrazak, M. (1999). *Directory of supplementary and mother-tongue supplementary classes 1999–2000.* London, UK: Resource Unit for Supplementary and Mother-Tongue Schools.

Kenner, C. (2007). *Developing bilingual learning strategies in mainstream and community contexts* (ESRC End of Award Report, RES-000–22–1528). Swindon, UK: ESRC.

Kramsch, C. (2006). From communicative competence to symbolic competence. *The Modern Language Journal, 90*(2), 249–252.

Kramsch, C., & Whiteside, A. (2008). Language ecology in multilingual settings: Towards a theory of symbolic competence. *Applied Linguistics, 29*(4), 645–671.

Li, W. (2006). Complementary schools: Past, present and future. *Language and Education, 20*(1), 76–83.

Li, W. (2007). Chinese. In D. Britain (Ed.), *Language of the British Isles* (pp. 308–325). Cambridge, UK: Cambridge University Press.

Li, W. (2011). Multilinguality, multimodality and multicompetence: Code- and mode-switching by minority ethnic children in complementary schools. *The Modern Language Journal, 95*(3), 370–384.

Li, W., & Martin, P. (Eds.). (2009). Tensions and conflicts in classroom code-switching [Special issue]. *International Journal of Bilingual Education and Bilingualism, 12*(2).

Li, W., & Wu, C. (2008). Codeswitching, ideologies and practices. In A. E. He & Y. Xiao (Eds.), *Chinese as a heritage language: Fostering rooted world citizenry,* (pp. 225–238). Honolulu, HI: National Foreign Language Resource Centre, University of Hawai'i.

Li, W., & Wu, C. (2009). Polite Chinese children revisited: Creativity and the use of codeswitching in the Chinese complementary school classroom. *International Journal of Bilingual Education and Bilingualism, 12*(2), 193–211.

Li, W., & Wu, C. (2010). Literacy and socializational teaching in Chinese complementary schools. In V. Lytra and P. Martin (Eds.), *Sites of multilingualism: Complementary schools in Britain today* (pp. 33–44). Stoke on Trent, UK: Trentham Books.

Li W. & Zhu, H. (2010a). Changing hierarchies in Chinese language education for the British Chinese learners. In L. Tsung & K. Cruickshank (Eds.), *Teaching and learning Chinese in global contexts: Multimodality and literacy in the new media age.* London, UK: Continuum.

Li W., & Zhu, H. (2010b). Voices from the diaspora: Changing hierarchies and dynamics of Chinese multilingualism. *International Journal of the Sociology of Language, 205,* 155–171.

Llurda, E. (Ed.). (2005). *Non-native language teachers. Perceptions, challenges and contributions to the profession.* New York, NY: Springer.

Macy, M. W., & Skvoretz, J. (1998). The evolution of trust and cooperation between strangers: A computational model. *American Sociological Review, 63,* 638–660.

Martin, P. W., Bhatt, A., Bhojani, N., & Creese, A. (2006). Managing bilingual interaction in a Gujarati complementary school in Leicester. *Language and Education, 20*(1), 5–22.

Martin, P. W., Creese, A., Bhatt, A., & Bhojani, N. (2004). *A final report on complementary schools and their communities in Leicester* (ESRC R000223949). Leicester, UK & Birmingham, UK: University of Leicester/University of Birmingham..

May, S., & Aikman, S. (2003). Indigenous education: Addressing current issues and developments [Special issue]. *Comparative Education, 39*(2), 139–145.

McLaughlin, T. H. (1995). Liberalism, education and the common school. *Journal of Philosophy of Education, 29,* 239–253.

Moll, L., Amanti, C., Neff, D., & Gonzalez, N. (1992). Funds of knowledge for teaching: Using a qualitative approach to connect homes and classrooms. *Theory into Practice, 31,* 132–141.

Moll, L. C., & Gonzalez, N. (1994). Lessons from research with language-minority children. *Journal of Reading Behavior, 26*(4), 439–456.

Nicholls, C. (2005). Death by a thousand cuts: Indigenous language bilingual education programmes in the Northern Territory of Australia, 1972–1998. *International Journal of Bilingual Education and Bilingualism, 8*(2&3), 160–177.

Nunan, D. (1988). *The learner-centred curriculum: A study of second language teaching.* Cambridge, UK: Cambridge University Press.

Ossowski, S. (Ed.). (1999). *Co-ordination in artificial agent societies: Social structures and its implications for autonomous problem-solving agents.* Berlin, Germany: Springer.

Pennycook, A. (2010). *Language as a local practice.* London, UK: Routledge.

Perry, T., & Delpit, L. (1998). *The real ebonics debate: Power, language, and the education of African-American children.* Boston, MA: Beacon Press.

Saxena, M., & Martin-Jones, M. (2003). Bilingual resources and "funds of knowledge" for teaching and learning in multi-ethnic classrooms in Britain. *International Journal of Bilingual Education and Bilingualism, 6*(3/4), 267–282.

Shoham, Y., & Tennenholtz, M. (1994). *Co-learning and the evolution of social activity* (Report No. STAN-CS-TR-94–1511). Stanford, CA: Stanford University, Department of Computer Science.

Shoham, Y., & Tennenholtz, M. (1997). On the emergence of social conventions. Modeling, analysis and simulations. *Artificial Intelligence, 94*(1–2), 139–166.

Smitherman, G. (2000). *Talkin that talk: Language, culture and education in African America.* New York, NY: Routledge.

9

BEYOND MULTILINGUALISM: HETEROGLOSSIA IN PRACTICE

Adrian Blackledge, Angela Creese, and Jaspreet Kaur Takhi

In recent times, scholars in sociolinguistics have found that language use in late modern societies is changing. Rather than assuming that homogeneity and stability represent the norm, mobility, mixing, political dynamics, and historical embedding are now central concerns in the study of languages, language groups, and communication (Blommaert & Rampton, 2011). As large numbers of people migrate across myriad borders, and as advances in digital technology make available a multitude of linguistic resources at the touch of a button or a screen, so communication is in flux and in development (see also García & Flores, this volume; Norton, this volume). In these conditions the notion of separate languages as bounded systems of specific linguistic features may be insufficient for analysis of language in use and in action (Jørgensen, Karrebæk, Madsen, & Møller, 2011; cf. Block, this volume; Ortega, this volume). The idea of "a language" therefore may be important as a social construct, but it is not suited as an analytical lens through which to view language practices. Blommaert and Rampton (2011) propose that "it is important to avoid the a priori separation of 'first' and 'second' language' speakers" (Blommaert & Rampton, 2011, p. 15). They point to a need for careful clarification of links and incompatibilities in the idioms commonly used to analyze *heteroglossia* (see below) on the one hand and standard second language learning on the other. Reporting a linguistic ethnographic study of language practices in and around a Panjabi school in England, this chapter responds to some of the limitations of an approach to language teaching and learning that relies on the naming and separation of languages—that is, an approach that relies on the concept of *multilingualism* to describe the language competence of speakers in the context of language contact. We tentatively propose that a return to literary scholar Mikhail Bakhtin's theoretical and practical notion of heteroglossia offers potential to go beyond multilingualism and develop language-learning pedagogy that is rooted in the communication patterns of students in late modern societies. First, however, we briefly review some recent developments in the study of multilingualism.

Multilingualism

Sociolinguistic study of multilingualism in the West has recently moved away from a view of languages as separate bounded entities to a view of communication in which language users employ whatever linguistic features are at their disposal to achieve their communicative aims as best they can (Jørgensen et al., 2011). Blommaert and Rampton (2011) argue that languages are ideological constructions historically tied to the emergence of the nation-state in the 19th century (cf. May, this volume). Rather than taking the named language as the unit of analysis, Blommaert and Rampton propose that "it is far more productive *analytically* to focus on the very variable ways in which linguistic features with identifiable social and cultural associations get clustered together whenever people communicate" (Blommaert & Rampton, 2011, p. 1). Makoni and Pennycook (2007) argue for an understanding of the relationships between what people believe about their language (or other people's languages), the situated forms of talk they deploy, and the material effects—social, economic, environmental—of such views and use (Makoni & Pennycook, 2007, p. 22).

Recently, a number of terms have emerged as scholars have sought to describe and analyze linguistic practices in which meaning is made using signs flexibly. These include, but are not limited to: "flexible bilingualism" (Creese et al., 2011); "codemeshing" (Canagarajah, 2011); "polylingual languaging" (Jørgensen, 2010; Madsen, 2011); "contemporary urban vernaculars" (Rampton, 2011); "metrolingualism" (Otsuji & Pennycook, 2011); and "translanguaging" (Creese & Blackledge, 2010; García, 2009; García & Flores, this volume). The shared perspective represented in the use of these various terms considers that meaning making is not confined to the use of languages as discrete, enumerable, bounded sets of linguistic resources (see also Block, this volume). Rather, signs are available for meaning making in communicative repertoires (Rymes, 2010) that extend across languages and varieties that have hitherto been associated with particular national, territorial, and social groups. For García (2009), a translanguaging approach to teaching and learning is not about code-switching but rather about an arrangement that normalizes bilingualism without diglossic functional separation. García argues that bilingual families and communities must translanguage in order to construct meaning. Similarly, flexible bilingualism (Blackledge & Creese, 2010; Creese et al., 2011) represents a view of language as a social resource without clear boundaries, which places the speaker at the heart of the interaction. This leads us away from a focus on languages as distinct codes to a focus on the agency of individuals engaging in using, creating, and interpreting signs for communication.

Blommaert (2012, p. 2) argues for a recognition that the contemporary semiotics of culture and identity need to be captured in terms of *complexity* rather than in terms of multiplicity or plurality. Indeed, he argues that "a vocabulary including 'multi-lingual', 'multi-cultural', or 'pluri-', 'inter-', 'cross-', and 'trans-' notions all suggest an a priori existence of separable units (language, culture, identity), and they suggest that the *encounter of such separable units produces peculiar new units:* 'multilingual' repertoires, 'mixed' or 'hybrid' identities and so forth." Blommaert argues that a perspective that focuses on code-switching is emblematic of this view. Bailey (2012) engages with the limitations of an approach to linguistic analysis that emphasizes code-switching, arguing that a focus on "constellations of linguistic features that are officially authorized codes or languages, e.g. 'English' or 'Spanish' can contribute to neglect of the diversity of socially indexical resources *within* languages" (Bailey, 2012, p. 501). Bailey points out that, if the starting point is social meanings rather than the code or language in use, it is not central whether a speaker is switching languages, alternating between a dialect and a national standard, register shifting, or speaking monolingually in a variety that highlights language contact. Language, whether monolingual or multilingual, carries social meanings through phonological, lexical, grammatical, and discourse level forms: "these forms index various aspects of individuals' and communities' social histories, circumstances, and identities" (Bailey, 2012, p. 506). The stem "hetero-" may, of course, be viewed as contiguous with "multi-," "pluri-," and so on. However, whereas previously sociolinguistic research has tended to refer to fixed bounded languages, we adopt heteroglossia to refer not to languages but to the heterogeneity of signs and forms in meaning making.

What we are suggesting in this chapter is that just as the traditional distinction between languages is no longer sustainable, so the distinction between monolingual, bilingual, and multilingual speakers may no longer be sustainable. Canagarajah and Liyanage (2012) have noted that even so-called monolinguals "shuttle between codes, registers and discourses" (Canagarajah & Liyanage, 2012, p. 50), and can therefore hardly be described as monolingual. We therefore argue that the questions we need to ask are not limited to which languages are in use in an interaction and why. We also need to attend to the ways in which linguistic resources are deployed in our societies and how this deployment of linguistic resources reproduces, negotiates, and contests social difference and social inequality (Heller, 2011). In order to shift our focus we need to develop an analytic gaze that incorporates recent scholarship on multilingualism, polylanguaging, and translanguaging but that goes beyond them to include the sociohistorical and ideological bases of language meaning and use. In doing so, we turn to Mikhail Bakhtin and the notion of heteroglossia.

Heteroglossia

It was with remarkable prescience or serendipity that Bakhtin wrote, in the 1930s, what appears to be a description of the era in which we live almost a century later:

> In the most sharply heteroglot eras, when the collision and interaction of language is especially intense and powerful . . . aspects of heteroglossia are canonized with great ease and rapidly pass from one language system to another . . . In this intense struggle, boundaries are drawn with new sharpness and simultaneously erased with new ease; it is sometimes impossible to establish precisely where they have been erased or where certain of the warring parties have already crossed over into alien territory. (Bakhtin, 1981, p. 418)[1]

These notions of the construction and demolition of boundaries, of the canonization of language resources and features, and of mobility and movement across national, linguistic, and symbolic territories, are key dimensions of language in action, and in use, in contemporary societies.

Recently, scholars in sociolinguistics have engaged with Bakhtin's term heteroglossia to illuminate understandings of the diversity of linguistic practice evident in late modern societies. However, the meaning of heteroglossia is not universally or straightforwardly agreed. Busch (2013) notes that Bakhtin did not use the singular term heteroglossia to set out his thinking about the stratified diversity of language and points out that a heteroglossic approach "does not only imply acknowledgement of the presence of different languages and codes (*raznojazyčie*) as a resource, but also entails a commitment to multidiscursivity (*raznogolosie*) and multivoicedness (*raznorečie*)." Madsen (2013) similarly argues that heteroglossia is a concept created by the translators of Bakhtin's work to cover the three concepts of diversity in speechness, diversity in languageness, and diversity in voicedness. Madsen notes that, as a cover term for these aspects of linguistic diversity, heteroglossia "describes how language use involves various socio-ideological languages, codes, and voices" (Madsen, 2011, p. 4). Pietikäinen and Dufva (2013) also view heteroglossia as a term chosen for the English translation, rather than a term used by Bakhtin himself. They point out that in the original Russian texts Bakhtin speaks of "intralingual diversity," the internal stratification present in one national language that also testifies to different ideological positions, a usage that has been rendered in English as heteroglossia. At the same time, Bakhtin acknowledges the presence of various languages and dialects in the community, that is, "language plurality," referring to linguistic-level phenomena. Bailey (2012) similarly notes that Bakhtin coined the term "raznorečie" specifically to refer to intralanguage variation within Russian, "varieties with competing social and political implications, and the term is translated as 'the social diversity of speech types' rather than 'heteroglossia'" (Bailey, 2012, p. 499). Heteroglossia as a theoretical term, then, is by definition heteroglossic. As such it reflects the mobility and flux that is often said to be characteristic of the late modern age. However, if heteroglossia is to be a useful heuristic in illuminating understandings of language in use and in action in our societies, it may be necessary to pin it down a little while incorporating diverse aspects of its meanings. In order to more precisely address Bakhtin's theoretical development of (what we now call) heteroglossia, we can group together his writings where consistent and repeated themes emerge. In this chapter, we propose to discuss Bakhtin's thinking about heteroglossia in relation to "indexicality," "tension-filled interaction," and "multivoicedness."

Indexicality

Bakhtin (1981) argued that language in use and in action represents "specific points of view on the world, forms for conceptualizing the world in words, specific world views, each characterized by its own objects, meanings and values" (Bakhtin, 1981, p. 291). That is, language points to, or "indexes" a certain point of view, ideology, social class, profession, or other social position (cf. Canagarajah, this volume). Bakhtin saw that "language is stratified not only into linguistic dialects in the strictest sense of the word, but also—and for us this is the essential point—into languages that are socio-ideological: languages of social groups, 'professional' and 'generic' languages, languages of generations and so forth" (Bakhtin, 1981, p. 271). Lähteenmaki (2010) notes that Bakhtin's notion of heteroglossia accounts for "the social, functional, generic, and dialectological variation within a language" (Lähteenmaki, 2010, p. 26). For Bakhtin, stratification and diversity within a language derive from its social nature, reflecting the social and ideological differentiation in society. Bailey (2012) points out that Bakhtin's notion of heteroglossia overlaps with the semiotic and linguistic anthropological notion of "non-referential indexicality" developed by Peirce (1955) and Silverstein (1976, 2003). Both heteroglossia and indexicality rely on notions of intertextuality, in which "meanings of forms depend on past usages and associations of those forms rather than on arbitrary referential meaning inherent in the form" (Bailey, 2012, p. 500).

The relationship between the indexical form and meaning is brought into being through historical association. Agha (2007) summarizes this point: "behavioural signs (including features of discursive behaviour) acquire recognizable pragmatic values that come to be viewed as perduring 'social facts' about signs, and which, by virtue of such recognition, become effective ways of indexing roles and relationships among sign-users in performance" (Agha, 2007, p. 80). Bailey (2012, p. 501) offers as an example of an index a regional accent. The relationship between an accent and a region is established through the historical fact of speakers from that region speaking in a particular way, and "there is no inherent relationship between the indexical form and meaning, simply one of historical association" (Bailey, 2012, p. 502). Agha further argues that in the process of indexicality a semiotic register, a repertoire of performable signs, is "linked to stereotypic pragmatic effects by a sociohistorical process of 'enregisterment', which makes usable facts of semiotic value associated with signs" (Agha, 2007, p. 81). In the process of enregisterment, performable signs become recognized as belonging to distinct semiotic registers differentially valorized by a population. Thus the word may point to, belong to, or be recognized as representing a certain set of values, an ideology, a social group, a nationality, and so on (cf. Li Wei, this volume). That is, "different language-forms are connected with particular ideological positions and express particular world-views conceptualizing extra-discursive reality in their own unique way" (Lähteenmaki, 2010, p. 28). However, Bakhtin (1981) demonstrates that the word does not relate to its object in a singular way, but rather "there exists an elastic environment of other, alien words about the same object, the same theme" (Bakhtin, 1981, p. 276). We need to look carefully at the "complex play of light and shadow" into which the word enters, and "determine within it the boundaries of its own semantic and stylistic contours" (Bakhtin, 1981, p. 277). That is, we need to pay attention not only to the word, but to the social tensions within it.

Tension-Filled Interaction

Bakhtin (1981) consistently pointed out that language is characterized by social tensions: "on all its various routes toward the object, in all its directions, the word encounters an alien word and cannot help encountering it in a living, tension-filled interaction" (Bakhtin, 1981, p. 279). Bakhtin argued that within a single (national) language exists "a multitude of concrete worlds, a multitude of bounded verbal–ideological and social belief systems; within these various systems (identical in the abstract) are elements of language filled with various semantic and axiological content and each with its own different sound" (Bakhtin, 1981, p. 288). Indeed, Bailey (2012) argues that what is distinctive about heteroglossia "is not its reference to different kinds of linguistic signs and forms, but rather its focus on social tensions inherent in language" (Bailey, 2012, p. 508).

A central trope for Bakhtin (1981) in his description of the social tensions in language is that of the opposing pull of "centrifugal" and "centripetal" forces. Whereas the centripetal force constitutes the pull towards the "unitary language," homogeneity, standardization, and correctness, the centrifugal force pulls towards heteroglossic disunification and decentralization. These forces are rarely free of each other, however, as the centripetal forces of language operate in the midst of heteroglossia, and alongside them centrifugal forces carry on their uninterrupted work: "Every utterance participates in the 'unitary language' (in its centripetal forces and tendencies) and at the same time partakes of social and historical heteroglossia (the centrifugal, stratifying forces)" (Bakhtin, 1981, p. 272). This point is elaborated by Pietikäinen and Dufva (2013), who argue that, in order to understand the dynamics and dialectics of heteroglossia, we need to note that normativity and pressure towards uniformity are also part of language use. Pietikäinen and Dufva suggest that characterizing language as heteroglossic is to say that there are also in play practices that aim at homogenizing language. In Bakhtin's analysis, a unitary language is constantly opposed to the realities of heteroglossia, and "makes its real presence felt as a force for overcoming this heteroglossia, imposing specific limits to it, guaranteeing a certain maximum of mutual understanding and crystallizing into a real, though relative, unity—the unity of the reigning conversational (everyday) and literary language, 'correct language'" (Bakhtin, 1981, p. 270).

What, then, does language look (or sound) like when it is filled with social tension? Link, Lipinoga, and Wortham (2013) point out that utterances echo with the voices of others. The use of certain words in a certain way indexes some social position(s) because these words are characteristically used by members of a certain group: "A voice is a social position from the stratified world, as presupposed by stratified language" (Wortham, 2001, p. 50). In this way, speakers inevitably position themselves with respect to others, making indexical associations and metalevel evaluations. This focus on the interrelationship between our own word and the word of the other—in discourse that is dialogic—leads us towards a third aspect of heteroglossia: *multivoicedness*.

Multivoicedness

For Bakhtin (1981), language is something that is historically real:

> a process teeming with future and former languages, with prim but moribund aristocrat-languages, with parvenu-languages and with countless pretenders to the status of language—which are all more or less successful, depending on their degree of social scope and on the ideological area in which they are employed. (Bakhtin, 1981, pp. 356–357)

Not the least of the historical context of languages and varieties is their hierarchization and indexical and ideological associations. Bakhtin (1981) pointed to the dialogic nature of the word, which is "shaped in dialogic interaction with an alien word that is already in the object" (Bakhtin, 1981, p. 279). The word is shaped not only by other words in the past and present, but also by the anticipated word of the other. Therefore language "lies on the borderline between oneself and the other. The word in language is half someone else's" (Bakhtin, 1981, p. 293). Hall, Vitanova, and Marchenkova (2005) argue that for Bakhtin the utterance is always a two-sided act: "In the moment of its use, at one and the same time, it responds to what precedes it and anticipates what is to come" (Hall, Vitanova, & Marchenkova, 2005, p. 2). Bakhtin saw that what we talk about most are the words of others such that our speech is overflowing with other people's words. In doing so we weigh, evaluate, refute, repudiate, celebrate, affirm, and so on not only the words of others but also the political/ideological position represented by those words. Bakhtin argued that the object has already been articulated, disputed, elucidated, and evaluated in various ways, and various views and trends cross, converge, and diverge within it. Any utterance, in addition to its own themes, always responds in one form or another to others' utterances that precede it, and speech inevitably becomes the arena where viewpoints, world views, trends, and theories encounter each other.

Bakhtin (1986) noticed that whole utterances and individual words may repeat the words of others in a way that re-accents and changes them, "ironically, indignantly, reverently, and so forth," and in particular "intonation is especially sensitive and always points beyond the context" (Bakhtin, 1986, p. 91). Bakhtin (1984) elaborated on this notion, arguing that metalinguistics has a role to play in providing a full and exhaustive classification of dialogic discourses, which "incorporate a relationship to someone else's utterance as an indispensable element" (Bakhtin, 1984, p. 186). Examples of dialogic discourse in Bakhtin's typology include stylization, parody, irony, hidden polemic, internal polemic, and hidden dialogicality—all varieties of discourse shaped by the word of the other. By re-accenting others' voices, narrators and ordinary speakers establish positions for themselves (Wortham, 2001). In this way, "the unmergedness of individual voices is expressed . . . in which two meaning-positions come into dialogical contact within one utterance" (Lähteenmaki, 2010, p. 24). Each type of dialogic speech has an analytical role in understanding language in use and in action in late modern societies.

Bakhtin (1981) defined stylization as "an artistic representation of another's linguistic style, an artistic image of another's language (Bakhtin, 1981, p. 362). In stylization, two individual linguistic consciousnesses must be present: the one that represents (the stylizer) and the one that is represented (the stylized). Madsen (2013) describes stylizations as "linguistic activities that put on display the simultaneously unique and socio-structural qualities of language" (Madsen, 2013). Rampton and Charalambous (2012) suggest that, in stylization, speakers shift into varieties or exaggerated styles that are seen as lying outside of their normal range, "and this disjunction of speaker and voice draws attention to the speaker herself/himself, temporarily positioning the recipient(s) as spectator(s)" (Rampton & Charalambous, 2012, p. 483). Rampton (2006) adopted the notion of stylization to analyze the accent shifts of young people moving between exaggerated "posh" and "Cockney" in moments of critical reflection on aspects of educational domination and constraint (see also Block, this volume). Rampton summarizes the stylized utterance as "a small, fleeting, but foregrounded analysis, suggesting that the person, event, or act that occasions the switch-of-voice can be classified and understood as the instance of the more general social type that the different voice evokes" (Rampton, 2006, p. 225). The stylized voice necessarily relies on a kind of common knowledge shared by the stylizer and the interlocutor or recipient of the utterance. That is, the style of the stylized voice should be recognizable; moreover, the social, political, and historical ideologies associated with, or represented by, the stylized word should be recognizable and shared, as the recipients identify what image of another's language the stylized word is supposed to be (Rampton, 2006).

In the study reported here, multilingual speakers frequently engaged in talk that portrayed the words of the other parodically. Bakhtin (1984) argues that in parodic talk the speaker again reiterates someone else's discourse, but "in contrast to stylization, parody introduces into that discourse a semantic intention that is directly opposed to the original one" (Bakhtin, 1984, p. 193). Now "discourse becomes an arena of battle between two voices" (Bakhtin, 1984, p. 193), as they serve opposing points of view. Irony, too, uses someone else's words to convey aspirations that are hostile to them. Bakhtin notes that "in the ordinary speech of our everyday life such a use of another's words is extremely widespread" (Bakhtin, 1984, p. 194). The words of another introduced into our own speech inevitably become subject to our evaluation. Another example of the ways in which the words of others shape our own speech is in what Bakhtin called "hidden polemic." Here, the other's discourse is not reproduced, is merely implied, but the entire speech is a reaction to another person's words: "The polemical colouration of the discourse appears in other purely language features as well: in intonation and syntactic construction" (Bakhtin, 1984, p. 195). A further category of dialogic discourse, internally polemical discourse, is also "extremely widespread in practical everyday speech, and has enormous style-shaping significance" (Bakhtin, 1984, p. 197). Included here is any speech that makes a dig at others with barbed words; speech that is self-deprecating and overblown; speech with a thousand reservations, concessions, and loopholes; speech that cringes in anticipation of someone else's reply. Analogous to internal polemic is a rejoinder that reacts to someone else's word. Bakhtin argues that, "[e]specially important is the phenomenon of hidden dialogicality" (Bakhtin, 1984, p. 197), a speech that appears to be a dialogue but from which one of the speakers is absent. The second speaker is present invisibly; his/her words are not there, "but deep traces left by these words have a determining influence on all the present and visible words of the first speaker" (Bakhtin, 1984, p. 197). Although the second speaker is not present, "each present, uttered word responds and reacts with its every fibre to the invisible speaker" (Bakhtin, 1984, p. 197).

In summary, Bakhtin (1984) views the word not as a material thing but rather "the eternally mobile, eternally fickle medium of dialogic interaction" (Bakhtin, 1984, p. 197). For Bakhtin, the life of the word is contained in its transfer "from one mouth to another, from one context to another context, from one social collective to another, from one generation to another generation" (Bakhtin, 1984, p. 202). Bailey (2012) summarizes heteroglossia as "the simultaneous use of different kinds of forms or signs, and the tensions and conflicts among those signs, on the sociohistorical associations they carry with them" (Bailey, 2012, p. 504). What we propose, then, is an analytic gaze that explicitly joins the linguistic utterance in the present and the sociohistorical relationships that give meanings to those utterances, a gaze that takes as its focus speakers as social actors using heteroglossic linguistic resources to negotiate the social world. Such an analytic gaze "encourages us to interpret the meanings of talk in terms of the social worlds, past and present, of which words are part-and-parcel, rather than in terms of formal systems, such as 'languages', that can veil actual speakers, uses, and contexts" (Bailey, 2012, p. 502). In the remainder of this chapter, we adopt the lens of heteroglossia to examine the speech of young people in an English city.

Methods

The study reported here is the Birmingham, United Kingdom section of an international linguistic ethnographic research project, *Investigating Discourses of Inheritance and Identity in Four Multilingual European Settings* (09-HERA-JRP-CD-FP-051), a two-year collaboration in 2010–2011 between universities in Birmingham, Copenhagen, Stockholm, and Tilburg. The project aimed to investigate the range of language and literacy practices of multilingual young people in the four European settings, to explore the cultural and social significance of these practices, and to investigate how their language and literacy practices are used to negotiate inheritance and identities. In Copenhagen, researchers spent a year observing in a large secondary school with a multilingual student constituency; in Stockholm, researchers conducted detailed investigations in two bilingual schools (Swedish/Finnish and Swedish/Spanish); in Tilburg, researchers studied linguistic practices in a Chinese complementary school (cf. Li Wei, this volume). The focus of the present chapter, though, is research conducted in a complementary (also known as "community language" or "heritage language") school in Birmingham, United Kingdom. The main purpose of the school is to teach Panjabi to young people of Panjabi heritage. The school operates across two sites in Birmingham on Saturdays throughout the school year. Complementary schooling is additional to regular (full-time) schooling, and is largely funded by communities. Across the two sites at this school there are 15 teachers and teaching assistants, teaching 200 pupils who range from age 5 to 18 years old. The teachers do not have official teaching qualifications but do have recognized qualifications in Panjabi.

Angela Creese and Jaspreet Kaur Takhi spent five months observing in all classes in the school. During the observations they wrote detailed field notes. Following the observation sessions, the researchers compared and discussed their notes. At the end of this initial five months of observation, one class on each site was identified for closer observation based on the teachers' and students' willingness to participate in the research project. In negotiation with the teachers of these classes, two students and the teacher and teaching assistant in each class were identified as "key participants" for focused observation. After further observations in these two classrooms, the key participant students, teachers, and teaching assistants were issued with digital voice recorders so that they could audio record themselves during class time. The key participants were also asked to use the digital voice recorders outside of the classroom to record their (and their families' and friends') linguistic repertoires at home and in other environments. The researchers interviewed 15 key stakeholders in the schools, including the key participant teachers and administrators and the key participant children and their parents. In addition, classroom sessions on each of the sites were video recorded.

In this chapter, we will focus on a single lesson in one of the two classrooms where we conducted the majority of our observations. During the lesson, one researcher, Jaspreet Kaur Takhi, was present. There were 20 students, a teacher (Gurpal, male, 23 years) and a teaching assistant (Prabhjot, female, 19 years). Two students, Komal (female, 17 years) and Sahib (male, 17 years), and the teacher and teaching assistant all wore digital voice recorders during the lesson. In addition, the researcher wrote field notes as she observed the class. A third student, Gopinder, is also prominent in the audio recording. Other students are occasionally audible. In addition to the recordings, we also refer to interviews with the key participants. The focus on this lesson does not suggest that it is taken in isolation, but that it typifies the kind of interactions observed in and out of the school over the course of 10 months. For the purpose of clarity, transcribed excerpts from the 48-minute segment are presented chronologically in Table 9.1.

TABLE 9.1 Participants in the interaction

Name	Role in Panjabi school	Sex	Age	Place of birth	Employment/ parents' employment	Education
Gurpal	Teacher	Male	23	Birmingham, UK	Part time Special Needs Assistant in schools	Graduate; state school educated
Komal	Student	Female	17	Oxford, UK	Father is a doctor, mother a nurse	Independent (fee-paying) school student
Prabhjot	Teaching Assistant	Female	19	Birmingham, UK	Family run a clothing business	College student; state school educated
Sahib	Student	Male	16	Sandwell, UK	Father is a warehouse operative; mother works in a bank	Grammar (selective entry) school student
Gopinder	Student	Female	15	Birmingham, UK	Father is a financier in the City of London	Independent (fee-paying) school student

The names of participants have been changed to preserve anonymity.

Heteroglossia in the Classroom

Example 1 occurs at the beginning of class. In this interaction, a student, Gopinder (female, 15 years) is audible, along with Komal and the teacher, Gurpal.

Example 1: "what's a mustachio?"[2]

1.	Gurpal:	ok what's a mustachio?
2.	Komal:	a moustache
3.	Gurpal:	moonsh <*moustache*>
4.	Gopinder:	mooch mooch is a
5.	Komal:	oh moonsh <*moustache*>
6.	Gurpal:	[laughs]
7.	Komal:	moonsh moustache a mustachio what's a mustachio?
8.	Gurpal:	[to Gopinder:] not a pistachio
9.	Gopinder:	I didn't say mus
10.	Gurpal:	mustachio
11.	Komal:	mustach
12.	Gurpal:	[laughs:] mustachio
13.	Gopinder:	what is it?
14.	Komal:	what language
15.	Gopinder:	can you explain in English? no that's moochaa <*moustache*>
16.	Gurpal:	mustachio
17.	Gopinder:	is that what Indian people say? No-one says mustachio
18.	Gurpal:	mustachio
19.	Komal:	[laughs:] right
20.	Gurpal:	you've learnt a new word we'll start using mustachio from now on
21.	Gopinder:	I said it do you say moochaa <*moustache*> or
22.	Komal:	yeah I thought it was moochaa <*moustache*>
23.	Gopinder:	I say mooch for English
24.	Gurpal:	homework, where's your mustachio man
25.	Gopinder:	that sounds like Michelin Man that joke
26.	Komal:	right maybe he just can't read

The teacher introduces the lesson with a question that generically fits the context, asking what appears to be a request for the students to define an unfamiliar word: "what's a mustachio?" The purpose of the class, and of the school, is for the students to learn Panjabi. It might therefore be assumed that the teacher would request the meaning of a Panjabi word or the Panjabi translation of an English word. However, instead, he asks a question that has no readily available correct answer. *Mustachio* does not appear in the *Oxford English Dictionary,* although *moustachioed* is listed as deriving from the Spanish *mostacho* and the Italian *mostaccio.* Mustachio has a number of connotations in contemporary popular culture, including a luxurious handlebar moustache, the name of a night club in Birmingham, and a character in a best-selling video game (elsewhere, including in this lesson, Gurpal often referred to the names of video games). Gurpal's question fits the norms of the language teaching class, but it is a parody, or perhaps a pastiche, of the genre.

Rampton (2006) distinguishes between "parody grounded in moral and political criticism of the oppressive distortions of class," and "pastiche, pleasure in the play of voices" (Rampton, 2006, p. 235). Komal (l.2) recognizes the "language teaching" genre and volunteers an answer. Consistent with the structural norm of Initiation-Response-Feedback (IRF; see also Leung, this volume), Gurpal (l.3) offers what appears to be an answer to his question: "moonsh." However, this is a linguistic feature straightforwardly associated with neither English nor Panjabi (the norms for this classroom) but Hindi. Gurpal adds to the already heterogeneous nature of the interaction by introducing this word. In l.4 Gopinder volunteers an answer, "mooch," an Anglicized version of the Panjabi word "moochaa" (*moustache*). Komal meanwhile (l.5), recognizing the familiar IRF structure, dutifully accepts her teacher's offer.

In Bakhtin's (1981) terms, while the departure from expected linguistic norms pulls centrifugally, the adherence to structural norms pulls centripetally. The teacher's laughter (l.6) indicates his amusement at the game, which is neither random nor chaotic, but relies on all participants' shared knowledge of the genre. Komal (l.7) tries out three of the versions of the word currently in play, and repeats Gurpal's initial question. However, she does more than merely repeat the question, as in recontextualizing it, she portrays and evaluates it. Gurpal keeps up the game, saying to Gopinder, "not a pistachio." Gopinder, however, defends herself, again responding within the expected norms. Her refusal to have the "incorrect" term ascribed to her (l.9, "I didn't say") indexes her attitude to correctness and academic success, which we saw on many occasions in observing this class. Gurpal repeats the original term (ll. 10, 12, and 14), correcting Gopinder's (nonexistent) error, and again his laughter reveals his amusement. With some exasperation now Gopinder demands the correct answer: "what is it?" (l.13), and "can you explain in English?" (l.15), while Komal asks "what language?" (l.14). Gopinder corrects Gurpal, offering the normative Panjabi term "moochaa" (l.15). These interjections index the students' orientation to correctness and academic achievement as they attempt to pull the interaction round to the "right answer" (cf. Li Wei, this volume). The teacher's response is again to merely repeat the original word, prompting Gopinder to ask "is that what Indian people say?" In doing so, she distances herself from "Indian people," as if they may be so foreign that they use this alien word.

Komal, however, seems to tumble to the trick at l.19, her laughter and intonation in saying "right" expressing both shared amusement and scepticism. Gurpal continues, though, extending the parody or pastiche of the normative, generic discourse, "you've learnt a new word, we'll start using mustachio from now on" (l.20), and "homework, where's your mustachio man" (l.24). Here the informal "man" provides a signal that the homework task is not serious but is part of the pastiche. Komal ultimately suggests, in an aside apparently to herself, "maybe he just can't read." This apparent (but not serious) explanation of her teacher's behavior positions him as the very antithesis of her orientation to academic success.

Example 2 follows a few seconds after Example 1 and involves the same protagonists plus another student, Sahib (male, 16 years). The task set by the teacher is for the students to compose at least two sentences in Panjabi about what they did during their week's holiday. Field notes for the session note that "the kids have to write summaries day by day to explain what they did in their holidays. It doesn't have to be the truth, Gurpal says, and we have some far-fetched and funny sentences." As we pick up the interaction, Komal is asking for her teacher's attention, having made previous, unsuccessful attempts to gain an audience:

Example 2: "dasso ji"

1. Komal: how would, Sir
2. Gurpal: [exaggerated politeness:] hanji <*yes*>
3. Komal: am I allowed to ask a question now?
4. Gurpal: [exaggerated politeness:] dasso ji <*pray tell*>
5. Komal: really? Are you sure?
6. Gurpal: [exaggerated politeness:] dasso ji <*pray tell*>
7. Komal: ok. If you wanted to say I made something what would it be? banondee? <*am*
8.   *making*>
9. Gopinder: banai
10. Komal: banai
11. Gurpal: banaiyaa <*made*>
12. Komal: banaiyaa <*made*>
13. Gurpal: mair ki banaiyaa? <*what did I make?*>
14. Gopinder: [stylized Indian accent:] cake
15. Gurpal: mair roti banaiyee aa <*I made roti*>
16. Komal: daal vaalay parontha <*lentil stuffed flatbreads*>
17. Gopinder: [laughs]
18. Gurpal: mair cake banaiyaa <*I made a cake*>

19.	Komal:	[stylized Indian accent:] cake
20.	Gurpal:	mair gaddi banaiyee <*I made a car*> vroom vroom yeah
21.	Komal:	[laughs]: yay vroom vroom
22.	Gopinder:	[laughs]
23.	Sahib:	my dad did that actually
24.	Komal:	made a car?
25.	Gopinder:	you made a car?
26.	Sahib:	well he worked in er in Rover
27.	Komal:	but I've always wanted to be a grease monkey ever since, no I even wanted you
28.		know Megan Fox in erm Transformers I was like I wanna be like that [Komal
29.		and Sahib laugh]

In l.2 Gurpal responds to Komal with the polite form, "hanji." Gurpal maintains Panjabi, while Komal responds in English. Although the teacher speaking Panjabi as the medium of instruction was common in other classrooms in the school, it was not the normative pattern in Gurpal's class, where he usually spoke English. Rather than immediately moving to her question, Komal (l.3) asks the more or less redundant but playful question, "am I allowed to ask a question now?" In doing so, and in following up with the equally superfluous "are you sure?" (l.5), she metapragmatically (Silverstein, 1993) and ironically draws attention to her previously unsuccessful attempts to capture her teacher's attention. Each of Gurpal's three responses (ll. 2, 4, and 6) is exaggerated; his intonation elongating the honorific suffix, "ji." Gurpal's stylized "dasso ji" is hyper-polite and exaggeratedly solicitous, adopting a linguistic form that is out of place here, but in place because it is a parody of another anonymized voice. Now Gopinder takes the role of the teacher, providing an answer (l.9: "banai") to her classmate's question. Gopinder and Komal frequently took the teacher role throughout the 48-minute interaction, often answering other students' questions and correcting their errors. Komal initially accepts (by repetition) Gopinder's answer, but then shifts to Gurpal's version (l.12). Gurpal seeks to extend the activity by asking questions related to the students' newly composed sentences, for example, "mair ki banaiyaa?" <*what did I make?*> (l.13). Gopinder adopts a stylized "ethnic Indian" accent to answer the question. He ignores this and offers a model answer: "mair roti banaiyee aa" <*I made roti*>. Komal offers her own attempt, but without including the verb. Gurpal provides another model sentence, now picking up Gopinder's "cake" and incorporating it. Komal repeats Gopinder's "ethnic Indian" stylization of "cake," although this equally may be a parodic repetition of Gurpal's use of the same word. Gopinder's and Komal's artistic representation of the "Indian" voice appears to be evaluative ("we don't speak like this"), humorous ("how funny this sounds"), and, probably, affectionate ("older members of our families speak like this").

The artistic performance of the Indian voice portrays a familiar stereotype, at one and the same time playing with it and negatively evaluating it. Now Gurpal offers a further model sentence and takes the opportunity to join in with the humorous exchange: "mair gaddi banaiyee" <*I made a car*> "vroom vroom yeah." Here Gurpal's discourse is double voiced, as he both progresses the learning activity and is willing to usurp it. Komal, delighted by this child-like departure, immediately repeats "vroom vroom." Sahib, as usual more sober than some of his classmates, explains that his father made cars when he worked at the local Rover car factory. Here Sahib's mini-narrative indicates his social class, or at least that of his father, which is different from that of Komal and Gopinder. Rampton, Harris, Collins, and Blommaert (2008) point to evidence that as the children and grand-children of immigrants grow up using English, they acquire both class-marked features and a style-shifting capacity tuned to the sociolinguistic stratification tra-ditionally linked to class hierarchy (cf. Canagarajah, this volume). Komal's response (ll. 27–29) to Sahib's intervention is to claim that she always wanted to be a car mechanic ("grease monkey"), but this quickly segues into her aspiration to be a glamorous Hollywood actress ("Megan Fox") rather than a factory worker.

Example 3: "numquam is never"

Example 3 was recorded 18 minutes into the lesson and again involves students Komal and Sahib and teacher Gurpal. As before, Komal asks the teacher for the Panjabi vocabulary she requires to complete the task.

1. Komal: sir how do you say it?
2. Gurpal: say what?
3. Komal: I never actually did any work
4. Gurpal: mair koi kam nahin kita <*I didn't do any work*>
5. Komal: mair <*I*>
6. Sahib: what's never?
7. Gurpal: never?
8. Komal: [sings:] never say never
9. Sahib: no it's numquam
10. Komal: yeah umquam is ever numquam is never never ever (.) [to Gurpal:] Latin

In this brief exchange, Gurpal provides Komal with the requested sentence in Panjabi. Sahib queries the Panjabi word for "never," and this prompts two quite different indexical responses in the discourse of the students. First Komal sings a phrase (l.8: "never say never") from a song by popular entertainment artist Justin Bieber, who was performing in Birmingham at this time. Explicit discussion of Justin Bieber occurred on three occasions during the lesson, with Komal again singing phrases from this song, Prabhjot saying she was going to Bieber's concert with her little sister, and opinions about the artist sharply divided along gender lines (when Komal reprised her performance of the song extract, the boys in the class booed and jeered). Sahib, however, is more oriented to academic study than to American pop music, and he offers "numquam" as an answer to his own question. Komal is only too willing to engage with this, typically competing for the floor and outdoing Sahib's demonstration of his knowledge of Latin vocabulary (l.10). Here "numquam" and "umquam" are emblematic of a particular kind of education. Latin is rarely taught in the majority comprehensive (state) school sector in Britain, and is largely the preserve of the kind of selective (grammar) and fee-paying schools attended by Sahib and Komal.[3] As such, features of Latin are also emblematic of middle-class status, as the majority of students attending these schools are (broadly) from socioeconomically privileged families. That the Latin terms themselves are filled with social tension is made more clearly evident when Komal turns to her teacher and offers the explanation: "Latin." She assumes (and she may well be right) that Gurpal, educated in the comprehensive school system, has no preexisting knowledge of the Latin features in play here.

Example 4: "a dramatic word"

Example 4 takes place a little over a minute later. Now the teaching assistant, Prabhjot, is involved. Throughout the year we saw that Prabhjot was an important presence in the classroom, taking a co-teaching role in which she was as active and authoritative as Gurpal. This exchange once again features discussion of the word "never," which Sahib wants to include in his Panjabi sentence.

1. Sahib: I don't know how to say never though
2. Prabhjot: kabhi nahin <*never*>
3. Komal: it's not Hindi
4. Prabhjot: Hindi Hindi word but I just use it as Panjabi as well
5. Komal: my mum does that as well
6. Prabhjot: a dramatic word to say
7. Komal: [dramatically:] kabhi nahin kabhi nahin nahin <*never never no*>
8. Sahib: Star Plus
9. Komal: yeah
10. Sahib: Star Plus
11. Komal: [in a stylized Indian accent:] Star Plus you know

Komal recognizes (l.3) that Prabhjot's offer of the word for "never" is a feature associated with Hindi rather than Panjabi and protests. Prabhjot's response, "I use it as Panjabi as well," suggests that, in this instance at least, heterogeneity is privileged above standardization and correctness. Although Prabhjot is comfortable with the labels "Hindi" and "Panjabi," and both she and Komal consent to what the labels connote, she seems to argue that linguistic features are interchangeable in action. Rather than continuing to protest, Komal endorses this perspective ("my mum does that as well," l.5). Prabhjot extends her point, metapragmatically explaining that the Hindi word is "a dramatic word to say" (l.6). Komal now (l.7) becomes the embodiment of Prabhjot's point of view, putting on a dramatic Bollywood-style performance of the Hindi linguistic feature. Sahib (l.8) associates this performance with the Hindi television channel, "Star Plus," repeating the name for emphasis and perhaps to offer Komal a cue. Here discourse shifts from the negotiation of the Hindi/Panjabi word for "never" to a point of view that proposes that "Hindi does drama." The name of the television channel, Star Plus, carries with it connotations of a particular (Bollywood) type of drama, which is common ground for Komal, Sahib, and Prabhjot. Komal's "ethnic Indian" stylization (l.11) is an artistic representation of the view that "Hindi does drama," portraying and evaluating it, indexically linking the "ethnic Indian accent" to the kind of people ("us" but at the same time "not us") who watch Star Plus.

Example 5: "hanji"

Towards the end of the lesson, Prabhjot is leading on the closing activity, in which the students are required to read out to the class the Panjabi sentences they have written. Himmat (male, 12 years) makes an appearance. Prabhjot says to the class: "say two sentences each and then if it's wrong we are going to ask everyone if it's right, and then someone else has to correct it for you, ok? Say two sentences, the most interesting ones." As we rejoin the protagonists, Prabhjot reprimands Komal and Sahib for talking while the other students are presenting their sentences to the class.

1. Prabhjot: [to Sahib and Komal:] hey hey hey your turn will come
2. Komal: [exaggerated baby voice:] hanji <*yes*>
3. Himmat: [speaking his sentence:] mair Will Smith baahar gaya si <*I went out Will Smith*>
4. Prabhjot: Will Smith?
5. Komal: [exaggerated remorse:] sorry
6. Gopinder: he's lying he didn't really
7. Prabhjot: he lives in England?
8. Komal: did you whip your hair back and forth? [Komal and Sahib laugh]

9.	Sahib:	[sings:] (xxx)
10.	Komal:	[sings] nod your head
11.	Prabhjot:	acha <*right*> ok your problem ok [to Sahib and Komal:] youse two you like
12.		talking too much, I am going to correct your sentences as well
13.	Komal:	[stylized, high-pitched:] ok
14.	Prabhjot:	if they're wrong
15.	Komal:	oh is it me next?
16.	Sahib:	yes
17.	Komal:	ok shall I say my longest one?
18.	Prabhjot:	yep
19.	Komal:	it's probably the longest one (.) budhvaar te mair atay meri chotee pehn chotee
20.		pehn cinema gaye si assi Paul dekhdee si oh film bahut mazaakh hai <*on*
21.		*Wednesday me and my younger sister younger sister went to the cinema we see*
22.		*Paul that film is very joke*>
23.	Prabhjot:	dekhiya si <*saw*>
24.	Komal:	dekhiya <*saw*>

Komal's stylized "baby voice" is high-pitched, submissive, and apologetic in the polite form of agreement, "hanji" (l.2) and exaggeratedly remorseful in "sorry" (l.5). This "stylized voice of inauthentic agreement" (Madsen, 2013) is double voiced, indexing both Komal's identification as a model student and as one who is merely putting on the clothes of a model student. That is, the stylized voice enables her to both apologize and to perform an artistic representation of the apology, reflexively commenting on her own utterance. The stylization indexes both authenticity and inauthenticity, as Komal identifies as model student and as commentator on her social identification. Komal's remorse does not last long. Prabhjot creates an environment in which comment on the newly composed Panjabi sentences is encouraged (e.g., in l.4 and l.7 she asks questions in English of Himmat). Komal responds to Himmat's (and Prabhjot's) reference to U.S. film and television actor Will Smith to allude to a song recorded by Smith's daughter, Willow: "did you whip your hair back and forth?" (l.8) (The song *Whip My Hair* bears the refrain "I whip my hair back and forth."). Sahib briefly attempts to sing, and Komal then sings a phrase, possibly misremembering the lyrics of *Whip My Hair* (l.10). Prabhjot's acceptance of comments on students' Panjabi contributions is tested, and she reprimands Komal and Sahib more firmly now (l. 11), with the emphatic "acha." She admonishes them directly, "youse two you like talking too much." The pluralization of the second-person pronoun is a feature of working-class "Brummie" (Birmingham) dialect (Clark & Asprey, 2012; Trudgill, 1990), probably originating in Dublin, Ireland, and appearing in Birmingham with the arrival of large numbers of Irish migrants to the city in the twentieth century. Here it probably indexes a directness and forthrightness that Prabhjot reserves for this sort of occasion. The reprimand induces a further demonstration of submissive behavior from Komal ("ok"), still double-voiced, as high-pitched intonation and "baby voice" again indicate inauthentic authenticity. When she realizes it is her turn to perform her Panjabi sentences she asks "shall I say my longest one," and claims, "it's probably the longest one." Here again she presents herself as the model student before performing her first sentence with aplomb, if not without correction, from Prabhjot.

Discussion

This 48-minute lesson in Gurpal's class was very similar to the many other classes we observed in this Panjabi school in 2010–2011. It also bears many similarities to audio recordings the young people made outside of school, with easy movement across linguistic boundaries being the norm. However, the defining characteristic of the speech of the students, their families, teachers, and teaching assistants, was not that they used features of more than one language in a single utterance or interaction (which they did) but that they used linguistic signs to socially identify themselves and others and that these signs were suffused with the voices of others and with social tensions. Although our three layers of analysis, indexicality, tension-filled interaction, and multivoicedness overlap considerably, we may be able to adopt them to frame some of our thinking about heteroglossia in use and in action in this class.

We suggested earlier that different language forms and signs connect with, and point to (index), particular ideological positions and world views. In the discourses of Komal, Sahib, and Gopinder, emblematic linguistic features point to a wider ideology (set of beliefs and practices) associated with academic success and achievement. Their unsolicited performance of knowledge of Latin vocabulary is indexically linked to this academic orientation. Elsewhere in the lesson, but not included here, Komal and Sahib engaged in informed discussion of the details of the Latin examination syllabus. Komal and Gopinder, students at elite independent (fee-paying) schools, and Sahib, a student at a much sought-after selective grammar school, were all students of Latin. Although the introduction of Latin features was fleeting, it was nonetheless emblematic of a particular orientation to study. Moreover, it was emblematic of difference, as a minority of students in nonselective state schools in England study Latin, and Latin itself has therefore come to symbolize selection in the schooling system according to meritocratic and economic criteria. Komal's one-word explanation to her state comprehensive-educated teacher ("Latin") further points to the emblematic status of these semiotic features. Bakhtin (1981) argued that language is stratified in ways that are socio-ideological, so that some linguistic features come to be associated with some social groups, professions, and so on (Bakhtin, 1981, p. 271). For these young people, some linguistic signs were indexically linked to their beliefs about, and practices of, educational achievement. We also saw students insisting on norms of standardization and correctness (cf. Norton, this volume; Li Wei, this volume), norms enregistered through years of schooling, in which questions have answers, and answers will be found or given. In her interview, Komal expressed definite opinions about pedagogy for language learning: "I like be to be taught, personally I like being taught how to do it, like I can write it down and refer to it later, so it's in my head clearer about how to say it." This was the model with which she was familiar in learning foreign languages at school. She expressed reservations about the pedagogy at the Panjabi school, which she saw as informal, and lacking attention to grammar and tense. Gurpal, on the other hand, told us that his philosophy of teaching was flexibility in the classroom: "some teachers . . . try to follow rigid lesson plans, . . . [b]ut as soon as you start doing that, forcing this child to do what you want to do, . . . the way you want them to do it, it's not going to work."

If a word points to a particular set of beliefs and practices, that is not to say that it points in only one direction. Komal's exaggerated remorse when she is reprimanded by Prabhjot points one way lexically but points another way phonologically. The word ("sorry") itself is authentic apology, but "intonation is especially sensitive and always points beyond the context" (Bakhtin, 1986, p. 91), and the high-pitched "baby voice" adopted for the apology points away from authenticity, identifying (momentary) tensions within the teacher–student interaction. We have seen that social tensions in language may be played out at the interstices between the centripetal pull towards homogeneity, standardization, and correctness and the centrifugal pull towards heteroglossic disunification and decentralization. This tension was starkly and amusingly evident in the teacher's linguistic play with the invented word, "mustachio," as he pedagogically unsettled his students' enregistered norms and teased them with heterogeneous possibilities. Similarly, Komal's commentary on Prabhjot's interchangeability of Hindi and Panjabi signs points to a social tension about what is permitted in the language class. Although Komal acknowledges that interchanging these signs is commonplace, her first response is that the language of the class is "not Hindi." She expects the classroom to be an environment that imposes specific limits to heteroglossia, "guaranteeing a certain maximum of mutual understanding and crystallizing into a real, though relative, unity—the unity of . . . 'correct language'" (Bakhtin, 1981, p. 270). Here "boundaries are drawn with new sharpness and simultaneously erased with new ease" (Bakhtin, 1981, p. 418), as Komal and Prabhjot interact in, and comment on, Hindi and Panjabi. It takes concurrence of views about Hindi as indexical of the dramatic word to move on, as Komal becomes the embodiment of "Hindi as drama."

There are myriad voices in play in the course of this class, as students and teachers stylize, parody, pastiche, and in other ways portray and re-accent the voices of others. The source of the represented voice is not always immediately evident, and we should be cautious in our analysis. The teacher's exaggerated politeness in responding to Komal may have been situated in a shared history or understanding, but that history is not immediately evident. Also, the stylized ethnic Indian accent adopted by the students on a number of occasions probably points to a range of social identifications. Komal's stylized "Star Plus you know" relies on her interlocutors' common knowledge not only of the television channel but of the kind of Bollywood-type programs broadcast by the channel and, perhaps, awareness of a stereotype of the kind of people who watch Star Plus. The voice here may be that of (a stereotype of) a character in a Bollywood-style Hindi language drama. However, it could equally be the voice of (a stereotype of) the Star Plus audience. It is "an artistic representation of another's linguistic style, an artistic image of another's language" (Bakhtin, 1981, p. 362). In the several stylized representations of the ethnic Indian voice here, the social, political, and historical ideologies associated with, or represented by, the stylized word are no doubt recognizable and shared by the recipients (Rampton, 2006). However, they are unlikely to be unitary or straightforward, as on the one hand a stereotype is portrayed and evaluated and on the other hand an ironic distance from the "Indian" voice is maintained, and the stereotype perpetuated.

What we have seen in adopting a heteroglossic lens to examine this language classroom is that the most important question is not which language is in use, but rather what signs are in use and action, what do these signs point to, what are the tensions and conflicts among those signs, and how are the voices of the participants represented in them (cf. Block, this volume). We do not propose a heteroglossic pedagogy for language teaching here, although for excellent examples see Busch (2013), Busch and Schick (2007), and García (2009). We agree with the central tenet of this volume in emphasizing the multiple competencies of multilingual learners as the basis for successful language teaching and learning. However, multilingual approaches do not in themselves guarantee critical engagement with localities, histories, and identities. There may be much to learn from a heteroglossic orientation to language teaching that incorporates multilingualism and goes beyond it to ensure that imperatives towards standardization, centralization, and correctness are held in balance with the acceptance and incorporation into learning environments of linguistic signs and voices that index students' localities, social histories, circumstances, and identities (Bailey, 2012). Our argument is that this should hold true for all learners. As we travel, we might leave aside the monolingual/multilingual divide and adopt a heteroglossic perspective on the signs and forms in use and action as meanings are made.

Notes

1. Dates refer to the publication of English translations of Bakhtin's works.
2. Transcription key:

   (.) pause of less than a second
   speech transcribed speech
   <*speech* > translated speech
   CAPITALS loud speech
   (xxx) speech inaudible
   [ ] stage directions/commentary

3. In 2010, 60% of independent (fee-paying) schools and 15% of state secondary schools in the United Kingdom offered Latin as a subject. 60% of selective schools offered Latin, while 12% of nonselective secondary schools offered Latin. In Birmingham the proportion of nonselective secondary schools offering Latin was 7.4% (Cambridge Schools Classics Project, 2010).

References

Agha, A. (2007). *Language and social relations.* Cambridge, UK: Cambridge University Press.

Bailey, B. (2012). Heteroglossia. In M. Martin-Jones, A. Blackledge, & A. Creese (Eds.), *The Routledge handbook of multilingualism* (pp. 499–507). London, UK: Routledge.

Bakhtin, M. M. (1981). *The dialogic imagination. Four essays.* In M. Holquist (Ed.), C. Emerson, & M. Holquist (Trans.). Austin, TX: University of Texas Press.

Bakhtin, M. M. (1984). *Problems of Dostoevsky's poetics.* In C. Emerson (Ed. & Trans.). Manchester, UK: Manchester University Press.

Bakhtin, M. M. (1986). *Speech genres and other late essays.* In C. Emerson & M. Holquist (Eds.). Austin, TX: University of Austin Press.

Blackledge, A., & Creese, A. (2010). *Multilingualism, a critical perspective.* London, UK: Continuum.

Blommaert, J. (2012). Complexity, accent and conviviality: Concluding comments. *Tilburg Papers in Culture Studies*, *26*. Tilburg, The Netherlands: Tilburg University.

Blommaert, J., & Rampton, B. (2011). Language and superdiversity. *Diversities*, *13*(2), 1–22.

Busch, B. (2013). Building on heteroglossia and heterogeneity: The experience of a multilingual classroom. Manuscript submitted for publication.

Busch, B., & Schick, J. (2007). Educational materials reflecting heteroglossia: Disinventing ethnolinguistic differences in Bosnia-Herzegovina. In S. Makoni & A. Pennycook, (Eds.), *Disinventing and reconstituting languages* (pp. 216–232). Clevedon, UK: Multilingual Matters.

Cambridge Schools Classics Project (2010). *Access to Latin in UK secondary schools.* Cambridge, UK: CSCP.

Canagarajah, A. S. (2011). Codemeshing in academic writing: Identifying teachable strategies of translanguaging. *The Modern Language Journal*, *95*, 401–417.

Canagarajah, S., & Liyanage, I. (2012). Lessons from pre-colonial multilingualism. In M. Martin-Jones, A. Blackledge, & A. Creese (Eds.) *The Routledge handbook of multilingualism* (pp. 49–65). London, UK: Routledge.

Clark, U., & Asprey, E. (2012). *West Midlands English: Birmingham and the Black Country.* Edinburgh, UK: Edinburgh University Press.

Creese, A., & Blackledge A. (2010). Translanguaging in the bilingual classroom: A pedagogy for learning and teaching. *The Modern Language Journal*, *94*, 103–115. doi: 10.1111/j.1540–4781.2009.00986.x

Creese, A., Blackledge, A., Barac, T., Bhatt, A., Hamid S., Li, W. . . . Yagcioglu, D. (2011). Separate and flexible bilingualism in complementary schools: Multiple language practices in interrelationship. *Journal of Pragmatics*, *43*(5), 1196–1208. doi:10.1016/j.pragma.2010.10.006

García, O. (2009). *Bilingual education in the 21st century*. Oxford, UK: Wiley Blackwell.

Hall, J. K., Vitanova, G., & Marchenkova, L. (2005). Introduction: Dialogue with Bakhtin on second and foreign language learning. In J. K. Hall, G. Vitanova, & L. Marchenkova (Eds.), *Dialogue with Bakhtin on second and foreign language learning* (pp. 1–10). Mahwah, NJ: Lawrence Erlbaum.

Heller, M. (2011). *Paths to post-nationalism*. A critical ethnography of language and identity. New York, NY: Oxford University Press.

Jørgensen, J. N. (2010). *Languaging. Nine years of poly-lingual development of young Turkish-Danish grade school students*. Copenhagen, Denmark: University of South Copenhagen, Faculty of Humanities.

Jørgensen, J. N., Karrebæk, M. S., Madsen, L. M., & Møller, J. S. (2011). Polylanguaging in superdiversity. *Diversities*, *13*(2), 23–38.

Lähteenmaki, M. (2010). Heteroglossia and voice: Conceptualizing linguistic diversity from a Bakhtinian perspective. In M. Lähteenmaki & M. Vanhala-Aniszewski (Eds.), *Language ideologies in transition. Multilingualism in Russia and Finland* (pp. 17–34). Frankfurt, Germany: Peter Lang.

Link, H., Lipinoga, S., & Wortham, S. (2013). Faux Spanish in the new Latino diaspora. Manuscript submitted for publication.

Madsen, L. M. (2011). Social status relations and enregisterment in contemporary Copenhagen. *Working papers in urban language and literacies, paper 72*. London, UK: King's College Publications.

Madsen, L. M. (2013). Heteroglossia, voicing and social categorization. Manuscript submitted for publication.

Makoni, S., & Pennycook, A. (2007). Disinventing and reconstituting languages. In S. Makoni & A. Pennycook (Eds.), *Disinventing and reconstituting languages* (pp. 1–41). Clevedon, UK: Multilingual Matters.

Otsuji, E., & Pennycook, A. D. (2011). Social inclusion and metrolingual practices. *International Journal of Bilingual Education and Bilingualism*, *14*(4), 413–426.

Peirce, C. (1955). *Collected papers II. Philosophical writings of Peirce*. New York, NY: Dover.

Pietikäinen, S., & Dufva, H. (2013). Heteroglossia in action: Sámi children's rap about text books. Manuscript submitted for publication.

Rampton, B. (2006). *Language in late modernity*. Cambridge, UK: Cambridge University Press.

Rampton, B. (2011). From "multi-ethnic adolescent heteroglossia" to "contemporary urban vernaculars". *Language & Communication*, *31*, 276–294.

Rampton, B., & Charalambous, C. (2012). Crossing. In M. Martin-Jones, A. Blackledge, & A. Creese (Eds.), *The Routledge handbook of multilingualism* (pp. 482–498). London, UK: Routledge.

Rampton, B., Harris, R., Collins, J., & Blommaert, J. (2008). Language, class and education. In S. May & N. H. Hornberger (Eds), *Encyclopedia of language and education* (2nd ed., Vol. 1, pp. 71–81) . New York, NY: Springer Science & Business Media LLC.

Rymes, B. R. (2010). Classroom discourse analysis: A focus on communicative repertoires. In N. Hornberger & S. McKay (Eds.), *Sociolinguistics and language education*. Avon, UK: Multilingual Matters.

Silverstein, M. (1976). Shifters, linguistic categories, and cultural description. In K. Basso and H. Selby (Eds.), *Meaning in anthropology.* Albuquerque, NM: University of New Mexico Press.

Silverstein, M. (1993). Metapragmatic discourse and metapragmatic function. In J. Lucy, (Ed.), *Reflexive language.* New York, NY: Cambridge University Press.

Silverstein, M. (2003). Indexical order and the dialectics of sociolinguistic life. *Language and Communication, 23,* 193–229.

Trudgill, P. (1990). *The dialects of England.* Oxford, UK: Blackwell.

Wortham, S. (2001). Ventriloquating Shakespeare: Ethical positioning in classroom literature discussions. *Working Papers in Educational Linguistics, 17*(1–2), 47–64.

AFTERWORD

Stephen May

This volume has (necessarily) covered a lot of ground—theoretically, empirically, and contextually. It has, first and foremost, tried to bridge the existing disciplinary divides between SLA, TESOL, and bilingual education in discussing the turn towards multilingualism in applied linguistics. While each contributor brings their own disciplinary background(s) to the wider discussion, there are clear and significant synergies across the various chapters. Ortega's advocacy of usage-based linguistics, for example, resonates with Canagarajah's notion of performative competence, as well as the discussion and analysis of heteroglossia by Blackledge, Creese, and Takhi. Leung's argument for a more contextually grounded notion of communicative competence that acknowledges participatory involvement also closely accords with this. Meanwhile, the implications for language assessment in English-language teaching that Leung outlines are usefully corroborated by García and Flores. The indexical links between language(s) and identity(ies), and their impact on teaching and learning, resonate throughout the various chapters, particularly Norton and Li Wei's, while the issues of embodiment, voice, and multimodality are also clearly evident, most notably in Block and Blackledge et al.

But there is still much left to do; the wider conversation has just begun. In this sense, a second key aim of the volume has been to extend existing discussions of multilingualism within critical applied linguistics beyond the recent (at least in the West) recognition and valorization of the multilingual repertoires of urban migrants. This work is important but it tends still to focus on quotidian, and primarily spoken, language usage in multilingual contexts. It has had less (and sometimes, nothing at all) to say about how we might actually harness these repertoires more effectively in both our pedagogical and assessment practices. Addressing this combination requires us to ally our growing understanding of the complexity, reciprocity, and porosity of multilingual repertoires with the ongoing need for access to standardized language varieties and to the achievement of bi/multiliteracy, given that both are essential to the long term educational and wider success of bi/multilingual learners. This is not to underestimate in so doing the ongoing structural inequalities that many of these learners face and which necessarily impinge upon, and often delimit, their educational and wider opportunities. Multilingualism, in itself, is no panacea and is always situated for the individual contextually in terms of their existing and current language experiences, and the roles and/or functions their language varieties play (or are allowed to play) in their daily lives.

But acknowledging those contexts, and their effects, should not deter us from the crucial task of resituating the bi/multilingual repertoires of learners more centrally, even foundationally, in our language curriculum, pedagogy, and assessment practices. In that, and much else besides, we still have much to learn in addressing the multilingual turn in applied linguistics but we hope this volume has at least provided a useful place to start.

CONTRIBUTORS

Adrian Blackledge is Professor of Bilingualism in the School of Education and Director of the MOSAIC Centre for Research on Multilingualism, University of Birmingham. His recent publications include *The Routledge Handbook of Multilingualism* (with Marilyn Martin-Jones and Angela Creese, Routledge, 2012), *Multilingualism, A Critical Perspective* (with Angela Creese, Continuum, 2010), and *Discourse and Power in a Multilingual World* (John Benjamins, 2005). His homepage is http://www.birmingham.ac.uk/staff/profiles/education/blackledge-adrian.aspx.

David Block is an ICREA (*Institució Catalana de Recerca i Estudis Avançats*) Research Professor in Sociolinguistics in the *Department de Anglès i Lingüística* at the *Universitat de Lleida* (Spain). His main interests are the impact of globalization on language practices of all kinds, migration, and the interface between identity and language learning and use. He is especially interested in how political economy can inform thinking about globalization and identity, and in his more recent work he has focused on neoliberalism as the dominant ideology in contemporary societies and class as a key dimension of identity. He has published articles and chapters on a variety of applied linguistics topics, including SLA, multilingualism, and identity. He is the author of *The Social Turn in Second Language Acquisition* (Georgetown University Press, 2003), *Multilingual Identities in a Global City: London Stories* (Palgrave Macmillan, 2006), *Second Language Identities* (Bloomsbury Academic, 2007), and *Social Class and Applied Linguistics* (Routledge, 2013), and coauthor (with John Gray and Marnie Holborow) of *Neoliberalism and Applied Linguistics* (Routledge, 2012). His homepage is http://www.dal.udl.cat/personal/professorat/Block.html.

Suresh Canagarajah is the Edwin Erle Sparks Professor and Director of the Migration Studies Project at Pennsylvania State University. He teaches World Englishes,

Second Language Writing, and Postcolonial Studies in the departments of English and Applied Linguistics. He has taught before in the University of Jaffna, Sri Lanka, and the City University of New York (Baruch College and the Graduate Center). His book *Resisting Linguistic Imperialism in English Teaching* (OUP, 1999) won Modern Language Association's Mina Shaughnessy Award for the best research publication on the teaching of language and literacy. His subsequent publication *Geopolitics of Academic Writing* (University of Pittsburgh Press, 2002) won the Gary Olson Award for the best book in social and rhetorical theory. His edited collection *Reclaiming the Local in Language Policy and Practice* (Erlbaum, 2005) examines linguistic and literacy constructs in the context of globalization. His study of World Englishes in Composition won the 2007 Braddock Award for the best article in the *College Composition and Communication* journal. He is currently analyzing interview transcripts and survey data from South Asian immigrants in Canada, the United States of America, and the United Kingdom to consider questions of identity, community, and heritage languages in diaspora communities. His homepage is http://www.personal.psu.edu/asc16/.

Angela Creese is Professor of Educational Linguistics at the School of Education, University of Birmingham. Her research and teaching cross references anthropology, linguistics, and education. She uses ethnography to investigate ideologies and interactions in educational and other social settings. She is coauthor of *Multilingualism: A Critical Perspective* (Continuum, 2010) with Adrian Blackledge. She is coeditor of the recently published collection *Routledge Handbook of Multilingualism* (Routledge, 2012) with Marilyn Martin-Jones and Adrian Blackledge. Her homepage is http://www.birmingham.ac.uk/staff/profiles/education/creese-angela.aspx.

Nelson Flores is Assistant Professor in Educational Linguistics at the University of Pennsylvania Graduate School of Education. His research agenda seeks to: problematize current trends in the education of language-minoritized students that reproduce oppressive language ideologies; develop new research methodologies for analyzing language practices of language-minoritized populations outside of these oppressive frameworks; and reimagine language education pedagogy in ways that resist these ideologies. He has collaborated on several studies related to the education of emergent bilingual students in New York City including a study of *Long Term English Language Learners*, a study of successful high schools of Latino emergent bilingual students and a study examining language use among teachers and students in two small schools that serve an exclusively Latino emergent bilingual population. He also served as project director for the CUNY-New York State Initiative on Emergent Bilinguals, a New-York-State-Education-Department-funded initiative that seeks to improve the educational outcomes of emergent bilingual students. His homepage is http://www.gse.upenn.edu/faculty/flores.

Ofelia García is Professor in the Ph.D. program of Urban Education and of Hispanic Literatures and Languages at The Graduate Center, CUNY. She has been

Professor of Bilingual Education at Columbia University´s Teachers College and Dean of the School of Education at Long Island University. Among her recent books are *Bilingual Education in the 21st century: A Global Perspective; Educating Emergent Bilinguals* (with J. Kleifgen, Wiley-Blackwell, 2009); *Additive Schooling in Subtractive Times* (with L. Bartlett, Vanderbilt University Press, 2011). Her recent coedited books include *Bilingual Community Education and Multilingualism* (with Z. Zakharia and B. Otcu, Multilingual Matters, 2012); *Handbook of Language and Ethnic Identity* (Volumes I and II, with J. Fishman, Oxford University Press, 2011*); Negotiating Language Policies in Schools* (with K. Menken, Routledge, 2010). She is the Associate General Editor of the *International Journal of the Sociology of Language* and has been a Fulbright Scholar and a Spencer Fellow of the U.S. National Academy of Education. Her homepage is http://www.ofeliagarcia.org.

Constant Leung is Professor of Educational Linguistics in the Centre for Language Discourse and Communication, Department of Education and Professional Studies at King's College London. He also serves as Deputy Head of Department. He was the founding chair of the National Association for Language Development in the Curriculum (NALDIC), a national subject association for teachers of English as an Additional Language in the United Kingdom. His research interests include additional/second language curriculum, language assessment, language policy, and teacher professional development. His most recent publication is *English: A Changing Medium for Education.* (with B. Street, Multilingual Matters, 2012). He is Associate Editor of *Language Assessment Quarterly* and Editor of Research Issues for *TESOL Quarterly.* His homepage is http://www.kcl.ac.uk/sspp/departments/education/people/academic/leungc.aspx.

Li Wei is Professor of Applied Linguistics at Birkbeck College, University of London, UK, where he is also Pro-Vice-Master and Director of the Birkbeck Graduate Research School. His research interests are in the broad field of bilingualism and multilingualism. He is Principal Editor of the *International Journal of Bilingualism.* Amongst his numerous publications are the best-selling *The Bilingualism Reader* (2nd ed. 2007, Routledge) and *The Blackwell Guide to Research Methods in Bilingualism and Multilingualism* (with Melissa Moyer, 2008) which won the 2009 British Association of Applied Linguistics (BAAL) Book prize. He is an Academician of the Academy of Social Sciences, UK and Chair of the University Council of General and Applied Linguistics (UCGAL), UK. His homepage is: http://www.bbk.ac.uk/linguistics/our-staff/li-wei

Stephen May is Professor of Education in Te Puna Wānanga and Deputy Dean Research in the Faculty of Education, The University of Auckland, New Zealand. He is also an Honorary Research Fellow in the Centre for the Study of Ethnicity and Citizenship, University of Bristol, United Kingdom. Stephen has written widely on language rights, language policy, and language education, including bilingual education, indigenous language education, and multicultural education.

To date, he has published eight books and over 80 academic articles and book chapters in these areas. His key books include *Language and Minority Rights,* which was originally published by Longman in 2001 and reprinted by Routledge in 2008. The reprinted edition was recognized as one of the American Library Association Choice's Outstanding Academic titles. He has since published a fully revised 2nd edition of *Language and Minority Rights* with Routledge in 2012. He has also recently edited, with Nancy Hornberger, *Language Policy and Political Issues in Education,* Volume 1 of the *Encyclopedia of Language and Education* (2nd ed.; Springer, 2008); and with Christine Sleeter, *Critical Multiculturalism: Theory and Praxis* (Routledge, 2010). He is General Editor of the 3rd edition of the 10-volume *Encyclopedia of Language and Education* (Springer, 2016), a Founding Editor of the interdisciplinary journal, *Ethnicities* (Sage) and Associate Editor of *Language Policy* (Springer). His homepage is http://www.education.auckland.ac.nz/uoa/stephen-may.

Bonny Norton is Professor and Distinguished University Scholar in the Department of Language and Literacy Education, University of British Columbia, Canada. Her primary research interests are identity and language learning, critical literacy, and international development. Recent publications include *Identity and Language Learning* (Longman/Pearson, 2000); *Critical Pedagogies and Language Learning* (with K. Toohey, Cambridge University Press, 2004); *Gender and English Language Learners* (with A. Pavlenko, TESOL, 2004); and *Language and HIV/AIDS* (with C. Higgins, Multilingual Matters, 2010). In 2010, she was the inaugural recipient of the Senior Researcher Award by the Second Language Research SIG of the American Educational Research Association (AERA) and in 2012 was inducted as an AERA Fellow. Her homepage is http://www.educ.ubc.ca/faculty/norton/.

Lourdes Ortega is Professor in the Department of Linguistics at Georgetown University. Her main area of research is in second language acquisition, particularly sociocognitive and educational dimensions in adult classroom settings. She has also long-standing interests in second language writing and foreign-language education and has published widely about systematic research synthesis and epistemological and ethical dimensions of second language acquisition research. Her publications include the book *Understanding Second Language Acquisition* (Hodder, 2009) and several coedited collections with John Benjamins, Routledge, and Wiley. She served as area editor for *Language Learning and Teaching* for the *Wiley Encyclopedia of Applied Linguistics* (2012). She is the editor of *Language Learning* for the five-year term of 2010–2015 and serves on the editorial boards of a number of other journals. Her homepage is http://explore.georgetown.edu/people/lo3/?PageTemplateID=129.

Jaspreet Kaur Takhi is Research Fellow in the MOSAIC Centre for Research on Multilingualism, School of Education, University of Birmingham. She is a graduate of University of Birmingham. Her research interests include bilingualism and the education of bilingual learners of English. Her homepage is http://www.birmingham.ac.uk/staff/profiles/education/kaur-takhi-jaspreet.aspx.

INDEX

discourse: analysis of 136–7; bilingual 158; CCSS and 152; defined 61–2; dialogic discourse 198–9; generic discourse 204; language and 93, 206, 208, 210; monolingual 46; polemical discourse 199; relations between 14; social meanings through 193; TESOL discourse 11; translanguaging 155, 160
distributive rules 14–15
diversity and multilingualism 148–50, 156–8
Dominican English 55
Dominican Spanish 55
Dufva, H. 194
Duncan, Arne 149
dynamic bilingualism 79, 154–6
dynamic systems theory 39
Dyson, A. H. 109

El Amante Bilingüe (The Bilingual Lover) (Marsé) 67
ELT *see* English Language Teaching
embodiment notion 49n1, 56, 57–61
emergent bilinguals 150, 152
emergent grammar theory 39, 40
English: No Problems series 130
English as a lingua franca (ELF) 140
English as an additional language (EAL) 124, 136
English language 23, 48, 55, 132–3, 159
English Language Arts teachers 151
English Language Teaching (ELT): bilingual students and 156; communication and 85, 123–5, 141, 143; examination of 4; standards in 149; textbook role in 129
English second language (ESL) 21, 43
English–Somali bilingual 138
enunciation 66, 86, 95
Equipped for Future (EFF) concept 130
erasure 35–6
Eskildsen, S. 45
ethical challenges: in bilingualism 3, 33; in linguistic–cognitive SLA 45; in monolingualism 32, 35; of nonnativeness 36, 37
ethnocentrism 2
ethnolinguistic diversity 124, 136, 140, 143, 148

face-to-face situations 63–4, 66–70, 69, 81
Faneca, Juan 67–8
Federation of Chinese Schools (UK) 173

first-language acquisition: in classroom 124, 136, 138; experiential view of 59; research on 37, 42, 68; UBL and 39, 49n3
Firth, A. 16–17
"flexible bilingualism" 1, 192
Flores, Nelson 4
fossilization 7–8, 10
framing notion: communication and 134; overview 3, 12, 14–15, 87; psycholinguistics in 38; rhetorical framing 137; for SLA field 44
France 64
Freiburg Institute of Advanced Studies (FRIAS) 48n1
French conversations 66
funds of knowledge 171, 186

García, Ofelia 1, 4
gaze aversion 66–7
Gee, James 61
gesture mode 4, 62; in children 58; communication studies on 65–6; importance of 68–72; SLA research on 47; words and 85
globalization: China and 187; diversity and 147; forms of 79; linguistics and 1, 78; research in 115
Global Scale descriptors 128
Goffman, Erving 62
Goodwin, Marjorie 71
grammar: communication and 123–5; competence in 55, 88, 134; contact zones and 83; dependence on 86–8; development of 45; emergent grammar theory 39, 40; explanation of 39–40, 80; knowledge of 42, 55; lack of attention to 211; principles of 18; of speakers 9; in teaching materials 129, 131, 132–5, 152
Gullberg, M. 68

habitus notion 12–14, 57, 91
Hakuta, Kenji 152, 153
Hanks, Williams 58
Harris, R. 9
Heller, M. 14, 17
heteroglossia: classroom examples of 202–10; discussion over 210–12; indexicality 195–6; methods 200–1; multilingualism and 192–3; multivoicedness 197–200; overview 5, 191–2, 194–5; tension-filled interaction 196–7
Hispanic Americans 149

lingual bias 56, 62, 68, 71; *see also* monolingual bias
linguistic birthrights 36, 41, 48
linguistic-cognitive SLA: changes driving 40–1; critical thinking from 33–4;
monolingual bias and 37–9, 41–4, 71;
multilingual turn in 39–40; opposition
to 68–9; overview 3, 9–10, 19; as self-
referencing and nonteleological 44–5;
theory for 38; UBL-oriented 43
linguistics: cognitive linguistics 33, 39, 41,
68; of community 85; competences 126;
defined 4, 62; ethnolinguistic diversity 124, 136, 140, 143, 148; input and
output 103; metrolinguism 1, 79, 192;
sociolinguistics 1, 126, 136, 154, 191; *see
also* monolingualism
literacy: home-language literacy 159;
multilingual literacy 107; photography
in literacy development 112–13; *see also*
identity, literacy, and multilingualism
Liyanage, I. 193
L1/L2 dichotomization in SLA 8–10, 16,
24, 54–5
Long-Term English Learners (LTELs) 150
ludic Englishes 79
Luke, A. 103

McCaffrey, S. G. 69–70
McNeill, D. 65–6
Madsen, L. M. 194
Makoni, S. 1–2
Mandarin speakers 174–81
Maori language 20–1
Marsé, Juan 67, 73n1
May, Stephen 48n1
metrolinguism 1, 79, 192
Mexican Americans 149
Mey, J. 18
migrants, skilled and unskilled 81–2, 94, 97
The Modern Language Journal (1997) 16
Monkeys Passage example 107–9, 114
monolingual bias: linguistic–cognitive SLA
37, 41–4, 71; overview 7, 11; research
on 32–3; in SLA 7, 33–7, 54; solution
needed for 33–7
monolingual discourse 46
monolingualism: cultural context 156;
ethical challenges in 32, 35; in immigrants 54; importance of 36; nativeness
and 32–4, 45–6, 48; overview 1, 3; translingual practice and 79; in US school
system 160

monolingual (English) language 23
Mühlhäusler, P. 19
multidialectalism 55–7, 71, 73
multidiscursivity 195
multilingual embodiment in SLA: embodiment notion 57–61; multimodality
61–8; overview 54–7
multilingualism 55, 73; Common Core
State Standards 151–3; cooperative disposition 99–100; defined 147; diversity
148–50, 156–8; education and 167;
funds of knowledge 171–2; heteroglossia and 192–3; home communities 90;
overview 147–8, 216–17; receptive
multilingualism 85; scholarship on 193;
see also bilingualism; bi/multilingualism;
identity, literacy, and multilingualism;
translanguaging
multilingual literacy 107
multilingual turn: in identity, literacy, and
multilingualism 115–16; introduction
1–6; in language education 116–17; in
linguistic–cognitive SLA 39–40
multimodality 61–8
multivoicedness 195, 197–200

Nash, Caroline 66
National Curriculum in England 4, 124,
132–3
National Governors Association Center for
Best Practices 151
nationalism 2, 18, 25
Native Language Arts standards 160
nativeness: abandonment of 3; consequences of 41; language competence 80;
meaning of 36; monolingualism 32–4,
45–6, 48; norms of 80
native speaker 10, 34–5, 82–3
Netherlands 64
New Literacy Studies 153
New Zealand 20–3, 126
New Zealand Ministry of Education 22, 24
No Child Left Behind (NCLB) 149
nonnativeness 34–7, 41, 44–5, 80, 82
non-referential indexicality 195
nonverbal behavior (NVB) 66, 69
norms of use 124, 134
Norris, Sigrid 63–4
Norton, Bonnie 4

Okada, Hanako 64
one language at a time (OLAT) policy
172–3, 174